Keith F. Pecklers

LITURGY
The Illustrated History

Afterword by
INOS BIFFI

PAULIST PRESS

LIBRERIA EDITRICE VATICANA

Original edition published in Italy as
Atlante Storico della Liturgia
© by Editoriale Jaca Book SpA – Libreria Editrice Vaticana

The number outside the parentheses indicates the page number; the number enclosed
in parentheses indicates the illustration number.

Andre Held: 35 (3), 40 (6); Angelo Stabin: 182 (1), 183 (2), 233 (2), 242 (8); Archivio Centro Studi per la
Cultura Popolare, Bologna: 209 (4–7), 212 (13–16), 214 (20–22), 215 (25–27), 216 (29, 30), 217 (31);
Archivio Fotografico dei Musei Vaticani © Musei Vaticani: 7 (4–6), 48 (12), 123 (4);
Archivio Nigrizia: 189 (6, 7), 249 (8); BAMS photo Rodella: 14 (7), 15 (9), 21 (7), 26 (10), 27 (12), 51 (4, 5),
54 (10), 69 (6), 72 (12), 163 (16–18), 192 (10), 194 (9), 195 (11), 204 (16–18), 205 (19), 211 (11), 232 (1),
252 (4); Eric Davanzo: 195 (12); Matteo Di Michele: 193 (7, 8); Les Éditions du Cerf: 196 (13–16),
197 (17); Jon Erikson: 248 (6); Luca Mozzati: 73 (15); Periodici San Paolo, Alessia Giuliani: 171 (4),
253 (7, 8); Periodici San Paolo, Barontini/Giuliani: 175 (2); Periodici San Paolo, Enrico Belluschi:
225 (12); Periodici San Paolo, Giancarlo iGiuliani: 186 (1), 187 (2), 188 (4), 189 (5), 220 (5), 221 (7, 8),
222 (9), 250 (1), 251 (2, 3), 252 (5), 253 (6), 177 (1), 178 (2); Periodici San Paolo, Nino Leto: 243 (11, 12);
Mahmoud Zibawi: 231 (7); Maria Cabrera Vergara: 192 (4–6); Westminster Abbey: 223 (10, 11).

Images from the archives of Jaca Book: Arnaldo Vescovo/Jaca Book: 29 (3, 4), 30 (7, 8),
31 (10, 11), 33 (15), 34 (2), 36–37 (4), 46–47 (7), 47 (11), 80 (9), 82 (2, 3), 83 (4), 100 (5);
BAMS photo Rodella/Jaca Book: 20 (4), 53 (9), 110 (1–3), 111 (4–7), 120 (1), 133 (5),
138 (1), 139 (3, 6), 142 (12, 13), 143 (15), 206 (1), 210 (9), 211 (12).

All images not listed above are from the archives of Jaca Book.
© Le Corbusier by SIAE 2012
© Succession H. Matisse by SIAE 2012

Printed and bound by
Grafiche Flaminia, Foligno (Pg)

Design and color separation by
Graphic srl, Milano

ISBN 978-0-8091-0604-2

Published by Paulist Press, Inc.
997 Macarthur Boulevard
Mahwah, New Jersey 07430

www.paulistpress.com

To Rowan,
Archbishop of Canterbury,
"Strong, Loving, and Wise,"
whose ministry and leadership
is a gift for all the churches

CONTENTS

1. WHAT IS LITURGY?

1

2

3

1. Sacrificial scene in front of one of the columns of the monument that honors Tetrarchi, beginning of the fourth century. Roman Forum, Rome.

2. Solomon's Temple, fresco in the Dura Europos Synagogue, Syria, third century, Damascus National Museum.

3. Frankincense sacrifice, mural painting in the Dura Europos' Temple of the Palmyrene Gods, first century.

4–6. Details of The Universal Judgment panel painting, Vatican picture gallery, Vatican Museums. Looking at Christ portrayed with arms raised in the direction of the altar (4), the Instruments of the Passion converging with the Madonna's gaze, Saint Stephen with the the martyr's palm, and the innocent saints (5), while some clergy perform merciful works by giving drinks to the thirsty, visiting the incarcerated, and clothing the naked (6).

The ancient Greek term *leitourgia* already offers us some indication as to why the early church chose this word as an apt means of describing what Christians do when they gather together to offer praise and thanks to God. Literally, it means work or service (*ergon*) and something belonging to the people (*litos*). In the secular Greco-Roman world, liturgy was identified both with common, public projects done for the good of the community and also with the particular public office with which one became involved. Gradually in Greek society, the term came to be linked with various types of service: acts of kindness to a friend or neighbor, or even tasks done by slaves for their masters. However, it was in the second century when the term came to be associated with Christian worship. This secular term, which we might equate with public service, was also used in ancient Judaism, but in a more restrictive way. Nonetheless, the term appears 170 times in the Septuagint

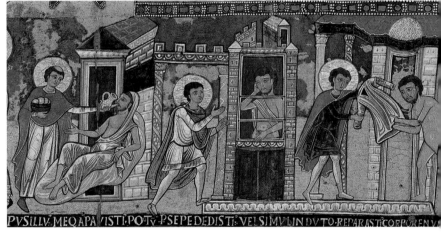

(the Greek version of the Hebrew Scriptures) as a way of describing religious rituals offered by priests. Perhaps it was employed because it seemed the most appropriate way of describing an official function or act done by religious leaders on behalf of the people. *Liturgy* appears much less frequently in the New Testament—a mere 15 times and with a more varied usage. For example, it is used in the Letter to the Romans 13:6 to describe a civic function or public servants whereas two chapters later in Romans 15:16, it is used to speak of Christians offering themselves spiritually. In the Letter to the Hebrews 8:2, the reference is to Christ's sacrificial offering on the cross. In the Acts of the Apostles 13:2, *liturgy* refers to the ritual celebrations of the Christian community at Antioch.

This varied terminology should surprise us especially since Christian worship grew out of already existing ritual structures. Whether adapting Jewish practices or those of the ancient Mediterranean religions such as the cult of Mithra, Christians gave new interpretations to these rituals and acts for its own purposes. Indeed, usage of the word *liturgy* in Christian texts offers a very early example of what will later be called "liturgical inculturation"—the borrowing of a term, concept, or symbol from outside the Christian context, reinterpreting it. Gradually, *liturgy* came to signify both service of God and the service of the community offering an early clue to understanding the integral relationship between liturgy and Christian charity or what will later become the relationship of liturgy and mission—the service of God's world.

By the fourth century, Eastern Christians used this term exclusively in reference to the Eucharist—"The Divine Liturgy"—as it continues to be used today. We see this, for example, in the liturgies of Saints Basil the Great, John Chrysostom, and Mark. In the West, terms like "Divine

7

8

Work" (*Opus Dei*) or "Divine Office" came to be used in place of *liturgy* until the sixteenth century, when it was introduced into the Western Church's vocabulary thanks to the influence of the Humanists. It was adopted by some churches of the Reformation in the seventeenth century, and introduced into Western Catholic literature in the eighteenth century by the first generation of liturgical scholars who used the term to talk of Christian sacraments. It was not until the pontificate of Gregory XVI (+1846), however, that the term was officially used in documents of the Roman Church. Later it appeared in the 1917 Code of Canon Law wherein it stated that the Holy See was responsible both for the ordering of the Church's liturgy and the approbation of its liturgical books (canon 1257). In the twentieth century, thanks to usage of the term within the liturgical movement, *liturgy* became a more normative term within the Church's vocabulary in the West.

In 1947 with Pius XII's promulgation of *Mediator Dei*—the first papal encyclical on the liturgy, the term is defined as "public worship which our Redeemer as head of the Church renders to the Father, as well as the worship which the community of the faithful renders to its founder, and through him to the heavenly Father. In short, it is the worship rendered by the Mystical Body of Christ in its entirety of its head and members" (no. 25).

At the Second Vatican Council (1962–65), the definition of *liturgy* became more systematic, affirming that Christian worship is enacted by the entire mystical body of Christ, head and members. It then described the goal of liturgy as the glorification of God and the sanctification of the liturgical assembly (*Sacrosanctum concilium* 7). This sanctification takes place and is signified by signs that the human senses can perceive. These signs and symbols include familiar gestures like the sign of the cross, the ancient *orans* gesture of praying with arms outstretched, or the laying on of hands that is performed by a liturgical minister at ordinations, in anointings, and in celebrations of the sacrament of reconciliation (penance). Also included are those symbols of the earth: bread and wine, oil, water and fire. In all these signs and symbols, the presence of Christ is encountered. Thus, even before we come to encounter the presence of Christ in the sacred scriptures or in the bread and wine that will be offered in the Eucharistic Prayer, the presence of Christ is recognized in the liturgical assembly, considered the primary liturgical symbol—the mystical body of Christ gathered together in praise and worship of God. The 1983 Code of Canon Law affirmed that liturgy is both the exercise of the priesthood of Jesus Christ who sanctifies all people and the public worship that is enacted by the Mystical Body of Christ (canon 834).

All of this invites our reflection on how ritual functions, the role of the non-verbal and the use of silence, and the ways in which we use our bodies in worship. Here, the church has been greatly helped by twentieth-century advances

9

10

8. Person at prayer, pictorial decoration on the walls of the oratory, in the Church of Saint John and Saint Paul, Rome.

9. Grape harvester, detail of floor mosaic from the fourth century, from the lower Church of Kaianos, 'Uyum Musa, Mount Nebo, Jordan.

10. Consecration of the candle, Exultet, circa 1136, Bibliothèque National de France collection, Paris.

11. Samaritan woman at the Fountain of Miracles, with the person born blind; scenes tied in with the symbol of water from the 1059–1071 Exultet, Capua. Museo dell'Opera del Duomo, Pisa.

11

within the social sciences—what the liturgical discipline could learn from anthropology, psychology, semiotics, and sociology. Late twentieth-century developments in the area of what is now called "ritual studies" made a further contribution to helping scholars understand how liturgy functions and how it leads believers into an encounter with the transcendent. Here, it must be said that Christians of the East are far ahead of their Christian counterparts in their use of the body with numerous processions and prostrations, as well as a fuller use of symbols that open worshippers to the mystical and transcendent. Indeed, the Eastern liturgical traditions have often been described as an experience of "heaven on earth." By contrast, Western Christians over the centuries have often approached Christian worship in a more cerebral and less corporeal manner that can easily weaken liturgy's symbolic power and impede the liturgical assembly's potential to encounter the triune God in spirit and in truth. This has been particularly evident in the post-conciliar Roman liturgy of the late twentieth century with an excessive use of comments throughout the liturgy explaining various aspects of the rite. While this has often been done in favor of greater intelligibility—helping people to comprehend and better understand—it has also been to the detriment of liturgy's ritual functioning.

Ultimately, liturgy is beyond us: it is first and foremost God's gift to the church with the acting subject of the

12

liturgy Christ himself—the only one competent to bring our work to God that the people might thus be sanctified. As members of the liturgical assembly, we respond to that gift through our participation in the liturgical action but the initiative is purely with God who draws us into that holy assembly in the first place. God's initiative and our response form the dialogical nature of all Christian liturgy, which extends beyond our places of worship and even beyond the church, to embrace the whole world. In this way, Christian worship imitates the pattern of our salvation that began with God's initiative and engendered our response—both individually and corporately. Moreover, Christian liturgy is also Trinitarian and doxological as it is dialogical, for the church always prays *to* the Father, *through* Christ, *in* the Holy Spirit. At its most basic level, liturgy and doctrine are fundamentally intertwined, mediated by church dogma. "Jesus is Lord" is both an acclamation and an assertion

As the public worship of the church, Christian liturgy by its very nature is both evangelical—directed toward mission—and eschatological—looking toward the future of God's reign. This dying and rising is brought to Christ in the liturgy, and Christ brings it to God as together the Christian community is healed and transformed. Vatican II stated clearly that liturgy is both the source and summit of the church's life (*Sacrosanctum concilium* 10), offering a clear indication of the intrinsic relationship between liturgy and life. Prior to the Second Vatican Council there was a sense that we would leave the world for an hour each week to enter the tranquility of the church for Sunday worship, and then return to the labors of daily life. But the council reminded us that when the Christian community

14

12–13. Liturgy of the Angels, detail of sixteenth-century frescoes at the Philanthropinon Monastery on the island of Giannina: Christ appears in bishop's, Eucharistic, officiant's, and sacrificial garments.

14. *Fresco, circa 1318, at the Gračanica Monastery: Christ with Luke and Cleophas, the Emmaus Altar, and the relating of the encounter with Christ to the apostles, acknowledged by the breaking of bread.*

gathers each week it brings with it all that has happened in the previous week—the good and bad, our successes and failures.

At the same time, however, Christian worship is about infinitely more than our own personal struggles and joys, as important as they are. The Second Vatican Council makes this abundantly clear when it notes that liturgy is never a private function but rather a ritual celebration that necessarily belongs to the entire church (*Sacrosanctum concilium* 24). Indeed, as we gather to celebrate the liturgy—whether in East or West, whether as Anglicans or Orthodox, Lutherans, Methodists, Reformed, Roman Catholics, or any number of other ecclesial communities we might mention—we do so in union with the whole of God's world. We take care to be especially mindful of those places most in need of healing and redemption and of those individuals who live without hope and in the shadow of death. So as we gather to celebrate the paschal mystery of Christ day after day or week after week, we are aware that what we do in the liturgy is fundamentally about God's reign on this earth and God's mission within the world. And as participants in those sacred rites, we are also charged with the task of embodying that reign of God not only within the liturgy, but even more importantly in our daily places of life and work where we are called to become the body and blood of Christ. Christian Liturgy, then, is ultimately about praising and thanking God as we recall God's mighty deeds and as we come to rediscover our own membership within Christ's mystical body in the world, enabling us to look upon God's world with God's eyes.

2. The Origins of Christian Worship

1. *Meeting tent in the city of Shiloh, detail of a miniature of the Octateuch of Constantinople, seventh century, Vatican Apostolic Library.*

2. *Map of Palestine showing worship sites and sanctuaries erected along the road of the patriarchs' disorderly retreats.*

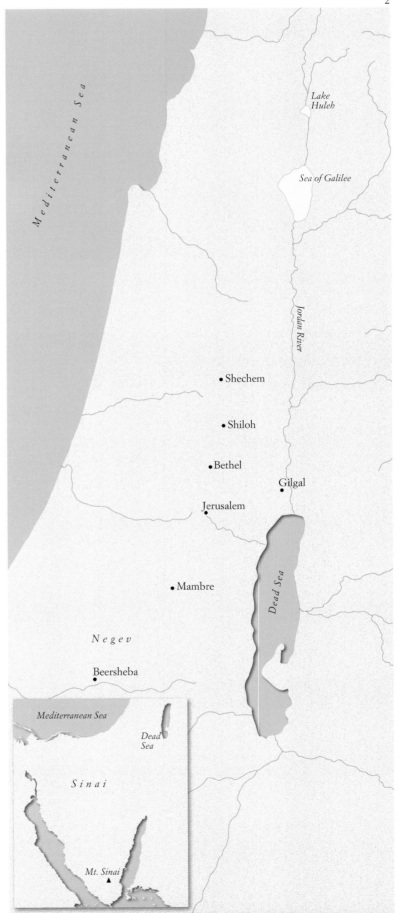

What liturgical scholarship of the past forty years has revealed is that we are left with more questions than answers in our attempt to discover the origins of Christian worship. Of course, since Christianity emerged from Judaism it follows logically that the origins of Christian worship are to be found within ancient Jewish worship. But this relationship also needs to be nuanced for it is clear that while early Christians carried forth certain Jewish ritual practices, they did not do so uncritically. Jesus himself embodied the balance between the old and the new—a faithful Jew who participated in the feasts of the Jewish liturgical year (Passover, Pentecost, the Feast of Tabernacles, and Dedication of the Temple) yet was not enslaved to Jewish law or tradition. Rather, true worship of God "in spirit and truth" needed to include service to others even on the Sabbath when Jews were to refrain from all activity.

At first Israel had no temple. The God of the patriarchs disclosed himself to them in places along the way of their journey to their new country. The routes of the patriarchal journeys were dotted with wayside shrines or sanctuaries whose foundations the Israelites attributed to the patriarchs (e.g., Shechem, Bethel, Mambre, Beersheba, Gilgal, Shiloh). Then, when Israel was led out of Egypt, the people assembled before the holy mountain of Sinai to receive a theophany—the revelation of God's will in the Torah. The stone tablets on which the Commandments were inscribed were then carried in a portable box called the "ark of the covenant." Throughout the forty years in the wilderness, the ark rested in a temporary sacred space, a desert sanctuary for a people on the move, called the "tent of meeting."

Once Israel was settled in the Promised Land, King David centralized the Israelite cult in Jerusalem. His son Solomon built the first temple there that became the center of the sacrificial cult and supreme symbol of God's

5–6. Map of Jerusalem that shows the principal biblical sites (5) and reconstruction of the Temple design (6).

presence among the people. Solomon's Temple was the first of three, the second being that of Zerubbabel after the Babylonian Exile, and the last (although known as the Second Temple) being built by Herod the Great. The basic structural design of each of the successive temples remained consistent. There was always a courtyard or courtyards in the temple complex to accommodate the assembly of various groups and gates of access; a court in front of the temple proper with the altar of sacrifice and the bronze "sea"—an immense water container. The temple proper was the building at the heart of this complex of courtyards. It comprised a porch leading to the Holy Place, which was a hall housing the golden altar of incense, the table of the "showbread" (twelve loaves representing the twelve tribes of Israel, which were changed every Sabbath). Beyond it was the most sacred part of the temple—the Holy of Holies, which contained the ark of the covenant.

The temple order of service was conducted by the high priest, the priests, and the Levites, and involved a complex round of prayer and sacrifice. Although teaching took place within parts of the temple precinct, the temple in

3. Saul's sacrifice in Gilgal, miniature from the Books of Kings, eleventh century, Constantinople, Vatican Apostolic Library.

4. Baetylus (holy rock), standing in the area that surrounds the Har Karom Mountain in Palestine.

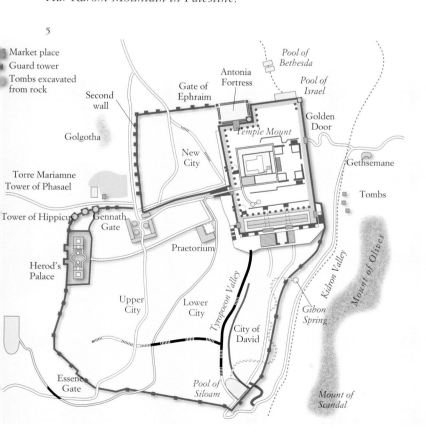

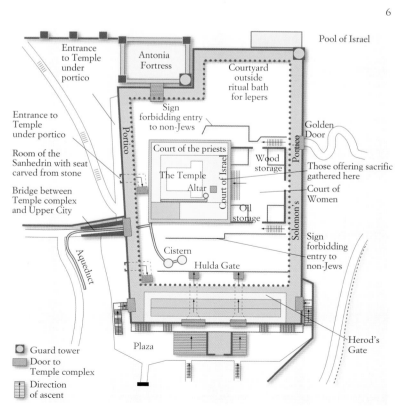

7

Jerusalem was primarily concerned with sacrifice; its altar was the place of sacrifice and sacrifice was the principal act in Israel's cult.

The sacrifices in the Jerusalem temple were varied. Holocausts—burnt or whole offerings—were a form of sacrifice in which the entire victim was burnt and nothing was given back to the offerer or to the priest. In communion sacrifices, the victim was shared between God, the priest, and the person offering the sacrifice. The purpose of expiation sacrifices was to re-establish the covenant with God when it had been broken by the sin of an individual. There were also unbloody sacrifices involving flour, oil, corn, bread, and incense.

Especially regarding temple worship and its sacrificial emphasis, many texts within the Hebrew Scriptures reveal the development of the notion of the importance of a more spiritualized form of worship, namely that the soul of true and genuine worship is shown in faithfulness to the covenant—not so much in ritual actions or, more precisely, in ritual formalism (i.e., strict or excessive adherence to prescribed ritual forms). By faithfulness to the law of the covenant, Israel proves that its worship is genuine and that it has no other God but Yahweh. The saving God of the Exodus and giver of the Ten Commandments is holy and demands that the people who would be molded into a priestly nation also be holy.

8

7. *Panoramic view of modern-day Jerusalem.*

8. *The Chariot of the Sun, detail of Hammath Synagogue floor mosaic, near Lake Tiberiade, end of third century.*

9. *Capharnaum Synagogue ruins.*

10. *Map of the Capharnaum archaeological zone:*
1) domus ecclesiae; 2) synagogue.

11. *Temple of Jerusalem, detail of Hammath Synagogue floor mosaic, near Lake Tiberiade, end of third century.*

12. *Map of Dura Europos, Syria:*
1) domus ecclesiae; 2) house of the scribes; 3) synagogue.

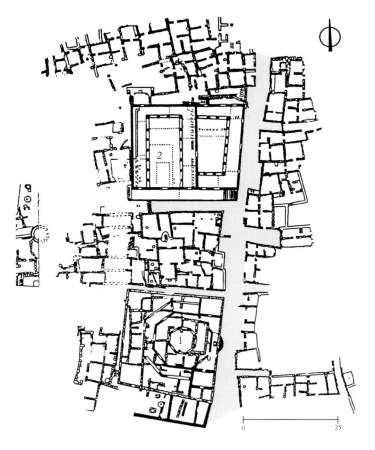

13. Procession of the Palms during the Sukkot Festival, *interior of Amsterdam Portuguese Jewish Synagogue, engraving by Bernard Picart, based on religious ceremonies and customs throughout the world, 1723–1737.*

A defining moment for Jewish worship was the destruction of that third Jerusalem temple in the year 70 CE—the one built by Herod the Great. That destruction brought with it the end of sacrificial worship of the old covenant. The temple had been an important point of reference, but in fact, the synagogue had more influence on both Jewish and Christian worship even as it had no standard liturgical form and any male congregant could lead the synagogue service. The liturgical context in this early period offers a similar diversity of practice and informality with precious little information as to the exact relationship between the synagogue service and Christian worship, for example. The reality of the destruction of the Temple along with the growing awareness that Jesus' return was not imminent as had been thought, led to the pastoral need for more organized structures within the Christian Church including the way in which it worshipped.

The synagogue was the place of assembly for prayer and instruction. The synagogue probably arose as a result of the destruction of the Jerusalem temple in 587 BCE and of the dispersion of the Jews to Babylon. A cult centered upon the temple ritual was impossible there and the synagogue was organized as a substitute to maintain Jewish unity in faith and worship. The earliest synagogues were doubtless purely private gatherings in private dwellings. By New Testament times, however, the synagogue was an established and essential part of Jewish life and cult. The synagogue had become a distinct building erected for a specific purpose; it was found in every Palestinian town of any size and in cities outside Palestine where there was a community of Jews. Its structure consisted generally of a rectangular hall designed to segregate men from women. There was a special place set aside for housing the scrolls of the law, and a tribune where the readers and preachers exercised their ministries.

Unlike the temple, the synagogue was not a house where the deity dwelt, but a meetinghouse for prayer and the study of the law. It was also the setting for the instruction and initiation of converts to Judaism. The government of the synagogue was entrusted to a group of elders, and its management, maintenance, and order of the services were the responsibilities in particular of an *archisynagogus* or "head of the synagogue." More than any other single factor, the synagogue was responsible for the survival of Judaism as a religion and of the Jews as a distinct people against the powerful assimilative forces of Hellenism. It was not only a place where the law and the traditions were preserved and explained; it was also a meeting place of the Jewish community, a preserver of its identity and a guardian of its values.

The synagogue maintained its vital importance in the origins and growth of Christianity. Jesus attended the synagogue regularly and made it one of the places in which he taught. Paul also began his preaching in the synagogue of Damascus and on his journeys, he would go first to the synagogue of the city where he would be invited to give an address, often ending in heated debate and sometimes in violence. The synagogues were abandoned by Christians only when the Jews repudiated and expelled them.

All of this background makes it abundantly clear that the Christian communities of those early years were closely linked primarily with the Jewish communities of Jerusalem and throughout Palestine, Asia, and elsewhere, despite growing differences. Even when Christianity went its own way, the Jewish influence was indelibly present. No more so than with regard to the liturgy for at the source of the Christian liturgy lies the Jewish liturgy. Christian worship inherited classic elements of praise, thanksgiving, and intercession from the Jewish tradition, along with the pattern of daily prayer at fixed times, the liturgy of the Word and sermon, the seven-day week, and the concept of a liturgical year, especially regarding certain feasts such as Easter and Pentecost. The Christian cult of the martyrs also finds its origins within Judaism. Other ritual traditions such as the laying on of hands, invitations such as "Let us pray," and doxologies to conclude prayers were also borrowed from Judaism. Even today, those same elements can still be found within contemporary Jewish worship.

At the same time, we must be careful not to draw too close a line between Jewish liturgical origins and early Christian ritual practice. The sacrament of baptism offers an interesting example. A number of scholars in the twentieth century attempted to show a direct link between Jewish ritual

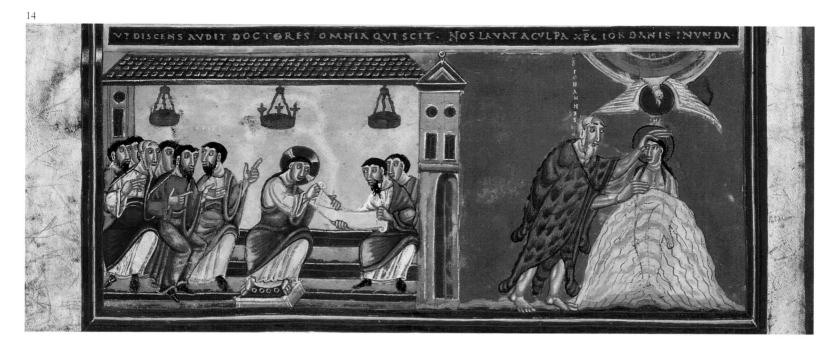

VT DISCENS AVDIT DOCTORES OMNIA QVI SCIT · NOS LAVAT A CVLPA XPC IORDANIS INVNDA ·

14. Baptism of Jesus, *detail of Codex Aureus by Echternach, 1020–1030, Germanisches Nationalmuseum, Nuremberg.*

15. *Qumran, basin for cleansing rituals.*

mentions Jesus baptizing others and makes no mention of his being baptized. Nevertheless, it appears that from early times it was the custom to initiate new converts into the church with a process that included baptism—perhaps in a river, pool, or domestic bathhouse. There are other questions about the origins of the anointings and imposition of hands and about whether infants were baptized with adults. There may also have been a preliminary period of instruction—a forerunner of the catechumenate. And it is presumed that there was some form of confession of faith in Jesus Christ.

The New Testament reveals a variety of interpretations as to just what baptism was to symbolize: forgiveness of sins and the gift of the Holy Spirit; birth to new life; enlightenment; union with Christ through participation in Christ's death and resurrection. Thus, all this leaves us with more questions than answers, which is why we cannot point to the New Testament to find quick solutions in our desire to arrive at the origins of Christian liturgical practice. Descriptions of the Eucharist and its understanding reflect a similar diversity of practice and theology. Indeed, in considering non-Jewish Christians of Greek origin, we can't presume that they would have automatically wanted to accept traditionally Jewish forms and structures of prayer. It would be enough to consider Acts 6, which recounts an early crisis in the Christian community between Jewish and Hellenist Christians over the treatment of widows; and the tensions at the Council of Jerusalem recorded in Acts 15 over male circumcision and Jewish dietary laws.

washings at Qumran and Christian baptism, for example. However, the fundamental problem with making such a link between Qumran and the Christian baptismal bath was that those were repeated washings at Qumran, not a one-time action like Christian baptism. In any event, whether the Christian adoption of baptism began with Jesus himself or only in the church after his resurrection cannot be easily resolved. The gospels of Matthew, Mark, and Luke record Jesus' baptism by John but say nothing of Jesus baptizing his followers while the Gospel of John only

3. LITURGY IN THE APOSTOLIC ERA

Consistent with synagogue worship, first-century Christianity did not emerge as what we would call today a formal religion. There were no shrines or temples; no sacrifices or public cult; and no celebrations of public feasts. Moreover, consistent with early synagogue practice there is no explicit first century evidence for the singing of psalms within Christian communities even as the psalms were frequently quoted. By the time of Tertullian (circa 200 CE) the custom was established of introducing antiphons and refrains in the psalms to be sung by the liturgical assembly. As the central Christian ritual had its origins in the domestic context of a meal, it continued to be celebrated in homes and residences for several hundred years, and those events were closed to the public. Of course, there were persecutions and obvious security risks. But even aside from that, some Christians defended their lack of altars and shrines by arguing that God's altar is the whole world and could hardly be contained in an edifice made by human hands.

Christian worship in those early years was thus quite informal. Indeed, the kinds of distinctions made today between sacramental and ordinary meals of the community would have appeared strange. We might think of the pious literature before Vatican II which spoke of Holy Thursday "when Jesus celebrated his first Mass," or artistic portrayals of Jesus distributing Communion at the Last Supper to his disciples who received on the tongue and kneeling! It seems certain that the Christian community's fraternal or *agape* meal was the context for the Lord's Supper until the end of the first century or the beginning of the second. This is evident in Paul's account of the Eucharist in 1 Corinthians 11). The Christian Scriptures offer four accounts of the institution of the Eucharist (Mark 14:22–24; Matthew 26:26–29; Luke 22:17ff; and 1 Corinthians 11:23–25). Already we see a cultural variance in these four different accounts as the texts were composed for different audiences. Paul's account in 1 Corinthians is significant in that he refers to the tradition that he handed on to the Corinthians: "For I received from the Lord what I also handed on to you, that the Lord on the night he was betrayed took a loaf of bread . . . " (1 Corinthians 11:23). Luke and Paul include the command: "Do this in memory of me," which is not included in either Mark or in Matthew. This institution of the Eucharist clearly takes place within the context of a domestic meal regardless of whether or not that meal was the Passover supper.

In those early years of the apostolic period, when the life and mission of the church took shape, we have little detailed information of just how the followers of Jesus worshipped or what they did when they gathered for common prayer. Regarding the celebration of the Eucharist in the first century, there are many more questions than answers

1. Bas-relief of Saint Peter and Saint Paul. Museo Paleocristiano, Aquileia.

2–3. Dieric Bouts' Last Supper Triptych, 1464–1468, Saint Peter's Church, Louvain: Passover (2) and Christian Easter (3). Depiction of the Last Supper and Christ himself, celebrating the liturgy of consecration.

because of a lack of evidence. What we can say is that the oldest form of the "breaking of bread" (Acts 2:46) took the form of a meal, leaving us only with the problem of determining how the new sacramental action was combined with the strictly Jewish meal. The assumption that the apostles merely repeated the rite of the paschal meal each week as Luke presents the Last Supper is not tenable. That rite was too complicated for frequent repetition, and according to Jewish law, was not permitted except during the actual celebration of the annual Passover feast. Eucharistic imagery can be found in numerous references in the Christian scriptures as in the account of the supper at Emmaus (Luke 24:13–35) when the disciples themselves recall how the risen Lord explained the scriptures to them and broke the bread. This imagery is especially clear in verse 30, which begins "While he was at table with them, he took bread, blessed and broke it. . . . "

It is more likely that the rite of the "breaking of bread" took place within the Sabbath meal, which had its own religious solemnity and symbolic significance. The Sabbath meal ritual was quite suited to combination with the Christian rite. The ritual of the breaking of bread at the

2

3

beginning of the meal and the cup of blessing after the meal were part of both the annual paschal meal and the weekly Sabbath meal. The apostles may have remembered the Lord and his death, then, in the action at the beginning of the meal—the blessing, breaking, and distribution of the bread—and in the action at the end of the meal—the blessing and distribution of the cup of thanksgiving. However, in certain other early Christian communities, namely those inclined to follow the traditions of Mark and Matthew, the two principal actions were no longer separated by the meal. Rather, they were joined and placed together either before or after the meal. The blessings over the bread and cup were eventually combined into one solemn prayer of thanksgiving, expanded from the form originally employed over the cup alone. Eventually in Christian practice, the meal itself was dropped altogether.

Like their Jewish forebears, early Christians continued the Jewish practice of praying three times daily: they gather at the third hour (9:00 AM) on the day of Pentecost in Acts 2; we hear of Peter's prayer on the roof at the sixth hour (noon) in Acts 10; and of the ascent of Peter and John to the temple at the ninth hour (3:00 PM) in Acts 3. Further

testimony on these three hours is given in the eighth chapter of the *Didache*, which suggests that the Lord's Prayer should be recited three times each day.

Another important dimension of first-century liturgical practice was its diversity. There was no one fixed form of liturgical practice in the New Testament. We know, however, that two important prayer forms for early Christians remained the doxology and blessing. Such diversity was reflected elsewhere, too. The mere fact that we have four gospels rather than one suggests this—and we have four accounts of the Institution narrative. Why? Because different cultural audiences demanded different approaches. For those early years, we have little detailed information on just how the followers of Jesus worshipped or what they did when they gathered. The second chapter of the Acts of the Apostles speaks of the "breaking of the bread." Eucharistic imagery can be found in numerous references in the New Testament as in the account of the supper at Emmaus recounted in Luke 24.

Baptism has its own liturgical references that signified a washing in water with God's word (Ephesians 5), and was performed in Christ's name for the forgiveness of sins. Of

4

the many baptismal references in the New Testament, however, only the account of the Ethiopian's conversion in Acts 8 describes the baptismal rite. We read of the apostles laying hands on those whom the community had commissioned to some form of service or leadership in Acts 6. Moreover, we read of praying over those who were ill and anointing them with holy oil in James 5.

One early document that does offer some important liturgical information is the *Didache* or "The Teaching of the Twelve Apostles." It was discovered only in 1873 and ranks as one of the most important discoveries of early Christian manuscripts. Written toward the end of the first century or early second century, it has been said to be perhaps the oldest non-canonical Christian document. It is an important liturgical source as it contains one of the earliest examples of a primitive "church order"—a book containing rules for the Christian life, church discipline, and liturgical forms. The text is a church order of a Jewish-Christian community, for it is replete with Jewish influence and makes substantial use of Matthew's gospel. The *Didache* was probably composed at Antioch in Syria and was destined as an instruction for pagan converts, although there is also some evidence to suggest that it came from Alexandria; both Clement of Alexandria and Athanasius make important use of the text.

The first six chapters, which constitute part one, offer a catechetical handbook and gives directions for imparting instructions to catechumens. Those preparing for baptism are taught of the "two ways"—the way of life and the way of death. This two-way device, which here becomes a basic method for training catechumens, was used in the Hellenistic synagogues to instruct proselytes. Part two, consisting of chapters 7 through 16, is the church manual proper. It opens with instructions concerning the actual administration of baptism—ideally done in living (i.e., running) water; describes baptized life as one of prayer and fasting on days different from those of the Jews; and of eucharistic "thanksgiving." The work then turns its attention to the ministries in the community, beginning with apostles and prophets followed by bishops and deacons. Oddly, placed between these is the short reference to the Sunday Eucharist. The *Didache* ends with comments related to the last days and the gospel warning to "watch over your life; your lamps must not go out nor your loins be ungirded; on the contrary, be ready."

The *Didache* represents an early attempt to break away from Judaism: prayer texts are deeply embedded in the Jewish tradition but they now center on Christ. Jewish practices of fasting and prayer are not rejected, but they differ in terms of time and form. The rite of the baptismal bath is devoid of any non-Jewish influence, but is briefly described in the way the Essenes of Qumran might have practiced their own ritual washings. Unlike Qumran, however, Christian baptism is never self-administered and is to be performed in the name of the Trinity. There is not yet

5

4. *Supper at Emmaus, architrave of the left portal at La Madeleine Church, Vézelay.*

5. *Dačani Monastery, frescoes stories from the life of Saint Paul: the apostle Philip gives instructions for the Ethiopian eunuch to be baptized, according to what is written in the Acts of the Apostles (8:26–39).*

6. *Page from the Didache, from an eleventh-century Byzantine manuscript.*

7. *Ethiopia: blessing of water during the Timkat Epiphany Festival, in commemoration of Jesus' baptism.*

6

7

any suggestion of rites like anointing or renunciation of sin. Thus, in this early period, we see a young church finding its way, establishing its own autonomy yet remaining linked to the tradition. We can observe a liturgical plurality and informality, largely conditioned by the particular local culture in which the liturgical celebration was enacted.

4. Cultural Adaptation in the Greco-Roman World

Emerging from the Jewish context, the church in the West faced the challenges of evangelization presented by the culture and religions of the Greeks and Romans. The missionary church needed to adapt to this new situation which would inevitably effect its worship. One major challenge came in the task of how best to calculate time since this, too, was culturally conditioned.

The Jewish calculation of time began as it still does, from sundown to sundown. Thus, the Sabbath began at sundown on Friday and concluded at sundown on Saturday. Predictably, Christian communities that emerged in the Jewish context observed the Lord's Day—Sunday—from sundown on Saturday until sundown on Sunday. The Greek calculation of time was quite different, however, calculating each day from sunrise to sunrise. Thus for Christians in the Greco-Roman context, their observance of the Lord's Day began at sunrise on Sunday and concluded with sunrise on Monday. The Roman calculation represented what we continue to employ today in secular life: time calculated from midnight to midnight. Of course, our liturgical horarium continues to follow the Jewish model—First Vespers on Saturday evening for Sunday and even the Vigil Mass on the eve of Sundays and feasts.

Such cultural diversity was even more evident in the practice of religion within the Roman Empire, which offered an extraordinary mix of cults existing alongside one another, a number of which included various superstitions. This was especially the case in Rome itself, which had numerous immigrants and visitors, some of whom, like Montanus of Phyrigia and his late second-century apocalyptic movement, led to erroneous notions. Those early Mediterranean religions were fascinated with signs and omens, ghosts, divination, and astrology. Cicero, for example, referred to the Roman rites of initiation as "those mysteries by which we are trained out of undiscipline to human ways."

"Those mysteries" included symbolic or sacramental actions: sacred meals and weddings; fertility and birth rites; baptisms; investitures with sacred garments; and rites of death and resurrection that took the form of symbolic journeys. Roman rites and priests were presided over by priests and mystagogues whose teaching was referred to as *mystagogy*. Indeed, one finds a great variety of religious cults responding to the vast amount of people in the Roman Empire. As long as the tranquility of the state was not disturbed, those new religions were allowed to continue and grow. Christianity was no exception in the early period. Its growth was helped at least in part by the fact

1. Detail of the House of the Centenary Lararium fresco, Pompeii.

2. Detail of the Barberini Mitraeum, Rome.

3. Mithras Tauroctonous, mural, circa 225–250, Mithraeum, Santa Maria Capua Vetere. The Mithraic cult used to baptize its followers in a bath of warm bull's blood instead of water.

3

that some saw it as an outgrowth of Judaism, which was already widely diffused throughout the Empire with synagogues in every town.

In this early period there was a significant amount of contact between Roman Christianity and the presence of mystery cults such as Mithra—the Persian god of light and wisdom. Mithraism gradually spread throughout the Roman Empire in the first century and reached its peak in the third, until it gradually faded in the fourth century with the legalization of Christianity. Unlike other early Mediterranean religions, Mithraism shared a special relationship with Christianity: both religions evolved at the same time and grew within the same geographical regions, embodying two distinct responses to the same cultural challenges and issues. In some cases, Christian apologists such as Justin and Tertullian criticized or even mocked the ritual practices of such non-Christian cults. Tertullian mocked the initiation baths of Isis and Mithra, which accomplished nothing, he argued, despite their elegance and expense. By contrast, the rites of Christian initiation brought purification and salvation with few words and at no expense. There were also some distinct ritual differences. For example, the cult of Mithra baptized its followers in a bath of warm bull's blood rather than water.

Even despite the Apologists' criticisms, however, and clear distinctions in ritual practices, Christian rites gradually incorporated cultural elements into them, some of which were taken from the mystery cults themselves, reinterpreting them for Christian usage. Anointing rites entered the Roman baptismal liturgy since the practice had long been known in the Greco-Roman world. Foot washing of the newly baptized with the kissing of the feet was borrowed from non-Christian rites and then incorporated into the rites of Christian initiation. Acts of renunciation and acclamation were graphically portrayed in the Christian baptismal ritual and related to similar corporeal gestures in the cult of Mithra and other Roman religions: turning to the West—the region of darkness—to renounce Satan; turning to the East—the region of light—to acclaim Christ. Worshipping toward the East—*ad orientem*—was also a common practice in the cult of Mithra as followers prayed toward the rising sun.

We can find other examples of cultural and religious borrowing in this early period, especially regarding the ritual development of Christian baptism, which made use of the term *enlightenment,* for example, a term that was also used to describe initiation into the cults of Isis and Mithra. We can also note a common vocabulary in terms such as washing,

4. Cult of Isis, mural at Ercolano,
Museo Archeologico Nazionale, Naples.

4

5

6

initiation, and illumination. The Initiation rites themselves exhibit a similar sharing of terminology and ritual components: the scrutinies; learning of sacred formulas; fasting; stripping naked for immersion at the font; baptism by immersion; the putting on of the white garment; the meal of initiation; and the post-baptismal period of mystagogy. Similarly, there was a borrowing from or adapting to secular culture. A mixture of milk and honey that came to be given to the newly baptized was borrowed from the custom in ancient Rome when the *paterfamilias,* or head of the household, welcomed the newborn child into the family. That rite, however, also had a superstitious dimension as a protection against evil spirits. In Roman noble households, the newborn was placed before the father of the family to be judged. If the child was deformed, or sometimes even just a girl when the parents wanted a boy, that newborn could be rejected and then given to the servants to raise. When the baby was finally accepted, however, the mixture of milk and honey was offered. Tertullian mentions this practice in the rite of Christian initiation in North Africa, using the Latin term *susceptio* or *munus susceptionis*—a juridical term which signified, among other things, the father's legal acceptance or recognition of the newborn infant presented to him as his own. In the mind of Tertullian, after baptism the newborn was accepted (*susceptus*) by the church as one of her own. The mixed drink was offered as a sign of welcome and recognition. Several centuries later, the *Apostolic Tradition* would also refer to this mixture of milk and honey offered to the neophyte. Not surprisingly, this ritual component lent itself easily to the biblical reference of the Promised Land "flowing with milk and honey"—a land into which the neophyte had entered through the waters of baptism.

7

9. Saint Peter's Chair, gift of Charles the Bald to Pope John VIII in 875, on the occasion of his coronation. Symbol of the Roman bishop's supremacy.

9

8

5. Maran, Hatrene divinity, head crowned by rays of sunlight. Archeological Museum, Mosul, Iraq.

6. Altar dedicated to the Invincible Sun, mid-first century. Museo Gregoriano Profano, Vatican City.

7. The Roman Pantheon: erected during the first century, dedicated to the Blessed Virgin Mary and to Roman martyrs. The church is still called the Basilica of Saint Mary of the Angels and the Martyrs today.

8. Icon of the Virgin Hodegetria, the Pantheon, Rome. The dating of this icon is tied to the transformation of the Pantheon into a Christian church in 609.

scriptural readings and a homily given by the bishop, the Mithraic meal was preceded by a time for instruction in which followers were reminded of the story of how the world was saved by Mithra. Just as bread and wine are objects for consecration in the Eucharist, so in the Mithraic ritual meal the bread and water were presented for consecration. Some scholars suggest that wine might have been included as well, since we know that Mithraists did indeed drink it. As early church fathers were critical of the initiatory practices of those early Mediterranean cults, so too did they criticize ritual meals within those same cults. Justin, for example, in chapter 66 of his *First Apology*, accused the worshippers of Mithra of counterfeiting the Christian Eucharist in its initiatory meal of bread and water. Tertullian, whose father was probably a follower of Mithra, uses the term *oblatio* in denouncing the offering of bread within the Mithraic ritual meal—the same term he uses to describe the Christian Eucharist.

There was also a certain resemblance in eucharistic terminology. Inscribed on the walls of a Mithraic temple in Rome were the words: "You have saved us O Mithra through your most precious blood." Changing the word "Mithra" to "Christ," little more would be needed to appropriately render that expression within a Christian context. In an underground pagan basilica in Rome near the Porta Maggiore, one finds an interesting fresco. There is an altar depicted on which is placed bread and fish. Behind the altar stands a president with arms outstretched in prayer using the same classic *orans* position employed by early

The ritual meal of the Mithraists also bears a striking resemblance to the early Christian Eucharist. Just as the Eucharist was preceded by a service of the Word with

10. Stucco representation of the goddess Spes, Porta Maggiore Hypogeum, Rome.

11. Pope Victor I, Saint Paul Outside the Walls, Rome.

12. Table set with gifts for the victors at the Hellenic competitions, Porta Maggiore Hypogeum, Rome.

10

11

Christians in their rituals, wearing the same style of liturgical dress that would have been worn by Christians charged with the task of liturgical presidency. To the side of the altar are inscribed the words "food for the journey"—a ritual partaking of food for the dying to grant them safe passage into the next world, not unlike what Christians would later call *viaticum*—holy communion for the dying. Clearly, those linguistic and ritual elements meant different things in those different Mediterranean religions; nonetheless, the similarity in expression and style is most fascinating. One wonders how such liturgical and symbolic borrowing originated and who initiated the exchange.

The equinoxes and solstices were particularly sacred to the Mithraic tradition and Roman Christianity would soon develop its own feasts to contradict those of their non-Christian neighbors. This was especially the case in the fourth century with the decline of the Elysian rites, the Egyptian rites of Osiris and Isis, the Phrygian rites of Attis, and the Persian rites of Mithra. For example, the fourth-century choice of December 25 as a date for the annual festival of Christmas was not by accident. As disciples of the sun god, followers of Mithra celebrated the feast of the invincible sun at the winter solstice—the shortest day of the year. In claiming Christ as "that sun which never sets," Christians carefully chose to celebrate Christ's birth at the same time. The Eastern Christian feast of the Epiphany on January 6 was likewise a replacement for the pagan feast of the virgin birth of Dionysius and related legends of various epiphanies of pagan gods recalled on that day. Some years later, toward the end of the fourth century, the feast of the birth of John the Baptist was also observed on June 24 around the summer solstice. Given John's relationship to Christ as forerunner, it is probable that the two feasts were chosen in harmony.

We have yet another example of the Christianization of pagan feasts in the February feast of the Chair of Saint Peter, which celebrates the primacy of the Bishop of Rome. The twenty-second of that month had traditionally been a pagan feast remembering Roman ancestors. Each year during the month of February, Romans celebrated an eight-day feast called the *Parentalia* in which the ancestors were recalled with homage paid to deceased family members and relatives. During the annual festival of *Parentalia* a ritual meal was celebrated called *Charistia* or *Cara cognatio* in which an empty chair was left at the table symbolically recalling the ancestors—both individually and collectively. To counteract that feast the Roman Church introduced the feast of the Chair of Saint Peter—our ancestor in the faith. Later examples of the reinterpretation of pagan elements include the seventh-century christening of the Pantheon in Rome. Built in the first century as a temple to all the gods, the church in the seventh century dedicated it as a Christian basilica to the Blessed Virgin Mary and the Roman martyrs; the Christian festival of All Saints on November 1 originated there to commemorate the christening. To this day, the Christian name of the Pantheon is the Basilica of Santa Maria *ad Martyres*.

The issue of liturgical language offered yet another challenge for the Christian community in the Greco-Roman world. *Koiné* Greek was spoken by a large part of the Roman Empire including in the city of Rome itself. Wisely, the Roman Church adopted *koiné* Greek as its own liturgi-

12

cal language since that was the language most accessible to the church members. Indeed, during the first two centuries ten out of fourteen bishops of Rome were Greek-speaking. The use of Latin within the liturgy originated with Pope Victor (+203). The result was a mixed liturgy that included Latin usage for the scriptural readings and a continued use of Greek for the prayers. (The first Latin version of the scriptures appeared around the year 250.)

Liturgical vocabulary in Latin was greatly enhanced thanks to writers like Cyprian, Tertullian, and Augustine. Tertullian, for example, borrowed military terms such as *sacramenti testatio* and *signaculum fidei* or promise of loyalty to the Roman emperor when he spoke of the baptismal profession of faith. As always, those cultural elements were given a new christological interpretation when they were introduced into Roman Christian worship, and Roman bishops used their mystagogical catecheses after they had baptized at Easter to explain the new symbolism. Nevertheless, Roman Christians continued to employ Greek for liturgical celebrations until the middle of the fourth century during the papacy of Pope Damasus I when the majority of Romans no longer understood Greek.

Interestingly, the Roman Church shifted to Latin for the liturgy as a cultural concession—what would later be called "liturgical inculturation"—so that those in attendance would be able to understand what they were celebrating. This bit of history is quite instructive in our own day, as some within the church have called for a return to Latin because it is "a more sacral language." Indeed, at the Council of Trent one bishop actually defended the continued use of Latin in the liturgy because "it was the language that Jesus used at the Last Supper with his disciples"! Of course, nothing could be further from the truth. Jesus, as we know, spoke the vernacular of his own day, otherwise his disciples would not have understood him. In and of itself, Latin is no more "sacral" than is Greek or Japanese. What perhaps gave Latin this sacral character was that it eventually came to be used only in the liturgy and was unintelligible to most worshippers. Today, Latin remains the official language of the Roman Catholic Church and of its worship, even though major vernacular concessions were granted at the Second Vatican Council (1962–65). In the seventh century, there was a brief return to Greek usage within liturgical worship, probably due to an increased number of immigrants to Rome coming from the East. That shift was to be short lived, however. Soon, the Roman liturgy would return to the exclusive use of Latin and the faithful would be further and further removed from the church's rituals because of an inability to understand Latin.

5. *DOMUS ECCLESIAE*: A HOUSE FOR THE CHURCH

1. Abandoned temple, detail of a fresco in the Dura Europos Synagogue, Syria, National Museum, Damascus.

2. Aedicule, probably of a Christian baptistery, from Dura Europos, circa 250, Yale University Art Gallery, New Haven, Connecticut.

3. Church of Saint John and Saint Paul (titulus Pammachii), Rome, south side facing the clivus Scauri: below, the lateral nave, built over the Roman domus.

4. Roman domus, fresco under the present-day Church of Saint John and Saint Paul, Rome.

1

2

Worship in the time of the apostles and of the early church took place in different locations: the Jewish temple, synagogue, and Christian houses. The practice of meeting in some Christian's homes continued throughout the next several centuries. The worship space made available in the larger homes of the wealthier members of the community came to be designated as the *domus ecclesiae*—the "house for the church" or "house church." At this time church property did not exist in law and buildings for the use of the Christian communities, therefore, remained the property of private individuals. Rich families offered their houses for the use of the *ekklesia*, the gathered worship community. Because of their physical plan these houses lent themselves easily to the liturgical needs of the community. With few adjustments these houses were transformed into fitting spaces for worship. Adopting the setting of the Roman house with its noblest traditions of family life, the church was able to celebrate its worship in a personal and intimate atmosphere.

A good example of a house-church is found at *Dura Europas* in Mesopotamia, a city that was an ancient military Roman colony on the right bank of the Euphrates which was destroyed by fire in 265 CE and was never rebuilt. It is a Hellenistic house, constructed around the year 232 CE and transformed into a *domus ecclesiae* for Christian gatherings in the 240s CE, only to be destroyed when the city was burned down. It had rooms allocated to the different needs of worship and was decorated with examples of early Christian art. One room on the ground floor was created from two after removing the partition wall and could accommodate a group of about sixty people. At the east end there was a raised platform presumably for the altar. Another room was used for catechetical instruction and a third room was redesigned as a baptistery, replete with images of the baptism of Jesus by John in the Jordan River. Interestingly, on the same street as the house-church was found a synagogue dating from the same period. The mere presence of house-church and synagogue existing side by side in the middle of the third century would seem to indicate an ease between the two faiths as they existed one alongside the other in such close proximity.

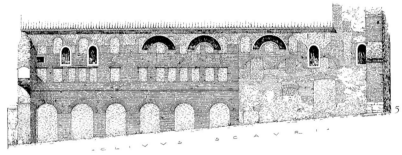

5. Reconstruction of the front of Imperial Age lodging rooms and storehouses along the clivus Scauri, incorporated into the foundation of the Church of Saint John and Saint Peter (by Gismondi).

6. Plan for Imperial Age lodging rooms and storehouses, on top of which the Church of Saint John and Saint Paul was built (by Krautheimer/Astolfi).

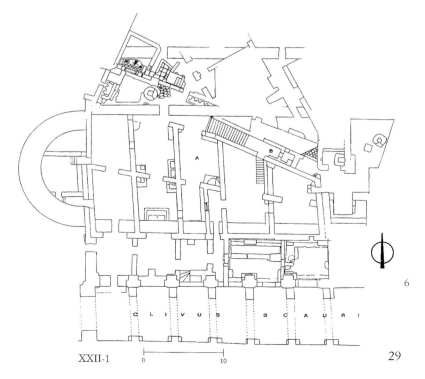

Roman places for regular Christian liturgical assembly were located within the city. These were also called *tituli* ("titles") deriving from the fact that they were private residences, each named after the one who owned the property whose name was inscribed on a plaque (*titulus*) and attached to the house, e.g., *titulus Byzantis; titulus Sabinae.* Each *titulus* was located in or near a populous district of

7. Saint Cecilia Church (titulus Caecilae Transtiberim), Rome, paleo-Christian era mural paintings in the church's baptistery.

8. Saint Cecelia Church, Rome, present-day atrium, with second-century cantharus, which came from the atrium of the paleo-Christian church.

9. Saint Clement's Church, Rome, plan for baptistery, built during the sixth and seventh century, which leans against the church's north side.

7

8

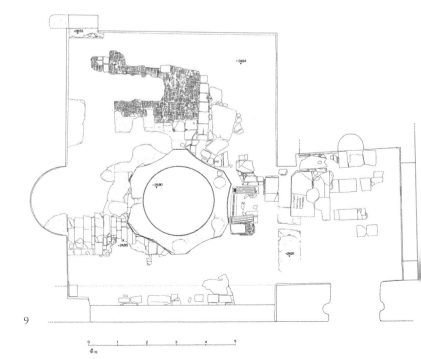

9

the city, but none would make much of a visible impact since they were ordinary residences provided for modest arrangements of worship. Such houses in Rome include those found under the present structures of the churches of SS. Giovanni e Paolo, Santa Cecilia, San Clemente, and Santa Pudenziana, to name a few. These houses must have continued to multiply throughout the whole of the third century since it is estimated that Christians in the city numbered between 10,000 and 30,000 in the middle of the third century and perhaps 200,000 worldwide according to some estimations.

Eusebius of Caesarea described the development of communities and the construction of buildings during the period of religious peace that followed the Edict of Toleration of the Emperor Gallienus in 260 CE, then of their destruction as a result of the persecution of Diocletian from 303–304 CE. The last persecution of Diocletian witnessed the destruction of house-churches in three North African towns. But the fact that they were destroyed so easily sug-

10. *Lower part of Saint Clement's, Rome, Madonna and saints, fresco painted during the seventh and eighth centuries.*

11. *Saint Pudenziana Church (titulus Pudentis), Rome, north wall of the basilica, with old masonry, expansion carried out by Pope Adrian (772–795).*

12. *Plan for Saint Pudenziana Church (by Krautheimer).*

gests something of their modest size. Eusebius still uses the term "houses of prayer" but also speaks of "spacious churches." In Book 10 of his church history, he includes the text that he delivered on the occasion of the dedication of a new basilica built at Tyre.

The enlargement of the places of assembly led to the regulation of their arrangement as we can read in the third-century *Didascalia Apostolorum.* The words *church* and *house* are both used as in Eusebius. The document specifies more precisely how this arrangement should be with regard to the different groups of people within the community dealing with the placement of the bishop with his presbyters, then the laity. The advice continues with reference to young people, children, visiting laity, visiting bishops and presbyters, and the poor. This is among the first indications of a liturgical ordering.

Many examples of primitive Christian art emerge during this period, a great deal of which is found in the house-churches; some of it still survives in the Roman catacombs. A common range of subjects is displayed, depicting scenes both from the Hebrew and Christian scriptures. The primary intention is to show how events and persons of the Hebrew Scriptures are fulfilled in the person and work of Christ. In other words, the Christians wanted their art to present in a simple and symbolic way what the cult celebrated sacramentally in signs, namely the mystery of salvation.

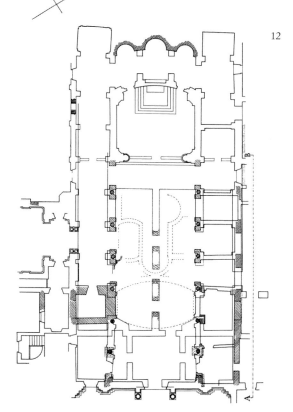

*13. Detail of the cupola's Exodus frescoes, Baghawat,
Kharga Oasis, Egypt: the Egyptians pursuing the Jews;
Jonah thrown overboard; the stories of Eleazar and Rebecca;
Isaiah's martyrdom, three young men in the furnace.*

*14. Right side of Brescian reliquary: apostles' medallions;
Moses' calling; three young men in the furnace; blind
man's recovery and Lazarus' resurrection; Jacob's cycle.
Civici Musei d'Arte e di Storia, Brescia.*

13

14

Biblical themes included depictions of Adam and Eve;
David and Goliath; the sacrifice of Isaac; Moses striking
the rock; Jonah; the three young men in the furnace; Daniel
among the lions; Mary with the child and a prophet; the
adoration of the Magi; the baptism of Jesus; the multiplication of the loaves; the saving of Peter from the stormy sea;
the Samaritan woman; the Good Shepherd; the five wise
virgins; the resurrection of Lazarus, and so forth.

The early church's decision to adopt the basilica form was
significant. Traditional temples were constructed as a sanctuary to house a cult object—a place in which only priests
would enter. As a "house for the church," Christian worship spaces would need to employ a different model since
they would need to accommodate groups of worshippers—
laity as well as clergy. Thus in the Judeo-Christian context,
early places of Christian worship relied more heavily on
synagogue structures than on the temple for the reasons
just stated above. In the Greco-Roman world, however, it
would be the basilica model that would win the day. As a
large public building, the basilica was originally intended

15

as the place to conduct public business—either a law court, imperial audience hall, or markets and other public gatherings. Thus, Christians transformed the basilica style by arranging the edifice on a longitudinal axis as evidenced in the fifth-century design of Santa Sabina on Rome's Aventine Hill. This open style easily lent itself to accommodating large numbers of people and to movement within the liturgy—processions. The central nave was flanked by two or four side aisles and there were numerous doors to further assist such movement. At the center of the apse was the bishop's throne surrounded by his presbyters seated on a bench to his left and right. The narthex served as a liminal space for catechumens and others who were not admitted to communion.

There was also what came to be called the *martyrium*—a basilica built over the tomb of martyrs, indeed, of Christ himself as witnessed in the Church of the Holy Sepulchre in Jerusalem. Within the *martyrium* was the shrine or *memoria* such as in the Vatican Basilica of San Pietro. In some cases, the *memoria* was located next to the basilica as in the case of San Lorenzo *fuori le mure*. These shrines were usually found in cemeteries and therefore outside the walls of a city.

The example of *Dura Europos* clearly demonstrates the importance of baptistries in relationship to the church building. The fact that candidates were baptized in the nude—removing one's clothing as a rejection of one's former way of living—a separate baptismal space was needed. These buildings were often octagonal in shape—symbolizing the eighth day—exceeding the perfect number of seven. Baptistries normally included smaller changing rooms—separate rooms for the women and men. The baptismal pool was located at the center of the room allowing for the full immersion of the candidate and often including a place outside of the font where the bishop would stand and pronounce the Trinitarian formula. As at *Dura Europas* these baptistries included rich iconography on the walls and in the dome of the room.

6. Liturgical Sources from the Patristic Era

1. *Antoninus Pius, his head concealed, celebrates twenty years of rule with a libation, bronze medallion, 158–159. Staatlich Museum, Münzkabinett, Berlin.*

2. *The Sacrifice of Melchizedek, who offers a basket of bread and a cup of wine. Mosaic in the Santa Maria Maggiore Basilica's main nave, Rome.*

3. *Heavenly Feast fresco in the Catacombs of Saints Peter and Marcellinus, Rome.*

In Rome the prohibition of evening gatherings of clubs and organizations may have led Christians to celebrate their eucharistic meal on Sunday mornings, no longer including the full ritual meal as described by Paul in 1 Corinthians 11, but rather limited to the offering of the bread and wine mixed with water. Around the year 150 CE, Justin Martyr in his *First Apology* reports to the Emperor Antonius Pius and Roman Senate of such a morning gathering.

Born in Samaria, Palestine, Justin converted to Christianity at Ephesus around the year 130 CE and became an itinerant philosopher. He came to Rome during the reign of Antonius Pius and opened a school to help pagan converts better appreciate the Christian faith in a simple, language with which they had been familiar prior to Christianity. This is the very approach he employs in attempting to explain to the emperor what Christians do on Sunday mornings as they gather for worship and the symbolic and religious significance of what is enacted. Justin was the first to use the Greek word *eucharist*, referring to what had previously been called "The Lord's Supper" and the "breaking of bread." In his *Dialogue with Trypho the Jew*, he also refers to this Eucharist as a sacrifice.

In his *Apology* Justin actually offers two descriptions of the Christian Eucharist. It is not clear whether he is reporting on the exact liturgical practice of the Roman Church or simply offering a more universal description of Christian worship. In chapter 65, Justin offers his first description of the Eucharist, which is appended to celebration of baptism. Here, the Eucharist is clearly seen as the culmination of Christian initiation, where the newly baptized are led into the assembly of believers, share the kiss of peace for the first time with other members of the church, participate in the prayers and the great thanksgiving prayer, and then share communion with the assistance of deacons who minister it to them.

The description found in chapter 67 provides an account of a typical Sunday morning service, which includes what we now call the liturgy of the Word and the liturgy of the Eucharist. The classic eucharistic action of taking, blessing (giving thanks), breaking, and distributing is evident as is a single blessing prayer and the importance of the assembly's "Amen" as an assent to what the president has proclaimed in the Eucharistic Prayer. There is also a very primitive description of the different liturgical roles that became standard in the tradition: lector, president (probably the bishop), assembly, and deacons. This diversity of ministries fostered the sense of liturgy as the work of the people.

In describing the Sunday Eucharist, he informs the emperor that whether in the city or the countryside, Christians gather "on the day of the Sun" and they read from the Acts of the Apostles and the Prophets "as long as time permits." There was not yet a fixed Lectionary and thus the readings

3

were probably read in a *lectio continua* (continuous reading) fashion. One might find it curious that no mention is made of reading from the Gospels. We know that in the second century the Gospels were increasingly accepted as sacred scripture and were gradually read within liturgical assemblies although Justin makes no mention of that here. A homily or "exhortation" follows the proclamation of the Word in which the president admonishes the assembly to imitate the holy example that they had just heard described in the readings. Following the homily Justin notes that the assembly stands and prayers are offered.

Bread, wine, and water are then brought forth by members of the assembly (presumably carried from their homes), and the president prays and gives thanks "according to his ability." This last reference refers to the fact that without any fixed liturgical texts, the president had to improvise in an *ex tempore* prayer, which is concluded by the people's strong "Amen." The gifts are then distributed and Justin notes that everyone shares in them without exception. Afterwards, the deacons carry those gifts to the absent members of the community, presumably the sick and elderly, although this might also have included other absentees who for one reason or another were unable to be present for the morning worship.

At the conclusion of the service there is an offering for the needy and a list is provided of those worthy of financial assistance: "orphans and widows, those in need because of illness or some other reason, those in prison, strangers and those visiting." Significantly, the collection is left with the president whose task is to oversee not only the spiritual but also the material life of the community, especially its *diakonia*—its social outreach to those at the margins. The deacons then assist with the distribution of those goods. Despite this primitive account of the Sunday Eucharist, we can already perceive something of that intimate link between Eucharist and justice; liturgy and life; liturgical participation and social outreach. Those members of the liturgical assembly who are financially stable are expected to sustain the less fortunate and it is the president of the liturgical assembly who both fosters and sustains that intimate bond between the two realities. Justin then offers the emperor a rationale for the choice of Sunday as the Christian day of cult, describing it as the first day in which God transformed darkness and matter and created the world, and the day when Christ rose from the dead.

The Apostolic Tradition

This early church order is rich in the liturgical information it offers, but quite complicated when we try to discern the text's authorship or provenance. Until fairly recently, the text was believed to have been composed by Hippolytus of

Rome at the beginning of the third century and it was thought that the work largely reflected Roman liturgical practice. Thanks to the work of liturgical scholars across denominational lines, it has now become quite clear that we can no longer be so confident in affirming the authorship, provenance, or dating of the text. Indeed, the document is more likely a redaction of several texts rather than a single composite and might well reflect the practice of various regions or geographical areas rather than one single Christian community. Portions of the *Apostolic Tradition* can be found in other fourth- or fifth-century church orders such as the *Apostolic Constitutions.* While the text was originally composed in Greek, it now survives only in a Latin translation found in a fifth-century manuscript and in Coptic, Arabic, Ethiopic, and other languages in subsequent centuries.

Despite the document's complicated origins, it has had significant influence on the liturgical reforms of the Second Vatican Council particularly in the restoration of the adult catechumenate and the celebration of Christian initiation—the Rite of Christian Initiation of Adults (RCIA) and the reform of the Catholic Mass. The important information that the document offers on the catechumenate and Christian initiation will be discussed in chapter 10.

The *Apostolic Tradition* also offers the rite for the ordination of bishops, presbyters, and deacons. Here we see ordination as a process involving several steps: election; laying on of hands and prayer; the kiss of peace; and the Eucharist. It is also important to note that the local community is present in all its components; indeed, members of that community are actively engaged in the choice of its leader; in the ordinand's process of preparation; and in the rite itself.

The text also presents the appointment of other ministries—widows, readers, virgins, subdeacons, and healers. Here, a clear distinction is made between ordination and installation. Those members of the community are not ordained but rather installed because with ordination comes a special charism through the laying on of hands which is not conferred upon widows, lectors, virgins, nor subdeacons.

There is important information offered on daily prayer at fixed times and the religious interpretation of praying at those determined hours. There are also certain observances of Christian life described here: the agape meal, a prayer for the blessing of the evening light (*lucenarium*), and a variety of other blessings.

Within the ordination rite of a bishop is found a eucharistic prayer that served as a base text for the Second Eucharistic Prayer currently found in the Roman Missal. It is christological in character, referring directly to God's action in Christ even as the prayer itself is directed to God the Father. There is no *Sanctus* nor are there any interces-

4

sions or commemorations of the saints. It is the first time that an Institution Narrative ("Take and Eat . . . " "Take and Drink . . . ") is included in a eucharistic prayer and also includes an anamnesis (memorial), epiclesis (calling down of the Holy Spirit), and a final doxology. The epiclesis is interesting in that it occurs after the Institution Narrative rather than before and combines the epiclesis over the bread and wine with the one over the assembly itself.

The Jewish *Birhat ha mazon*—the thanksgiving prayer at the end of a meal—clearly provides the pattern for this eucharistic prayer. But the Christian eucharistic prayer, in contrast to Jewish prayers of blessing from which it originates, celebrates the memorial of Christ's death and resurrection while also considering the themes of creation and salvation history begun in God in the Old Testament, and fulfilled in Christ. Accordingly, the Christian eucharistic prayer transforms the Jewish material both in terms of new content and according to a style more reflective of the hymnic religious prose of Hellenistic culture.

This is not an obligatory text but merely a suggested model and leaves intact the president's right to improvise freely, either by praying at length and offering a solemn prayer, or by pronouncing a shorter and simpler prayer provided that it be sound and orthodox. At the same time, the author of this particular part of the *Apostolic Tradition* regards the prayer as traditional, even "apostolic," and therefore to be taken as normative. One can imagine that this eucharistic prayer must have met a generally felt need as the age of the charismatics was ending.

4. Sixth-century triumphal arch mosaic in the Basilica of Saint Lawrence Outside the Walls, depicting a majestic Christ positioned between Saint Peter and Saint Paul; on the left, a bishop (Pope Pelagius II) and a deacon (Saint Lawrence), and on the right, another deacon (Saint Stephen) and the church elder Hippolytus form a circle around them.

and perhaps also a physician. The locale of its composition is generally regarded as northern Syria, perhaps near Antioch. Treating various members of the church (bishops, deacons, deaconesses, etc.) and several liturgical practices (baptism, penance, fasting), indeed, the *Didascalia* describes a well-developed penitential system but one with few signs of the rigorism characteristic of many Western churches of the time. It not only speaks of the role of the bishop and the community in the conversion and reconciliation of the penitent, but also indicates that the catechumenate was the model followed for the organization of the reconciliation rites. The descriptions of the phases of penance and the bishop's responsibilities emphasize the public nature of the ritual and the gathered community's intercessory role. Particular emphasis is also given to the healing aspect of the penitential system.

The text also offers us the earliest description of the Easter celebration—a precious witness to how the Pasch was celebrated liturgically. The text is not theological but rather practical and lacks good organization. Nonetheless, it is valuable particularly in what it offers on the ordering of the liturgical assembly and on the subject of liturgical hospitality. It stresses the importance of the bishop presiding at the Sunday Eucharist in his district, and his need to extend hospitality to visiting bishops by inviting his guests to share in the Eucharistic Prayer.

This theme of hospitality extends to the liturgical assembly itself. Members of the assembly should make room for one another. The young, for example, should give up their seats to the elderly if need be. Deacons should welcome church members at the doors and show them to their places especially if they arrive late. The bishop is to be the model of hospitality *par excellence*, especially to guests, foreigners, the elderly, widows, orphans, and the ill. Moreover, the bishop-president is to give the poor a special welcome. When a poor person arrives late for the Sunday Eucharist, the bishop is the one who should rise and greet the latecomer, not the deacon. In showing that person to his or her place if, by chance, no places remain within the assembly, then the bishop is to give the poor visitor his seat and then sit himself on the floor!

Several other interesting bits of information regarding this document are worth mentioning. The fifth and sixth chapters speak of the eventual offering of oil, cheese, and olives, which seem to have their place within the eucharistic celebration itself although it is not clear the exact usage or intent. Chapters 37 and 38 bear testimony to the practice of the faithful bringing home a small piece of the consecrated bread and taking a little each day as directed by the bishop—before eating any other food. Obviously, the concept of daily Eucharist had not yet become normative in the Western church, but this reference would seem to suggest a certain desire on the part of the faithful to be nourished by the Eucharist at various moments throughout the week apart from the regular Sunday celebration.

The *Didascalia Apostolorum*

The *Didascalia Apostolorum* or, according to its Syriac translation, the *Catholic Teaching of the Twelve Apostles and Holy Disciples of Our Redeemer*, was originally written in Greek; only fragments in that language survive. The full text is available in a Syriac translation which was perhaps redacted in the fourth century. About two-fifths of the work exist in Latin and are contained in a late fourth- or early fifth-century collection found at Verona. The document also exists in Arabic, Ethiopic, and Coptic translations.

The *Didascalia* most probably dates from the third century and is the work of an unknown author—certainly a bishop

7. DAILY PRAYER IN THE EARLY CHURCH

1. View of landscape and of excavated caves in Qumran, Palestine, where an Essene community settled at the beginning of the middle of the second century AD.

The New Testament offers numerous commands to "pray always" (1 Thess 5:17), to sing "psalms, hymns, and spiritual songs to God" (Col 3:17), etc. The *Didache* (chapter 8) states that Christians are to pray the Lord's Prayer three times each day but fails to indicate the precise times for that prayer. In the third century, Clement of Alexandria notes that it was already common for Christians to pray at the third, sixth, and ninth hours. He also mentions prayer at rising; before going to sleep; and before, during, and after meals. Clement also offers the first patristic witness of the eschatological nature of night prayer. Origen spoke of prayer in the morning, noon, evening, and night. In North Africa, Tertullian attests to an obligatory prayer at the beginning and end of each day with prayer also recommended at the third, sixth, and ninth hours and at night. Christians, moreover, should pray before meals, when they go to the baths, when they are with guests, indeed, during their various activities throughout the day. Cyprian of Carthage indicates a strong emphasis on the themes of light and darkness in the celebration of morning and evening prayer.

As already mentioned, *The Apostolic Tradition* offers a good deal of information on the patterns of daily prayer citing its importance: at rising and then at the third, sixth, and ninth hours; at the evening agape; before retiring; at about midnight; and at cockcrow. There is an interesting reference to night prayer for a couple in a mixed marriage whose wife is not yet baptized. If that is the case, then the believer is to rise from his bed and go into a separate room to prayer. Upon completing the prayer, he may then return to his matrimonial bed.

While these various examples give clear indication of daily prayer in the early church, they also make it abundantly clear that we can discern no fixed pattern as normative in this early period. While it is clear that the Christian concept of daily prayer was borrowed from the Jewish tradition we must be careful not to draw too close of a connection as we find a similar variance of style and practice within Judaism, as well. For example, at Qumran there was one pattern of daily prayer linked to Temple sacrifice—later in the morning and again at the ninth hour in the afternoon—

2. *Words of the Luminaries, fragment of the manuscript found at Qumran that contains a collection of hymns, one for each day of the week, starting with Sunday.*

3. *The Book of Psalms, Dead Sea Scrolls, Qumran.*

4. *Phylacteries found at Qumran. Phylacteries are small black leather boxes containing pieces of parchment on which are passages from the Law. Jews still wear them on their arms or foreheads during morning prayers.*

5. *The Temple of Jerusalem, with its sacrificial altar and offering table, detail of mosaic in the Theotokos Chapel in the Moses Memorial on Mount Nebo, first decade of the eighth century.*

and another pattern of prayer linked to the rising and setting of the sun. These two patterns of Jewish prayer appear to have been blended together into the rabbinic tradition of praying three times each day. This reality offers a helpful corrective to the more simplistic understanding of morning and evening prayer in the early church as in direct continuity with the synagogue tradition and the additional prayers at the third, sixth, and ninth hours as minor prayers intended mostly for private usage. All of this is to suggest that once again, there are more questions than answers here, and the most we can affirm is the fact that Jews and Christians had a tradition of praying at fixed times although the fixed pattern differed from place to place. Thus, while the liturgical reforms of the Second Vatican Council are correct in stating that Morning and Evening Prayer are the "two hinges on which the daily office turns" as we reflect upon our own day, we must not move too quickly to affirm that this was always the case. It certainly

was the practice in certain places, but we can find equally valid examples of communal prayer at the third, sixth, and ninth hours, which functioned not as two but as three hinges that offered a spiritual focus to the day.

This same diversity of practice came to be reflected in the diverse forms of prayer as exhibited in the cathedral, monastic, and urban-monastic offices as they evolved in both East and West especially in the fourth century. What was consistent in these fixed times of prayer was the desire to search out God's will in the various moments of the day and that the prayer itself was offered as a "spiritual sacrifice" or a "sacrifice of praise and thanksgiving." We have precious little information on the content of the first three centuries although one would presume that the use of psalms, hymns, and readings would have been standard fare. It also should be noted that Christians in the early church made little distinction between liturgical or private prayer; much depended on the place, the time, the context etc. Thus the rubric to pray facing the East, with arms outstretched, or kneeling, was employed whether one prayed privately at home or in the wider liturgical assembly. During times of persecution or days of work, this often meant that one prayed alone. In our own day we are accustomed to thinking of the "Liturgy of the Hours" as a pattern of daily prayer normally reserved to monastic and other religious communities and clergy, even as the laity are strongly encouraged to participate. What is quite evident in the early church, however, is the fact that daily prayer began as a lay movement that was gradually

6. *Woman at Prayer, called the "Veiled Lady," Velatio cubiculum, Catacomb of Priscilla, Rome.*

7. *Person at prayer, fresco in the Christian chapel located in the area of the Hospital of Saint John complex, Rome, fifth century.*

8. *People at prayer, box from Samagher, near Pola, fifth century. Museo Archeologico, Venice. The scene is inserted into a background that preserves the memory of the presbyteral order of worship in the Vatican basilica.*

9

10

9. *Figures of people at prayer. Coptic Art Museum. Old Cairo.*

10. *Two praying saints, detail of Saqqara fresco from the seventh and eighth century, the subjects of which are presumed to be Saint Apollo and Saint Fib.*

monasticized and only clericalized much later in the Middle Ages.

It is probable that the ancient evening hymn *Phôs hilaron* ("O Gladsome Light"), which was commonly used in the *lucenarium* of the fourth-century cathedral office, was already employed in the Evening Prayer of earlier centuries at least in certain places. Similarly, the classic Vespers Psalm 140/141, "Let my prayer rise before you as incense, O God, the lifting up of my hands as an evening sacrifice," which was constitutive of Evening Prayer in the Cathedral Office, might well have been used in earlier centuries given its thematic link to that particular hour. It is also probable that the *Laudate* psalms (147–150) became a standard element in Morning Prayer so much so that the term "Lauds" took its name from those psalms.

It was the great German liturgical scholar Anton Baumstark, who in 1948 uncovered the rich distinction between the "cathedral" and "monastic" offices of the fourth century. Baumstark stresses the term *cathedral* rather than *parochial* since the bishop's church was the center of the local church's liturgical life and the bishop was normally present for these offices. The cathedral office was popular in style with use of symbol and ceremony—incense, light (e.g., the *Lucenarium*) processions. The fourth-century Spanish pilgrim from Galicia, Egeria, provides a detailed account of such symbol and ceremony inherent within the cathedral office as she records what she observed in Jerusalem during her three-year sojourn there toward the end of the fourth century.

41

11. *Map of sites.*

12. *Exterior of a Cappadocian monastic church, with openings to cells along its rock walls.*

The cathedral office employed the responsorial mode of chanting psalms and hymns to allow for greater participation on a popular level; the assembly would simply repeat the antiphon or response that was first chanted by the cantor or choir. Moreover, psalms were usually chosen for thematic reasons (Psalm 62/63 for the morning and Psalm 140/141 for the evening) rather than sung continuously or in order, as was the case in the monastic tradition. The repetition of this limited number of psalms allowed for greater familiarity with both the text and tone of the chant. There was also a diversity of ministries present: the bishop, presbyters and deacons; readers; choir—all in proper liturgical vesture. These were offices of praise and intercession, not a Liturgy of the Word. In fact, there was normally no reading of Scripture in the cathedral office except in Egypt and Cappadocia.

In the early fourth century, the bishop and church historian Eusebius of Caesarea in Palestine was the first to give testimony to the cathedral office. He spoke of morning and evening prayer celebrated in the cathedral tradition, of the hymns and praises that are "truly divine delights," and emphasizes Psalm 140/141 as *the* classic psalm of Evening Prayer. In Egypt, the first testimony of the cathedral office comes from Athanasius of Alexandria who speaks of the night Vigil of the cathedral that is frequented by both monks and laity, and composed of readings, responsorial psalms, and prayers. A bit later, John Cassian, who was in Egypt from 380 to 390 CE, mentioned in his conferences that the abbot should exhort his monks to attend Morning Prayer in the cathedral.

In Cappadocia, testimony of the cathedral office came from one family: Basil the Great, Bishop of Caesarea in Cappadocia; his sister Saint Macrina, his brothers Gregory of Nyssa and Peter of Sebaste who was also a bishop; his mother and grandmother. They state that Evening Prayer began with the lighting of the lamps with the chanting of the *Phôs hilaron*; Psalm 140/141; readings followed by a homily; and Intercessions. John Chrysostom also attests to the chanting of Psalm 140/141 daily along with Psalm 62/63 as the classic psalm of Morning Prayer. Basil speaks of Vespers as dealing with God's forgiveness for whatever sins had been committed throughout the day.

While the East was largely known for the cathedral office, there was also the fourth-century Egyptian monastic office, which contained two daily offices: not Morning and Evening Prayer but rather one in the middle of the night at cockcrow and a second office in the early evening. From Monday to Friday monks prayed these offices privately in their cells or with whomever happened to be visiting them while on Saturday and Sunday the offices were prayed together in church. The core of these offices contained twelve psalms

with private prayer, prostration, and a collect prayer after each psalm. There was also the hybrid urban-monastic office that combined the simplicity of the cathedral office with the texts of the monastic office. There were diverse expressions of this form in Palestine, Antioch, and Cappadocia.

14

13. *Holy monk on a fresco in the Saint Mercurius Church, Old Cairo.*

14. *Saint Benedict positioned between Saint Sebastian and Saint Zosimus, eleventh-century fresco, San Sebastianello, Rome.*

of its existence in Rome, for example. We have significantly greater information on the growth of the monastic office beginning with the North African *Ordo monasterii* from the year 395 CE in Tagaste that was later incorporated into the Rule of Saint Augustine. In that office Psalms 62, 5, and 89 were commonly used for Lauds.

In the middle of the sixth century, "The Rule of the Master" (530–560 CE) provided the foundation for the Rule of Benedict, and offers much information on the Liturgy of the Hours. The oldest monastic foundation in Rome was the fifth-century Monastery of San Sebastiano on the old Appian Way, and the Old Roman Office that grew out of that monastery also influenced Benedict. Here we can see some cathedral influence in the development of Morning Prayer and that influence within Evening Prayer is virtually nonexistent.

13

In the West, the situation was somewhat different. While Ambrose does speak of the presence of the cathedral office in Milan citing the standard use of Psalm 140/141 at Evening Prayer, this office does not appear to have been as widespread as it was in the East. We have no information

8. THE LEGALIZATION OF CHRISTIANITY AND PUBLIC WORSHIP

Constantine the Great has gone down in history as the liberator of the Christian Church from the oppression of the preceding centuries, when the Christians were without any legal rights. After Constantine's victory over his rival Maxentius at the Battle of the Milvian Bridge (312 CE)—at which, legend has it, his army displayed a Christian motif on its shields—and the misnamed "Edict of Milan" (313 CE), all this changed. The edict, issuing from Licinius, Master of the East, and from Constantine, Master of the West, was framed in specially friendly terms granting Christians complete and entire freedom of worship and the immediate restitution of all confiscated goods.

Constantine continued to show active sympathy toward Christianity throughout the rest of his reign. He favored the clergy of the "Very Holy Catholic Church" with tax exemptions and the privileges previously enjoyed by members of pagan priesthoods. Gradually, the clergy acquired titles and insignia that state dignitaries once enjoyed. Pagan representations on the coinage were replaced with Christian symbols, a ready instrument of propaganda. Church leaders were assigned to pass judgment even in purely civil cases and their decisions were recognized as valid. Indeed, in the year 318 Constantine conferred on bishops civil jurisdiction over court litigations that involved Christians. Churches were granted the right to succeed to property, a measure that allowed them to increase their heritage; Christian slaves were freed by force of law. Christians for the first time rose to the highest civil posts. Constantine also passed legislation ordering "all the judges, the populations of the cities and all

1. Coin depicting Emperor Valentinian II (371–392), Aquileia. The emperor, with halo, holds in his left hand the labarum that has Christ's monogram on it.

2. Plan and elevation of the Holy Sepulchre complex, from the first Constantinian age, fourth century: on the left is the Anastasis Rotunda, with Christ's Tomb; on the right is the basilica used for liturgical worship, connected to a courtyard portico.

1

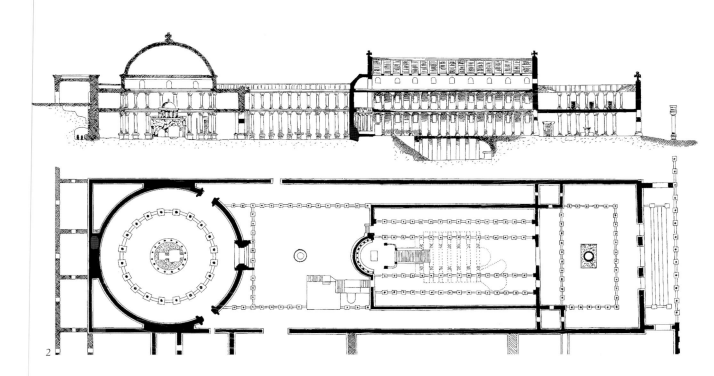

2

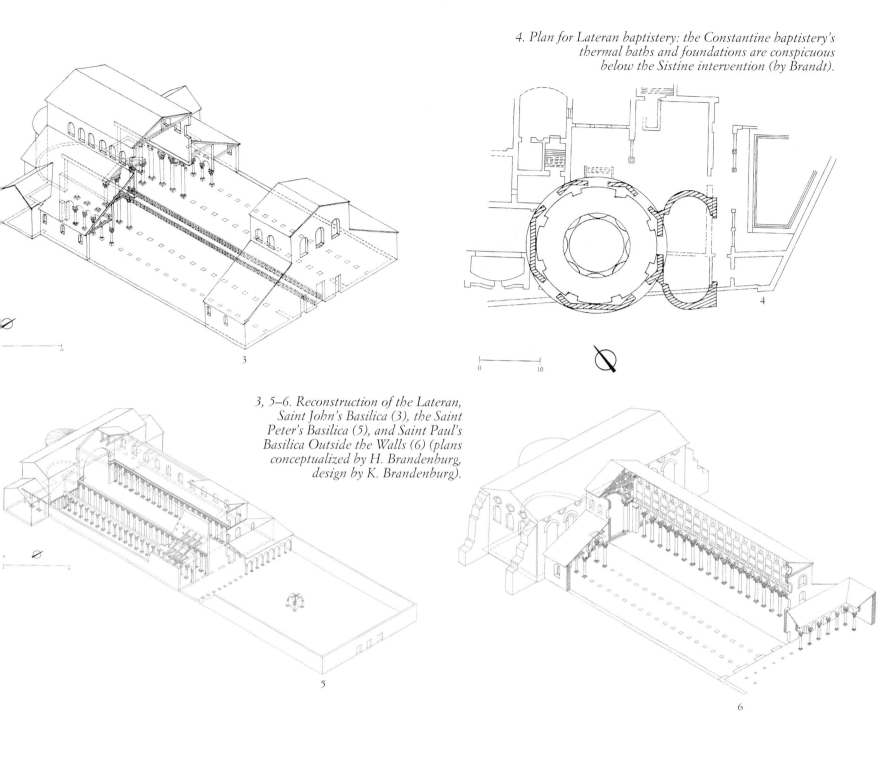

4. *Plan for Lateran baptistery: the Constantine baptistery's thermal baths and foundations are conspicuous below the Sistine intervention (by Brandt).*

3, 5–6. *Reconstruction of the Lateran, Saint John's Basilica (3), the Saint Peter's Basilica (5), and Saint Paul's Basilica Outside the Walls (6) (plans conceptualized by H. Brandenburg, design by K. Brandenburg).*

the trade associations [to] cease work on the venerable day of the sun. Nevertheless, that farmers devote themselves freely and without any hindrance to the cultivation of the fields . . . " Sunday thus came to be recognized as a public holiday. Gradually, successive laws and restrictive measures against pagan practices appeared, forbidding sacrifices to idols, magic, and the consultation of diviners.

Be that as it may, Constantine was also limited in the ways he could serve the church. In fact, the Roman Forum remained pagan territory even after the Peace of Constantine. The *Via Sacra* was erected between the years 337 and 341 with a series of pagan statues among which can be found some old deities. Similar developments were also found at Ostia Antica. Paganism was only definitively suppressed in Rome with the Christian Emperor Theodosius in the year

395. Then, the last members of the great families who had not yet become Christian were forced to do so even if they remained crypto-pagans. While Constantine couldn't abolish pagan cults, he could extend greater privileges to the bishops and clergy; while he could not destroy pagan buildings, he could build impressive ones for Christian worship. Some of these buildings were privately financed while others, like the Basilica of Golgotha in Jerusalem, were erected at public expense. Constantine's interest in this project was evidenced by his request that a progress report on the construction was to be made to him personally.

Thus, places of worship multiplied and it was in this period when the basilican architectural style already discussed came into common use for worship. The generosity of the Emperor and his family (the Empress Mother Helena and

45

7

7. *Basilica of Saint Stephen in the Round, Rome, panoramic view of interior. On the first floor to the left is a marble bench from the First Imperial Age, which was used later as a bishop's seat.*

8. *Basilica of Saint John Lateran.*
2 *Jerusalem's Holy Cross Church.*
3 *The Lateran—Saint John's Church.*
8 *The Vatican's Saint Peter's Church.*
10 *Lucina's Saint Peter's Church.*
16 *Saint Clement's Church.*
17 *Santi Quattro Coronati Church.*
20 *San Sisto Vecchio Church.*
22 *Sanata Balbina Church.*
25 *San Crisogono Church.*
26 *Damascus' Saint Lawrence Church.*
30 *Saint Pudenziana Church.*
35 *Saint Mark's Church.*
39 *Saint Anastasia's Church.*

9. *Reconstruction of the Saint Agnes Outside the Walls Basilica, with women's gallery, seventh century (plan conceptualized by H. Brandenburg, design by M. Bordicchia).*

10. *Structural reconstruction of the altar and apsidal podium at Basilica of Saint Peter in the Vatican, about the year 600 (by Ward-Perkins, Toynbee).*

8

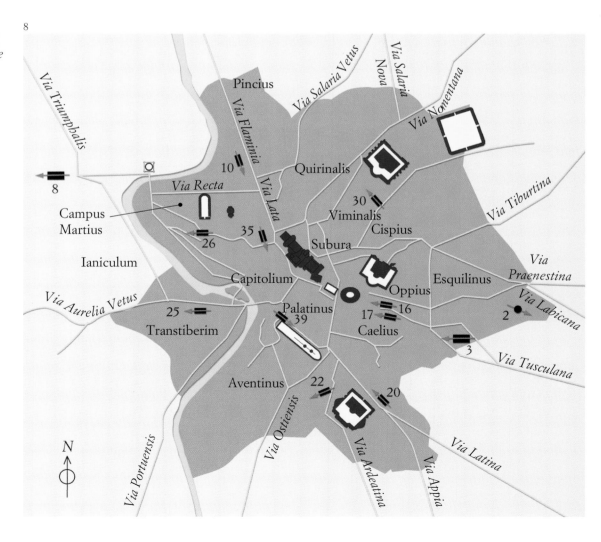

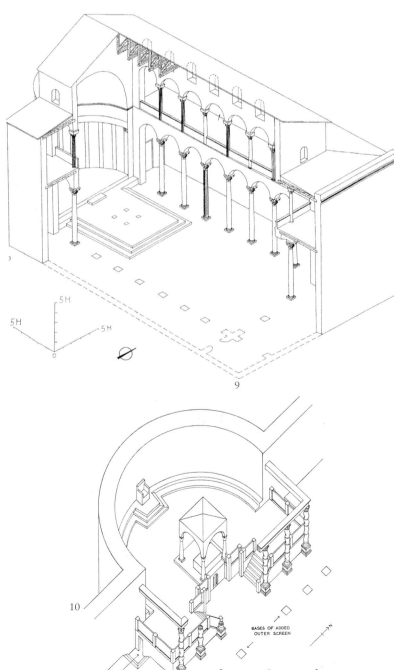

11. Saint Agnes Outside the Walls, view of interior, toward the eastern side of the basilica, with the women's gallery, built by Pope Honorius I (625–638).

Constantine's sisters—all Christians—permitted the construction and adornment of magnificent buildings. At Rome, those buildings included the Basilica of the Lateran where the adjoining palace, later the residence of the Pope, seems to have been placed at his disposal as early as 314; the Basilicas of San Pietro on the Vatican Hill; San Paolo on the road to Ostia; and of the Apostles (today San Sebastiano) on the Appian Way. Edifices for worship and shrines at sites traditionally associated with the life of Christ began to be constructed in the Holy Land, thus making Jerusalem in particular both a center of pilgrimage and a tribute to the new imperial order. Constantine enhanced Jerusalem with a magnificent group of buildings centered on the supposed sites of Calvary and the Holy Sepulcher. The new imperial capital, Constantinople (officially founded and dedicated in 330 CE), could also boast several Christian churches including the "Great Church" (later rebuilt as "Holy Wisdom" or *Hagia Sophia*), the basilica known as *Hagia Eirene* ("Holy Peace"), and the Church of the Holy Apostles under whose golden dome, Eusebius claims, were placed twelve coffins for the apostles with Constantine's own in the center. It was in this church that Eusebius describes the funeral and burial of Constantine.

The history of Christianity had now entered an entirely new phase, for the church had at last found a certain amount of peace in which to live and prosper. All the barriers, legal and material, which formerly prevented the spread of the Gospel, had been lifted; it could now make free and steadily more effective progress. In all parts of the Empire conversions multiplied as Christianity reached the masses and circles formerly hostile to it. Everywhere new episcopal sees were founded with the bishop's portrait hanging in public places where there was once a portrait of the Emperor or another government official. There was also intense theological activity and, of course, the church's liturgical life developed as well.

However, this period was not entirely favorable to Christianity; rarely did the Christian communities live in genuine lasting peace for two reasons. Firstly, there was an unending series of schisms and heresies (e.g., Arianism, Docetism, Apollinarianism, Nestorianism, Monophysitism). In the fourth century, the problem of the Unity and Trinity of God was confronted and resulted in the elaboration of the church's trinitarian doctrine with the solemn proclamation against the Arians of the equality of the Son with the Father, and consequently of his divinity at the Council of Nicea (325 CE). The First Council of Constantinople (381 CE) sought, among other things, to profess faith in the equality of honor and glory of the Holy Spirit with the Father and the Son. Nevertheless, the question remained: "Who is Jesus Christ?" The church in the fifth century and then in part also in the sixth sought to probe this question more deeply, involving itself in a series of christological debates which centered on issues such as the divinity of the Word, the complete and integral humanity of Jesus, and the relationship between the human and divine natures of Christ.

Secondly, the peace of the West was also damaged when it was ravaged by successive barbarian invasions of tribesmen seeking land and fleeing from the Huns in the steppes of central Asia (e.g., Goths, Visigoths, and Vandals). Those invasions decimated populations and eliminated their structures—political, cultural, and religious—almost completely annihilating the effects of the first evangelization. Christian communities very painfully felt this ruin and perceived the capture and sack of Rome in 410 by the Vandal leader Alaric as an outrage. Pagans blamed Christians, reproaching them for having banished the gods—protectors of the city—and for having abandoned their worship. Indeed, the population of Rome was only 800,000 at the time of Constantine while it had reached a million or even a million and a half at other times. In addition to the barbarian invasions, the fifth century also saw the arrival of malaria, cholera, and the bubonic plague. By the year 452 CE Rome's population fell to 500,000 and then again to only 100,000 in the year 500. After the invasion by the Goths, the population fell to 30,000 or perhaps even less. Despite those impediments, however, the church survived and its growth continued.

The changes which had taken place as a result of the Edict of Milan and Constantine's sympathy toward Christianity, the subsequent growth of patristic preaching and theology, and the insertion of the church in the cultural and sociopolitical streams of ancient civilization all had a profound influence on the development and future shape of the liturgy.

12

13

16

14

15

12. *Figure of person at prayer, detail of the back of Publius Caesilius Victorinus' sarcophagus, end of the third century. Vatican's Saint Rosa Necropolis.*

13. *Praying female figure, mosaic from the end of the sixth century. Federico Zeri Collection, Rome.*

14. *The Schola Juvenum, reused as a basilica for the Christian community in Maktar, Tunisia.*

15. *Altar in the Saint Marcel of Crussol Church in France, fourth century. On the table (at the top of the picture), two groups of doves converge toward a monogram of Christ; on the short side (at the bottom), two groups of birds are headed in the direction of a crown. National Archeological Museum. Saint-Germain-en-Laye.*

16. *Christ, as the new Orpheus and Good Shepherd, on the Aquileia baptistery's floor mosaic.*

From an intimate household liturgical celebration in the *domus ecclesiae* Christian worship evolved into something both solemn and regal in the splendor of the Constantinian basilicas. The bishop now sat in the throne at the center of the apse surrounded by his presbyters, which in a different context would have been the throne reserved for the Emperor. Not only the Roman Rite but also the Oriental Rites began to flourish, and had attained their specific forms by the seventh century.

Creativity and adaptation characterize this period. The church employed two methods of adaptation. One was substitution, the other, assimilation. Substitution was carried out by replacing pagan cultic elements with Christian ones in such a way that these practically abolished the pagan elements. By the method of assimilation, the church adopted elements of pagan rituals and gestures as we saw earlier, into which she could infuse a Christian meaning. Nevertheless, the Scriptures remained the principal source of inspiration for catechetical instruction and the composition of liturgical texts. The history of salvation was the context for the eucharistic prayers of this period: praise of God for the work of creation and for the promise of salvation and its realization in Christ. Attachment to traditional forms, however, was easily discernible, notwithstanding the frenzy of original creations and adaptations.

9. LITURGY IN FOURTH-CENTURY JERUSALEM

1. Saint Matthew the Evangelist and Saint John Crisostomo, the latter's homily manuscript. Saint Catherine of Sinai Monastery, Egypt.

2. The Christian East during Egeria's times.

1

2

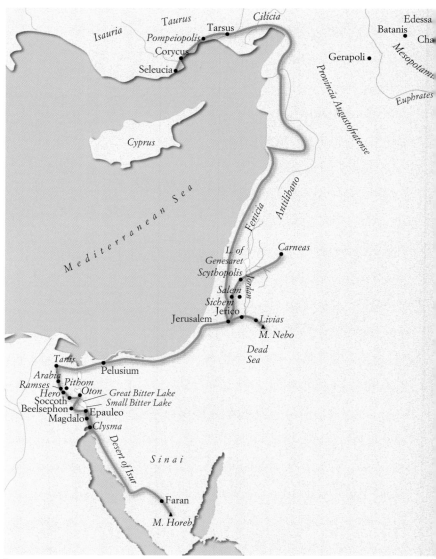

3

The Holy City of Jerusalem gained a new prominence in the time of Constantine and became an important center of pilgrimage. Gradually the liturgy of Jerusalem came to influence liturgical developments in the fourth and fifth centuries both in East and West. Indeed, the outstanding characteristics of the liturgy of Jerusalem became models for Christian worship: the structure and organization of the daily hours of prayer; the celebrations of festivals throughout the church year; and the Rites of Christian Initiation—Baptism, Confirmation, and Eucharist.

The baptismal homilies of Cyril of Jerusalem, Ambrose of Milan, John Chrysostom, and Theodore of Mopsuestia give us some insight into the local liturgies of the churches where they served since they often commented on those liturgical rites and texts in their homilies. Cyril of Jerusalem's catechetical homilies from the middle of the fourth century are

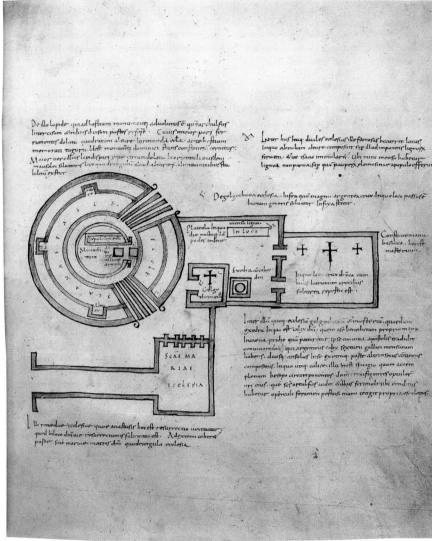

4

3. Egeria's Holy Land travel route.

4. Façade of the Holy Sepulchre Basilica, Jerusalem.

5. Calvary Chapel, Holy Sepulchre Basilica, Jerusalem.

*6. Plan for the Holy Sepulchre, designed by Arculfo in 680.
Badische Landesbibliothek, Karlsruhe.*

5

6

especially important because of the influence of the Jerusalem liturgies on those of other churches in this period and in the subsequent century. Bishops like Cyril took advantage of the large number of pilgrims who began visiting Jerusalem in this period, offering them liturgical models especially on feast days, which the pilgrims then brought home, attempting to imitate them.

One such pilgrim was the already mentioned Egeria, who visited Jerusalem perhaps from the years 381 to 384 and wrote a travel diary for her sisters back home in which she records with an extraordinary amount of detail the liturgical practice and customs that she witnessed there. Egeria begins with a description of the liturgies that were celebrated daily followed by Sundays, and then the great feasts of the church year that were celebrated annually. Egeria recounts an eight-week Lent observed in Jerusalem, but of particular

7. Plan for the Holy Sepulchre Basilica, with the liturgical routes for Monday, Wednesday, Friday, and Saturday of Holy Week. A: Anastasis; B: Holy Sepulchre aedicule; C: Holy Sepulchre Rotunda; D: atrium with three porticoes; E: Golgotha; F: Martyrium; G: east atrium; H: baptistery area (by Coro, 1980, redesigned by Kruger, 2000).

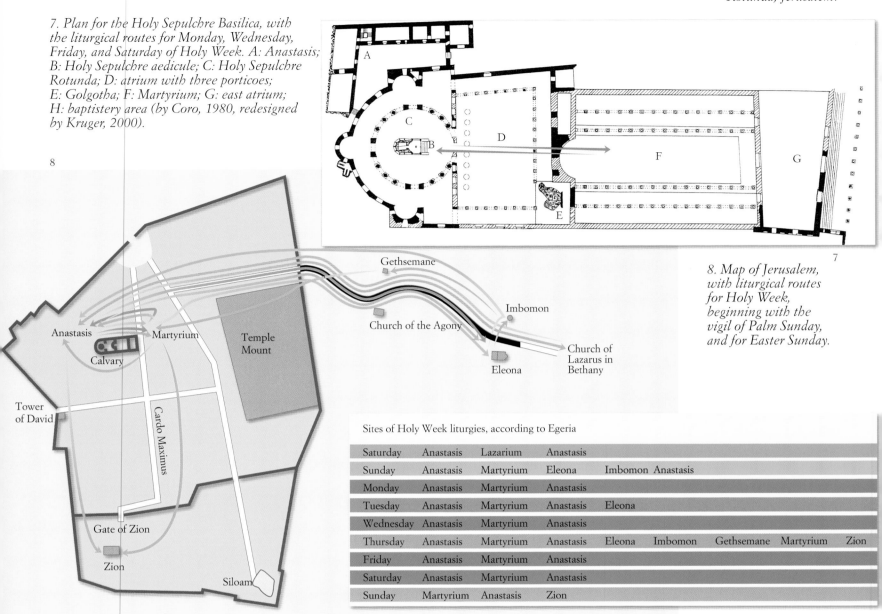

8. Map of Jerusalem, with liturgical routes for Holy Week, beginning with the vigil of Palm Sunday, and for Easter Sunday.

Sites of Holy Week liturgies, according to Egeria

Saturday	Anastasis	Lazarium	Anastasis					
Sunday	Anastasis	Martyrium	Eleona	Imbomon	Anastasis			
Monday	Anastasis	Martyrium	Anastasis					
Tuesday	Anastasis	Martyrium	Anastasis	Eleona				
Wednesday	Anastasis	Martyrium	Anastasis					
Thursday	Anastasis	Martyrium	Anastasis	Eleona	Imbomon	Gethsemane	Martyrium	Zion
Friday	Anastasis	Martyrium	Anastasis					
Saturday	Anastasis	Martyrium	Anastasis					
Sunday	Martyrium	Anastasis	Zion					

interest is her account of Holy Week, which she calls "Great Week." Here she offers precious information on the rites of Christian Initiation as they were carried out there. Her record is consistent with what we read in Cyril's baptismal catecheses. We find a similar agreement in their similar descriptions of the arrangement of the liturgical year, the buildings used on various days for various rites, and the readings that were proclaimed during such liturgies.

Indeed, Egeria's attention to detail is so extraordinary that one could almost reconstruct the plan of the Basilica of the Holy Sepulchre from her many references to how the liturgy was celebrated there. Moving from West to East one encounters the Anastasis—sanctuary of the Resurrection—a church in the round with the grotto of the Holy Sepulchre found at the center. The cathedral office was celebrated there daily. Then there was the atrium of the Holy Cross—an inner courtyard enclosed on three sides by porticos and on the east side by the Martyrium—the principal church of the complex where the Eucharist was normally celebrated on Sundays with crowds as large as those at Easter, prior to

a second Eucharist celebrated later in the day in the Anastasis. On the southwest corner of the courtyard was the Ante Crucem where there was a cross on the supposed site of the crucifixion. Nearby was the stational church called the Ad Crucem for certain rites during the liturgical year and for the daily rite of dismissal at the conclusion of the evening office. Behind the cross was the Post-Crucem Chapel where the Eucharist was celebrated on Maundy Thursday and the wood of the cross venerated on Good Friday.

Of particular interest is her description of one cathedral office—a special vigil of the resurrection which takes place on Sunday mornings at cockcrow in the Basilica of the Holy Sepulchre. After the bishop enters and goes into the cave of the Anastasis, the doors are all opened and the liturgical assembly enters as well. Once inside, one of the presbyters chants a psalm with a response by the whole assembly. This is followed by another psalm and prayer chanted by the deacon, then a third psalm by another member of the clergy. The bishop then takes the Book of the Gospels and stands at the doors of the Anastasis where

10. Aerial view of central Jerusalem, which takes in the Holy Sepulchre Basilica.

11. Lazarus' Resurrection, detail of the Holy Sepulchre's façade's right portal architrave. Rockefeller Museum, Jerusalem.

12. Octagonal shrine built by the crusaders in Jerusalem on the site known as Imbomon, also known as the Small Church of the Ascension.

13. Ruins of the Jerusalem basilica known by the name "Eleona" (olive grove). In the background is the modern Pater Noster Basilica.

10

12

11

he reads an account of the Lord's resurrection. As he begins reading, the text members of the assembly groan and lament aloud "at all that the Lord underwent for us." Having concluded the Gospel, the bishop then comes out "and is taken with singing to the Cross." The assembly goes with him where one final psalm is chanted with a prayer. He then blesses the people and dismisses them. As he leaves, everyone comes forward to kiss his hand.

Regarding Egeria's descriptions of eucharistic celebrations, the basic liturgical shape was clearly in evidence. What we can observe, however, is increased use of movement—processions at various moments in the liturgy—and the chanting of responsorial psalmody and litanies to accompany those movements. Whether one is considering the entrance procession of the bishop and clergy, the Gospel procession, or procession with the gifts, not to mention the procession at the moment of communion, one can imagine the large number of people present within those churches and the obvious pastoral desire to cover those movements with music. This responsorial style of singing allowed members of

13

the assembly to easily remember the antiphon that they would repeat numerous times during the procession.

Six churches played the most significant role in the liturgy according to Egeria's account: the Basilica of the Holy Sepulchre and the Church of Sion, both within the city walls; the two churches on the Mount of Olives: the Imbonon and the Eleona; the Basilica of the Nativity in Bethlehem; and the Church of the Lazarus or Lazarium in Bethany. Egeria never mentions the Basilica of the Nativity by name, but refers to services held in the Bethlehem church "where the grotto in which the Lord was born is located." The Lazarium served as a stational church particularly for the solemn liturgy of the Saturday before Palm Sunday called "Lazarus Saturday."

Apart from the specific information, which Egeria offers on the enactment of both eucharistic and non-eucharistic liturgical rites and how the various churches were used to facilitate processions and engage the assembly, her testimony outlines several basic principles that characterize the church's liturgical life in fourth-century Jerusalem. While maintaining a hierarchical style, the liturgy was very much communal. Clearly, the bishop plays a prominent role and is treated with great respect as he enters the worship space with the presbyters and deacons. However, those ministers also remained in the midst of the assembly with their own role of responding to the various litanies as they were chanted.

Egeria's account also bears witness to the growth of a monastic presence within the city and no longer just living as hermits in the countryside. She mentions both male and female monks who are present at the various liturgical offices gradually acquiring their own liturgical role, remaining in church after Morning Prayer for further communal prayer until the eucharistic celebration. Her description clearly reveals a liturgical continuity with what preceded it before the Peace of Constantine in terms of both the cathedral office style of worship but also the ways in which the Jerusalem Church observed the liturgical year through its celebration of its different feasts and fasts.

10. THE EVOLUTION OF THE CATECHUMENATE AND CHRISTIAN INITIATION

As we have already seen, in the *Didache* and in the *Apology* of Justin Martyr, we have early testimony of the church's desire to properly catechize those preparing to be initiated into the Christian Community. Ignatius of Antioch states that baptisms should only take place with the bishop's approval which would seem to suggest a certain, albeit primitive, process of discernment as to who would be accepted. Already in the late second and early third century we know that there was a private school of Christian education at Alexandria led by Clement and Origen. While Christian education at Alexandria appears to have been highly diversified both of these church fathers engaged in the instruction of adult catechumens. At roughly the same time the North African Tertullian of Carthage, in his treatise *On Baptism*, emphasized the three parts of the one rite of initiation: the baptism itself involving purification of water; anointing involving ordination into the priesthood of the baptized; and the imposition of hands that confers the gift of the Holy Spirit.

By the time we arrive at the *Apostolic Tradition*, it is clear that adult baptism had been combined with an extended period of instruction—longer than we would infer from the two above-mentioned texts. A closer look at the structure of the Rites of Initiation is in order. What can be discerned here is that the preparatory process toward Christian baptism appears clearly as a journey of faith with a developed liturgy involving the selection of candidates; catechesis; preparatory or initiatory rites including the first mention of a special anointing ("Confirmation"). This process of initiation culminates in the Eucharist that is celebrated throughout a Saturday night vigil until the morning of Sunday— presumably from Holy Saturday through Easter morning. This expanded period of instruction was necessary for several reasons. Firstly, with the expansion of Christianity into a pagan environment there was the desire to ensure the seriousness of conversions and to wean converts from their former ways of idolatry. Secondly, the severity in the choice of candidates can be seen as protection against spies or enemies of the church who might try to infiltrate the system under the guise of being catechumens. The fundamental question at stake was this: "Are these individuals who desire membership in the catechumenate capable of hearing the Word?" Inquiry was then made into the trades and professions of those who were brought to instruction. The catechumens were to give up any professions that were involved with idolatry (actors, idol makers, magic or sorcery, for example); killing (e.g., gladiators, military); or immorality (e.g., prostitution) Once accepted, they were to "listen to the Word" for about three years but the time period was negotiable depending on the individual case.

Once the catechumens had entered the final stage of preparation, there was a daily laying on of hands accompanied by a prayer of exorcism. On Holy Thursday, those to be baptized were to bathe and then fast on Good Friday. On Holy Saturday morning, the Bishop was to gather them all in one place for a profound prayer. They were then to kneel for another laying on of hands by the Bishop who "commanded the evil spirits to depart." He then made the sign of the cross on their ears and nose before inviting them to stand. They would then pass the entire night in vigil and prayer, accompanied by readings and instructions. Those to be baptized were to bring nothing with them "except what each person brings for the Eucharist."

The moment for Baptism arrived at cockcrow (i.e., at 3:00 AM). A blessing was said over the water and candidates were invited to remove their clothes. The men were baptized first followed by the women who were to remove all their jewels before descending into the baptismal pool. The Bishop then pronounced the prayer over the Oil of Thanksgiving and then over the Oil of Exorcism. The deacons then took the two oils and stood at the left and right of the presbyter who lead the candidates aside, turning toward the West to renounce Satan and evil whereupon they were anointed with the Oil of Exorcism. They then turned to the East to acclaim the risen Christ. The Bishop remained near the font as the deacon descended into the font with the candidate, pronouncing the triple baptism in the name of the Holy Trinity.

Coming out of the font having been clothed with the white garment, the Bishop then confirmed the newly baptized, imposed hands upon the head, pronounced the invocation, and poured the Oil of Thanksgiving over the head. He then signed the newly baptized on the forehead and offered them the Kiss of Peace. The neophytes in turn then offered the peace to the other members of the faithful.

The Eucharist then followed with the deacons presenting the offerings to the Bishop who then gave thanks for the bread; for the cup; for the mingled milk and honey; and finally for the water. The "breaking of Bread" followed and the distribution; there is no mention yet of communion. Deacons assisted with the distribution of the three cups if there were not enough presbyters present. The first cup of water was offered for purification; the second of milk and honey both to symbolize nourishment for newborn children and the "land flowing with milk and honey"; and the third cup of wine. The Trinitarian formula was used for the ministration of the three cups: "In God, the Father almighty: Amen; and in the Lord Jesus: Amen; and in the Holy Spirit and the Holy Church: Amen."

The fourth century is often called the "Golden Age of the Catechumenate" and rightly so. With the Peace of Constantine and the legalization of Christianity, the church grew significantly in membership. Christians ceased to be a minority vulnerable to persecutions but rather, began to

1. Baptismal scene from the third century. Terme Museum, Rome.

2. Detail of pictorial decoration in the Christian chapel in area of the Saint John's Hospital complex. The gesture of imposing the hand in the manner of protection is also interpreted as a gesture of holy unction.

3. Gregory Nazianzan, Homily. Biblioteca Ambrosiana, Milan.

enjoy a new privileged status. This was also the period of the great baptismal catecheses and the great mystagogues: Cyril, Bishop of Jerusalem; John Chrysostom; Theodore of Mopsuestia; and in the West, Ambrose of Milan. Such preaching and catechizing usually took place during a three-year instruction period. Catechumens had a special place reserved in church and were dismissed from the assembly before the "Prayer of the Faithful." It was for this reason that the first part of the Mass had been referred to as "The Mass of the Catechumens"—because they were present.

In Jerusalem, to judge from the eighteen catecheses given by Cyril, the teaching offered to catechumens was fairly straightforward even as it was supplemented with rich mystagogical post-baptismal teaching on the sacraments. The lectures followed the outline given by the creed and ended on Palm Sunday.

We can't presume, however, that in all the churches the catechumens were equally well taught. Gregory of Nazianzus warned wealthy converts against their ambitious plan to be baptized in Jerusalem, saying that grace depends not on places or important church leaders (e.g., the Bishop of Jerusalem) performing the baptism but rather on the Spirit of God. Nevertheless, the preparations for Baptism in

4. *Fourth-century circular baptismal pool, Tipasa, Algeria.*

5. *Spreading of Ambrosian baptistery typology to:*
A: Milan; B: Nevers; C; Fréjus, and; D: Marseilles.

4

Jerusalem were indeed elaborate. On the eve of the First Sunday of Lent, candidates for Baptism separated themselves from the rest of the catechumens and presented their names to the Bishop for inscription into this final stage of preparation. He then proceeded to question neighbors of the candidates, inquiring about their state of life and moral living; if something were found lacking then their candidacy was postponed. Each morning of Lent, from the first hour through the third, the Bishop personally gave the catechesis—an exegesis "of all the scriptures"— as well as teaching about the resurrection and the Christian faith in general.

At Alexandria, consistent with that earlier catechetical school that had been led by Clement and Origen, fourth-century catechumenal preparation tended to develop into a more sophisticated level of theological education under the leadership of Gregory of Nyssa, who was a great admirer of Origen. Thus, Gregory was as interested in addressing himself to the catechists as he was to the catechumens themselves. The teachers, he believed, needed a more systematic theology based on metaphysics and not only on the scriptures. So in his *Oratio catechetica magna* he devoted four chapters to the doctrine of the Trinity; twenty-eight chapters to the history of salvation in Christ; and four chapters to the sacraments and their relation to faith. Of course, such dense theological prose would have been lost on the catechumens but assisted greatly in the formation of the catechists.

As Gregory of Nyssa made his contribution to a more systematic theology of Christian Initiation, baptismal preachers like Theodore of Mopsuestia and Ambrose made their own significant contributions in providing accessible instruction to catechumens in their respective churches that was grounded in a rich theology. This is evident in Theodore's *Liber ad baptizandos* with ten homilies on the creed for use prior to baptism, and six mystagogical homilies on the Lord's Prayer, baptism, and Eucharist, for use in the post-baptismal Easter season. In Ambrose's *De mysteriis* we learn that during Lent the Bishop of Milan gave daily instruction on Christian morals and on the elements of Christianity.

In observing the evolution of the Catechumenate and the Rites of Christian Initiation in these early centuries of the church's life, we can note a certain degree of flexibility and modification, determined especially by the changing social conditions in the local churches. This was particularly evident in the rite called "scrutiny," which evolved in the fourth century along with baptism itself. In Rome and North Africa, for example, scrutiny was a rite involving re-

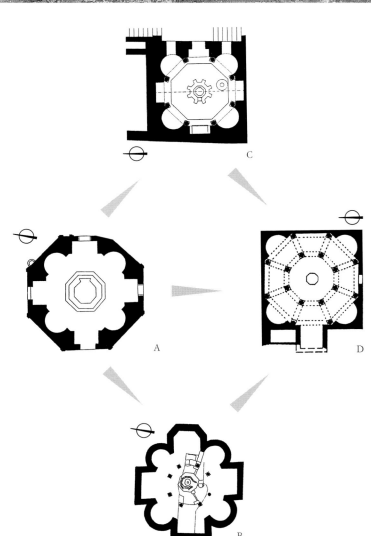

5

6. Saint Ambrose's Baptism, posterior face of the Golden Altar,
Saint Ambrose Basilica, Milan, mid-ninth century.

7. Baptism of babies, detail of the Exultet "Benevento," circa 969,
Biblioteca Casanatense, Rome.

6

7

nunciation of the devil, performed with exorcisms and intercessory prayer. At the end of the fifth century in Rome, however, John the Deacon stated that the purpose of the scrutiny was to examine the baptismal candidate with regard to scripture, salvation, and faith in God the Father. The rite was preceded by a period of instruction that clearly had its own theological significance.

Clearly, the catechumenate and the Rites of Christian Initiation played a crucial role in the formation of a new generation of Christians whose relationship to secular life and civil authority would inevitably be closer and consequently, there would be the danger of compromising with the secular world. During this period, infant children of Christian parents were enrolled in the catechumenate and could be baptized, confirmed, and given the Eucharist while still in infancy. However, baptism was the forgiveness of *all* sins without any penance, so the fear of children lapsing from the faith and not having another chance led many parents to defer baptism until their children had grown up and settled down. Sins after baptism were even worse than before. This was the case with Saint Augustine who waited until age 30 to be baptized. And his baptizer, Ambrose, was only baptized himself when he had been elected Bishop of Milan! John Chrysostom waited until he was 25; Basil of Caesarea until he was 26 years old; and Gregory of Nazianzus until he was 28. It wasn't until Augustine stressed the doctrine of original sin and the danger of children dying unbaptized that the situation began to change.

With the subsequent flood of infant baptisms in the fifth century, the adult catechumenate waned, as it no longer served a need: the majority of adults had all been baptized as infants. Moreover, as presbyters in the West came to be delegated with the ministration of baptism, since it was no longer physically possible for the Bishop to baptize the large number of those desiring the sacrament, he retained the sacrament of Confirmation for himself to complete the process of initiation and maintain some participatory role within it. Gradually, Confirmation was further and further removed from Baptism as it was delayed until the bishop was able to be present to confer it and the ancient structure of Baptism and Confirmation culminating in the Eucharist was lost. Only in the Christian East was that classic structure retained. Even today, infants in the Christian East receive all the Sacraments of Christian Initiation at the same time. In the West, as Confirmation now stands alone (with the exception of adults who are initiated at the Great Vigil of Easter), it has largely lost its theological import and is explained as a sacrament of Christian maturity and mission—a sort of rite of passage into Christian adulthood.

11. ORIGINS OF THE LITURGICAL YEAR

Regardless of religious tradition, most cultures in the ancient world celebrated spring festivals that focused on the tilling of the fields and the departure of flocks for their pastures, and autumn harvest festivals to celebrate the return of the flocks and reaping of the fruits that had been garnered. Indeed, from the beginning, human life has always attended to the cosmic dimension in one way or another—the way in which time was calculated; seasons were celebrated around summer and winter solstices and the spring and autumn equinoxes; and feasts were kept. The alternation of light and darkness, heat and cold, related to the play between sun and moon all figured into this equation. Twentieth-century anthropologists like Victor Turner, Mary Turner, and others, made us aware of the special role played by "rites of passage" in these ancient civilizations. At key moments in the life cycle—birth, puberty, marriage, and death—festal rituals marked those turning points—and those feasts were celebrated in public and kept by entire tribes and communities. Other rituals marking historical events; natural catastrophes; victories and defeats; birthdays; elections; and coronations, further led to the establishment of feasts and commemorations whether celebrated locally, nationally, or universally. Any discussion of the Christian liturgical year needs to be seen in this wider anthropological context.

The seven-day Christian week was inherited from Judaism, but the Jewish tradition of keeping the Sabbath on the seventh day of the week soon gave way to the choice of Sunday—the day of resurrection—as the preferred day on which Christians would gather for the celebration of corporate worship. As can be observed in the ancient Syrian manuscript, the *Didache*, dating to the late first or early second century, it was standard practice in the early church to maintain particular traditions inherited from Judaism but also to adapt the tradition so that it was distinctively Christian. For example, Christians continued the Jewish practice of fasting but chose to do so on different days: on Wednesdays and Fridays as opposed to the Jewish fast days of Monday and Thursday. In the West, Wednesday tended to decline in importance in later centuries leaving only Friday as the weekly fast day. In a similar way, Sunday came to be observed as the weekly day of rest and worship because of its association with the resurrection of Christ. Thus, Sunday came to be celebrated as the "Day of Resurrection."

Sunday and Easter

Sunday has often been described as "a little Easter," but the truth of the matter is that Easter would better be described as a "great Sunday." This is because the oldest and classic feast of the church is Sunday—the first day of the week, the day of the Sun, the day of Light, the eighth day, the day of the new creation. Together with the Wednesday and Friday fasting days already known in the *Didache*, the *dies dominica*—Sunday—appears to have constituted the original Christian week. Both fasting and kneeling for prayer on Sundays was soon forbidden as incompatible with what Sunday celebrated—the weekly commemoration of the Paschal feast. This was seen in Egeria's fourth-century description of the Resurrection vigil in Jerusalem early on Sunday mornings discussed earlier. Sunday was not so much a commemoration of a single past event (e.g., the resurrection of Christ) but rather an icon or symbol of ongoing and present communion with the risen Lord.

Similar to the move from Jewish Sabbath to Christian Sunday was the move from Jewish Passover to an annual celebration of Christian Easter, but this shift was more gradual and varied as it evolved, including a fair bit of tension over when the annual Easter festival should be celebrated. Scholars have had difficulty in determining if that annual feast took place on a Sunday or on a fixed date as would come to be the case with Christmas. Early scholarship tended to favor an early and near universal celebration of *pascha* but recent studies have argued the opposite. Modern liturgical scholars are moving increasingly to the position that the most ancient form of *pascha* (possibly even reflected in the New Testament itself) was not in connection with a Sunday but was an all-night vigil held in Asia Minor (and elsewhere) on the night of 14 Nisan, the day of Passover on the Jewish calendar and the calendar date of Jesus' death according to the chronology of John's Gospel. This was the equivalent of either March 25 or April 6 according to various versions of the Julian calendar, culminating in the celebration of the Eucharist at cockcrow, the conclusion of the Jewish Passover. Strongly eschatological in orientation as a vigil awaiting the return of the Lord, the overall emphasis of this Christianized Passover was the death of Christ the true paschal lamb. Consequently there is no record of any baptisms every having been part of that celebration.

The earliest Christian name for Easter, *pascha*, is the same as the Greek word for Passover, and the earliest theologies of Easter in the second century draw from the Jewish theology of Passover. Although the precise calculation of the annual *pascha* was not completely determined until the Council of Nicea in 325 CE, the Sunday celebration of Easter preceded by one, two, or six days of fasting became normative practice by the end of the second century around the year 185, which in some places had increased to a full week in the third century. Egeria referred to that week as "Great Week"—what came to be called "Holy Week" in the West. The feast was commemorated with a nightlong vigil, which drew upon the liturgical sources of the weekly vigil of the Resurrection beginning with the *lucenarium* or light service.

After the legalization of Christianity with Constantine's Edict of Milan in 312, and the corresponding wave of adult converts entering the church, those days of preparation took on greater significance as the time of immediate preparation for Baptism, which occurred during the Great Vigil of Easter on Holy Saturday night. This grew into a forty-day period of prayer and penance, which became the season of Lent, observed not only by catechumens preparing for baptism but for the whole Church. Leo the Great

1. *Angel before the Holy Sepulchre, detail of katholikon fresco, beginning of the twelfth century, Church of the Ascension of Christ at the Mileševa Monastery, Serbia.*

2. *Pentecost Gospel miniature from Egypt, 1249. Institut Catholique, Paris.*

1

2

appears to bear witness to a numbering of the forty-day period that began on the First Sunday of Lent and ran up until Holy Thursday, which began the Easter Triduum culminating in the paschal vigil. Easter was followed by a fifty-day period of rejoicing known as "Pentecost."

Along with this, an annual Sunday celebration with its natural association with Jesus' resurrection came to interpret *Pascha* as *transitus,* or passage. This would eventually suggest that the celebration of Easter was not only about the passage of Christ from death to life but also about Christian participation in this passage through baptism and Eucharist. The papal preacher Raniero Cantalamessa interprets this as a shift from seeing Christ as protagonist of the feast to seeing the assembled community as protagonist. Hence, in some places, especially North Africa and Rome, the paschal vigil would become the preferred occasion for Christian Initiation. By the fourth century, the Easter vigil lasted throughout the night as seen once again in Egeria's testimony. By the late sixth century, the vigil ended before midnight and Easter Day had its own Mass. By the eighth century, the vigil began even earlier and by the ninth century, it could begin by three in the afternoon! Also discernible in this period is a nascent but aliturgical paschal triduum. This included fasting from Friday through the end of the vigil; the development of Holy Week with the association of specific days with events in Jesus' last week; Lent (at least in Rome and possibly only three weeks in duration).

The concept of an Easter octave developed as an initial period of mystagogy for the newly baptized. This happened during the daily Eucharist in the eight days following the Paschal celebration and was also known as "White Week" because the neophytes wore their white baptismal garments throughout the week until the following Sunday—*domenica in albis*. However, by the seventh century the newly baptized already put aside their white garments on Easter Saturday, noting a symbolic link to Holy Saturday. That same century also introduced the practice of celebrating the anniversary of one's baptism but disappeared around the year 1000 CE

Pentecost came to be celebrated as a fifty-day period (*Pentekoste*—literally "fifty") during which, similar to Sundays themselves, fasting and kneeling were forbidden and alleluias were sung. However, these practices were not yet fully liturgicized according to any particular schema. So today, we speak of "Sundays of Easter" rather than "after Easter." This is what came to be known as the Easter Season—the great fifty days—after the Jewish Feast of Weeks—a time of thanksgiving. In the fourth century, Egeria still reports a unified feast of Ascension/Pentecost while other churches had already introduced a separate feast for the Ascension on the fortieth day. Augustine, for example, states that the Ascension is "celebrated all over the world." Technically speaking, Pentecost is the eighth Sunday of Easter. The fact that today red vestments are worn on this feast is a holdover from when Pentecost was viewed as a separate feast. Innocent I (+1216), for example, spoke of those red vestments as representing tongues of fire.

Advent and Christmas

The word *Adventus* is of pagan origin. Pagans observed a manifestation of the divinity that came to dwell in the temple at a certain time each year. That feast honoring the divinity was called *Adventus*. On those days, the temple that was normally closed was opened; sometimes a statue of the divinity would be moved into a space much larger than the small sanctuary where it was usually placed. The *Adventus* thus was a return each year, an anniversary. In the imperial context, the *Adventus* celebrated the return of the emperor. So the word was used by Christians to describe the coming of the Son of God in the temple of his flesh—his return—his visit. The word's usage came to be limited to what was considered the only true coming—the *Adventus* of the Lord. The origins of this season are Western focusing primarily on Spain and Gaul. The second half of December had been a conclusion of the agricultural year in Rome, and a theme of thanksgiving pervaded the days of the Roman Saturnalia from the 17th to the 23rd of December. In the canons of the Synod of Saragosa (380 CE) the laity are reminded to be in church from the 17th of December through the 6th of January. That observance would function as a Christian interpretation or countering of the pagan feast of Saturnalia.

In fifth century Gaul, we hear of an ascetical feast of three days each week beginning on our near Saint Martin's Day (November 11). What came to be called "Saint Martins' Lent" ran from November 11 until Christmas. Monday was added as a fast day to the traditional Christian fast days of Wednesday and Friday. None of this defends the theory that Advent served as a sort of catechumenal period for Epiphany baptism. Baptism, while celebrated in Spain on Epiphany, was also celebrated on Christmas Day in the 380s, much to the dismay of the Bishop of Rome. In any event, the pre-Epiphany, pre-Christmas fast dates from the sixth century as evidenced in the Synod of Tours (567 CE) and Macon (581 CE) lasted from Saint Martin's Day to Christmas. In the Gelasian Sacramentary, we find prayers for the five Sundays before Christmas and for Wednesdays and Fridays (fast days for Christians) of those five weeks. The season took on the nature of a penitential season paralleling Lent, using purple vestments, dropping the Gloria and Alleluia from the Eucharist, and the *Te Deum* from the Liturgy of the Hours. The Celtic penitential practices and rising emphasis on judgment influenced the shape of Advent along with the *Dies Irae* hymn, which was composed for the beginning of Advent.

Initially, Advent was linked exclusively to the final coming of Christ with a strong eschatological theme. Gradually, it was viewed more as a penitential time of preparation for Christmas. Pope Leo I (440–461 CE), for example, brought eschatological themes into his homilies at this time of the year, warning Christians against the excesses of Roman festivals, but nowhere does he refer to the coming festival of Christmas. The origins of Advent in Rome come later and appear to be a combination of Gallican influence and local tradition. There was already evidence of a pre-Christmas fast in the late fourth century. At the end of the sixth century, Gregory the Great reduced the practice of a six-week Advent to four weeks stressing the commemoration of Christ's birth rather than the judgment themes of the Gallican liturgies. This shift from six to four weeks was perhaps to highlight the difference between Lent and Advent. However, by the twelfth-century, Rome, too, was influenced by the penitential aspects of the Gallican Advent and dropped the Gloria from the Mass, retaining the Alleluia as a vestige of an earlier non-penitential approach to the season. The poetic "O Antiphons" were introduced in the seventh century, exemplifying the preparation for the solemnity, and by the eighth and ninth centuries, the sacramentaries reveal Advent rather than Christmas as beginning the liturgical year.

By the early fourth century, Christians in Rome and North Africa had begun to observe a feast of Christ's incarnation on December 25, while Christians in the East observed January 6 as a feast of Christ's epiphany or manifestation. In those early centuries, Christianity in Rome grew alongside the cult of Mithra whose annual feast of the "Invincible Sun" was celebrated at the winter solstice—the shortest day of the year in the northern hemisphere. It was not surprising, then, that Christians in Rome chose to observe the annual festival of Christ's incarnation at the same time as a certain antidote to the Mithraic feast. By the end of the fourth century, churches began to adopt both the feasts of December 25 and January 6 into their local calendars. Gradually other feasts were added to the cycle, corresponding to the celebration of Christ's birth on December 25: the Annunciation on March 25, exactly nine months before December 25; the commemoration of Presentation of Jesus in the Temple forty days after Christmas on February 2; and the birth of John the Baptist on June 24 at the summer solstice.

Christians in Rome began celebrating Christmas around the year 336 to counteract the Mithraic feast of the invincible sun—*Natale solis invicti*. Around the winter solstice on the shortest day of the year the Roman Church celebrated the incarnation of Jesus Christ—the true invincible sun. In the East, however, the Christmas feast continued to be linked to Epiphany and in fact, the Jerusalem Church waited until the year 549 CE to change from January 6 to December 25. Epiphany is a much older feast than Christmas and was observed as a celebration of Jesus' baptism. In Egypt, for example, Clement of Alexandria attests to this feast already in the second century, and also claimed that January 6 was known there as the feast of Christ's birth. When the Epiphany feast was eventually introduced in the fourth century, it lost its baptismal character and tended to focus more on the magi and the manifestation of Christ. From the second half of the fourth century Western Christians also kept the birth of John the Baptist on June 24 to counter the Greco-Roman feast of the summer solstice.

3. Fresco in the Nativity Chapel at Greccio, built in 1228. The fresco tells the story of Saint Francis' manger scene, along with the Eucharist celebration, and Christmas in the Bethlehem cave.

4. Baptism of Jesus, mural painting from the end of the third century, Saints Peter and Marcellinus Catacombs.

5. Gifts of the Magi, altar said to be that of Duke Rachis, from the eighth century. Saint Martin Church chapter house, Cividale del Friuli.

Helped by the Franciscans with their promotion of popular piety focused on the Christmas *presepio*, Advent and Christmas came to be viewed almost historically. Today, the biblical lessons and liturgical texts continue to maintain the eschatological dimension of the season although pastorally this is unfortunately often neglected. Moreover, it is an increasing challenge to maintain the spiritual character of the Advent season when the Christmas season in the secular world begins in early November with advertising, decorations in store windows, and Christmas music played on radios and in public buildings.

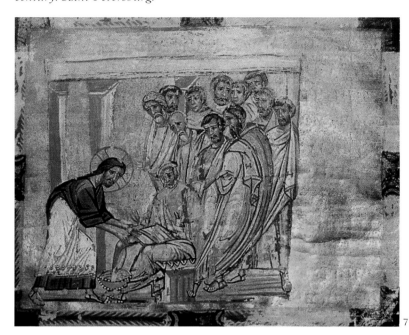

6. *Christ's Entrance into Jerusalem, Otto III's Book of Gospels, from about the year 1000, Richenau. Bayerische Staatsbibliothek, Monaco of Bavaria.*

7. *Washing of Feet, Trebizond Book of Gospels, from the tenth century. Saint Petersburg.*

Lent and Holy Week

Lent came to be seen initially as a time of immediate preparation for Easter baptism. By the Council of Nicea (325) Lent was already part of the liturgical calendar though its exact length differed from place to place— three weeks to four to six or eight—as we have already seen in Jerusalem. Gradually the whole church joined catechumens in this period of penance and fasting as a means of solidarity and support while recognizing its own ongoing need for purification. This period also became the time of intense preparation for public sinners who were then received back into the church on Maundy Thursday after a period of perhaps several years in the Order of Penitents. That program bore a certain resemblance to the catechumenate itself, except for the fact that those who participated were already baptized.

The Palm Sunday procession was already known in the eighth century but was not universally known until the twelfth. The observance of Maundy Thursday was in existence by the fourth century with the washing of the feet except for Rome, which waited until the fifth century to adopt the custom of foot washing. The practice of washing feet gradually faded in the West with the spread of the Roman Rite but was eventually recovered in monasteries. Indeed, the Rule of Saint Benedict states that when a guest arrives at the monastery the abbot should be called at once so that he may welcome the guest and wash the guest's feet as a gesture of hospitality. The Council of Toledo (694 CE) required that the washing of feet be done on Maundy Thursday by bishops and priests in Spain and Gaul. In Rome, the practice only became normative in the twelfth century. The 1570 Missal of Pius V puts the foot washing at the end of Mass; the 1955 Revised Holy Week Order

placed it after the homily with an emphasis on service of the needy and not ordination. In our own day, there can be a tendency in certain places to refer to this day as the anniversary of the priesthood. It is important to remember, however, that such a concept only dates back to the First Vatican Council at the end of the nineteenth century. The more ancient tradition notes the washing of feet with its implied service of the needy along with the institution of the Holy Eucharist as the two pillars on which Maundy Thursday was established.

The oldest witness to the Good Friday and Holy Saturday fast comes from Irenaeus of Lyon in the second century but without any special liturgy. In the late fourth century, Egeria reports that Jerusalem Christians gathered in the morning to venerate the cross and then again in the afternoon to hear the Word. We find more substantial information in the seventh century. The Pope, barefoot, carried the relic of the cross in procession. The relic was then venerated by everyone. This practice of the minister venerating the cross barefoot has now been restored and is included as an option in the Third Edition of the Roman Missal. Communion during the Good Friday liturgy is a late addition dating back only to the twelfth century. Even today, some argue for the value of fasting from the Eucharist on that day, as was the more ancient tradition.

Feasting the Saints

Very early in the church's history we already have evidence of martyrs' feasts being celebrated on the anniversary of their deaths, known as their *natale* or heavenly birthday. Intensely local in character, these feasts were inseparably linked to possession of a martyr's tomb, remains, or relics,

8

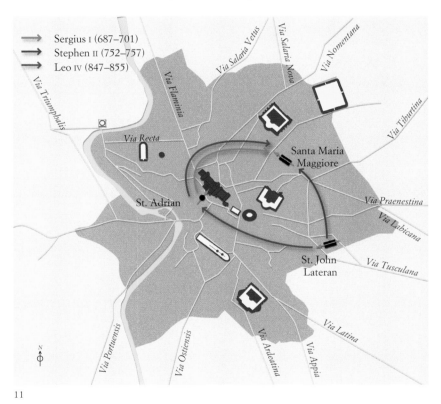

9   10   11

around which the community would assemble. Only later as relics were transferred to other churches would the cult of martyrs spread. The martyrs became concrete embodiments of Christ's own passion and death, hence the veneration of martyrs spread quickly given their role as intercessors.

Together with this developing cult of martyrs, there was also a growing devotion to the Virgin Mary in this period. The *Theotokos* possibly first used by Origen of Alexandria already appears in an early third-century liturgical hymn. The Marian feast of the Dormition (August 15) appears in the fifth-century Armenian Lectionary, and scholars believe that it reflects the Jerusalem practice which might date back to the first or second century. Indeed, some scholars believe that the Marian feast on August 15 was actually linked to the date of the conception of Isaac within a sectarian Jewish calendar known from the *Book of Jubilees* and Qumran documents.

The evolution of the liturgical year offers a clear example of how the various feasts and seasons were culturally conditioned. This continues to be the case today as one considers distinct traditions of preparation for Christmas in the Philippines and Mexico, for example, or the famous Holy Week processions in Seville and other cities in Andalusia, quite distinct from those of Corsica and southern Italy.

12. Liturgical Diversity in the Ancient Oriental Churches

In the course of the fourth to sixth centuries, patriarchates came into existence within the church. These were to play an extremely important role in the development of the liturgy, so much so that a rite came to be characteristic of and, indeed, almost synonymous with, each "union of churches" or patriarchate. "Rite" refers to the entire lived experience—liturgical, theological, and cultural—of a specific church and so must not be conceived too narrowly. In other words, it must be understood as the total spiritual heritage of a particular church—its liturgy, popular piety, spirituality, discipline, and theology.

The patriarchates grew up in the context of a major city. The bishop of a major city soon acquired a pre-eminence, which itself had been formed as a result of the relations of reciprocal dependence that had naturally grown up in the course of time between a major city and surrounding area. If the church in question actually possessed or claimed to have an apostle or a disciple of the apostle as its founder, it was regarded as a preserver and defender of authentic apostolic tradition. Thus, the bishops of such sees enjoyed a special prestige and primacy from a very early period. They presided over regional synods, ordained, and even deposed the bishops of their province, and arbitrated in disputes. The new patriarchal sees naturally proved to be liturgical as well as administrative centers and the various episcopal sees attached to each patriarch followed his lead. The result was the emergence of various liturgical families, within each of which only unimportant local differences were to be found.

The origin of all Eastern Christian liturgies is therefore closely linked to the development of the Eastern patriarchal sees, primarily Alexandria, Antioch, Jerusalem, and Constantinople, which sought to advance its own prestige among the others, as can be evidenced by canons of different ecumenical councils of the fourth and fifth centuries. The First Council of Constantinople (381 CE), for example, stated that the Patriarch of Constantinople would have the prerogative of honor after the Bishop of Rome because "Constantinople is the new Rome," given the fact that Constantine made it the new imperial capital in the year 330 CE. Unlike the West, whose liturgical diversity gradually waned because of a series of factors—political, sociological, and religious—the Christian East was much more successful in maintaining its rich diversity of liturgical families along with synodal structures of leadership within the local churches. In the development of the different Oriental liturgical families, we can speak of two major phases: an early period of establishment and a later period of consolidation. In the earlier period, two great liturgical branches were already quite distinct in the East at the beginning of the fourth century: the Syro-Antiochene branch and the Alexandrine branch. These two principle Eastern branches

gave rise to further differentiation. The Syro-Antiochene branch included an East-Syrian group with the Nestorian Rite (Iran), the Chaldean Rite (Iraq), and the Malabar Rite (India), and a West-Syrian group that was the primary heir to the Jerusalem tradition: the Syrian, Maronite, Byzantine, and Armenian Rites. The Alexandrian branch included both the Coptic and Ethiopian Rites. Today's Oriental liturgies, then, are descendants of those rites that grew in the major cities of the East. Today, the liturgical families of the East—the Alexandrian, Armenian, Byzantine, East and West Syrian rites—correspond with the territorial organization of the Eastern churches in the fifth century. No separate Jerusalem rite has survived.

1. Representation of patron goddesses of the cities of Rome and Constantinople, ivory diptych presumed to be from Constantinople, circa 500. Kunsthistorisches Museum, Vienna.

2. Eastern church's spreading of the word and liturgical variety.

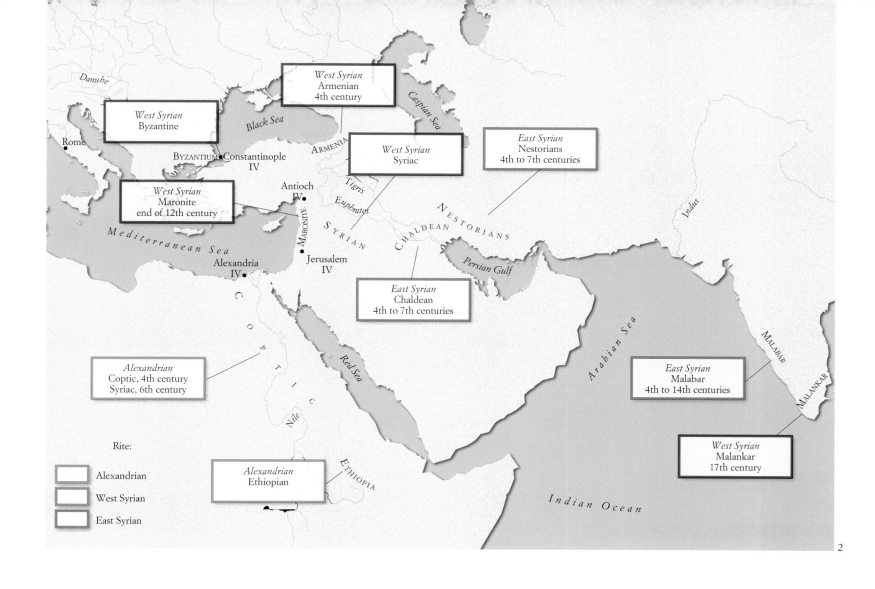

West Syrian
Byzantine

West Syrian
Armenian
4th century

West Syrian
Syriac

East Syrian
Nestorians
4th to 7th centuries

West Syrian
Maronite
end of 12th century

East Syrian
Chaldean
4th to 7th centuries

Alexandrian
Coptic, 4th century
Syriac, 6th century

East Syrian
Malabar
4th to 14th centuries

West Syrian
Malankar
17th century

Alexandrian
Ethiopian

Rite:

Alexandrian

West Syrian

East Syrian

Danube
Black Sea
Caspian Sea
Rome
BYZANTIUM•Constantinople
IV
ARMENIA
Antioch
IV
Tigris
Euphrates
MARONITE
SYRIAN
CHALDEAN
NESTORIANS
Indus
Mediterranean Sea
Alexandria
IV
Jerusalem
IV
Persian Gulf
C
O
P
T
I
C
Red Sea
Nile
Arabian Sea
MALABAR
MALANKAR
ETHIOPIA
Indian Ocean

2

3. Saint Cyril of Alexandria, fresco, Monastery of Saint Moses the Ethiopan, Nabak, Syria.

3

The Alexandrian Family

Within the Alexandrian branch, the foundation for the Coptic (i.e., Egyptian) Rite is the ancient liturgical tradition of Alexandria. While that liturgy was celebrated in Greek in the Hellenized cities, rural areas began using Coptic as early as the fourth century. In the sixth century the Alexandrian liturgy underwent reform with clear Antiochene influence when it was reorganized in the monasteries of Scetis with the help of Syrian monks. A period of liturgical renewal followed in the eleventh and twelfth centuries where some Byzantine elements were introduced into the sacraments. Arabic was gradually introduced and by the fourteenth century was firmly established. The number of anaphoras (eucharistic prayers) was limited to three in the twelfth century. Today, while the ancient Alexandrian anaphora of Saint Mark is still used in a redacted form using the name of Cyril of Alexandria, the more commonly used anaphora is that of Saint Basil. The anaphora of Gregory

4. Christ in Glory, mural from Bawit, seventh century. Coptic Museum, Old Cairo.

5. The Wedding of Cana, illumination of Coptic tetra gospel, from 1179–1180. Bibliothèque Nationale de France, Paris.

6. Jesus' Entrance into Jerusalem, painted mural in the Debre Selam Saint Michaels's Church, near Atsbi, Ethiopia.

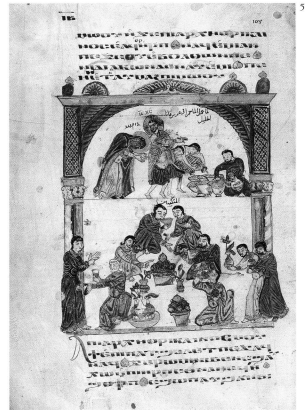

of Nazianzen is reserved for solemn feasts of the Lord. The Coptic eucharistic rite employs four New Testament readings—Paul, Catholic Epistles, Acts, Gospel—and uses a form of the General Intercessions similar to the style used in the Roman Rite on Good Friday. Within the liturgy are two rites of reconciliation with the solemn formulas of absolution addressed to the Son and the Father. Another form of reconciliation is found in the cathedral office discussed earlier in which the offering of incense becomes its own rite of reconciliation with absolution in morning and evening prayer. The Ethiopian Rite is the other liturgy in the Alexandrian branch and grew largely in monasteries beginning in the sixth century. Interestingly, the Ethiopian Church remained dependent on the Coptic Church until 1951. Over the centuries, liturgical books brought from Egypt were translated from Greek, then Coptic or Arabic, into Ge'ez and then enriched by liturgical elements garnered from other sources. Since the bishops there were largely foreigners who seldom spoke the language, the evolution of the Ethiopian Rite lacked the sort of leadership it needed to

7. Large drums are played during Ethiopan religious ceremonial rites, in Mdhame Alem, Sokota, 1991.

8. The sistrum is an instrument that still is used during Ethiopian ceremonial religious rites.

create a unified liturgical practice. The Rite underwent various forms of renewal in the fifteenth and seventeenth centuries with a revision of the liturgical calendar and a newly composed Liturgy of the Hours. The structure of the eucharistic liturgy closely resembles that of the Coptic Rite but the Creed has a form proper to the Ethiopian Church. Moreover, the use of drums, sistra, and indigenous music gives the liturgy a particularly inculturated feel.

9. Saint Peter opens the gate to Paradise while incense is burned, detail of The Last Judgment, Monastery of Saint Moses the Ethiopian, Nabak, Syria.

10. Virgin Hodegetria (Our Lady of the Way), 1318, refurbished during the eighteenth century, Our Lady of Balamand Patriarchal Monastery, Lebanon.

The East Syrian Family

Within the East Syrian family, the Chaldean Rite evolved in Persia in the fourth through seventh centuries. Even today, the Chaldean liturgy is largely that which was codified in the seventh century after the Arab conquest. The ritual reforms of that period include the approval of only the standard anaphora of Addai and Mari, or those of Mar Theodore, and Mar Nestorius; the adaptation of the rites of Christian Initiation for the baptism of children; the reorganization of the liturgical calendar; the establishment of norms for the lectionary system; and the systemizing of the various hours of prayer within the cathedral office. Psalm prayers for Vigils and Matins were later added along with a liturgical book of poetic hymns and antiphons. Unlike other Eastern rites, the Chaldean liturgy is characterized by a certain simplicity in its celebration of the Eucharist and other sacraments having maintained a number of archaic features from the rite's earliest form. Today, while Syriac remains the official liturgical language, Arabic may also be used in the Liturgy of the Word for the prayers and the four readings from the law, prophets, apostle, and gospel. The Malabar Rite evolved in Kerala, southwest India. Tradition states that Saint Thomas evangelized South India, thus the name "Thomas Christians" took hold. Nevertheless, we know that from the fourth century on, the churches of South India were linked to the Persian church until the arrival of Portuguese missionaries in the sixteenth. The liturgy found there by the European missionaries was a form of the East Syrian Rite along with some Hindu practices reinterpreted for Christian usage. With the help of the Jesuits, the Latin liturgy was imposed on South India at the end of the sixteenth century, leaving only traces of the original liturgical tradition: the Syriac language; the Liturgy of the Hours; and the essential shape of the eucharistic liturgy into which numerous Western liturgical elements were added. Only the Anaphora of Addai and Mari was approved for usage but with the addition of the words of Institution added which had not been in the original text. Unleavened bread was now required for the Eucharist and the chalice would no longer be offered. Regarding the Anaphora of Addai and Mari, it is important to note that the Holy See recently issued an extraordinary affirmation of that prayer's authenticity and orthodoxy, despite the absence of the words of Institution. For the celebration of other sacraments, a sixteenth century Portuguese ritual was translated into Syriac as was the Roman Pontifical. Old liturgical books were destroyed to prevent their being used.

Work at the restoration of the oriental character of the Malabar Rite began with Pope Pius XI in 1934 and the Syrian *Qurbana* (eucharistic offering) was once again approved for usage by Pius XII in 1957 and introduced in 1962. The Malabar Rite has continued to undergo liturgical revision despite certain resistance from some corners of the Malabar Church. Today Malayalam has replaced Syriac as the liturgical language employed in the rite.

The West Syrian Family

The West Syrian family includes the Syrian, Maronite, and Malankara Rites. The Syrian Rite is used by the Syrian Orthodox and Syrian Catholic churches and is based on the ancient liturgy of Antioch. The liturgical celebrations were in Greek in the cities but in Syrian in the countryside where the liturgy was gradually influenced by Syriac culture, arriving at its classic shape in the twelfth century. The Syriac Liturgy has had as many as eight anaphoras including the Anaphora of the Twelve Apostles related to the Byzantine anaphora of Saint John Chrysostom, as well as the Anaphora of Saint James, which comes from the Jerusalem tradition. The Liturgy of the Word has six readings from books of Law; Wisdom; Prophets; Acts or the Catholic Epistles; Paul; and a Gospel. The primitive Syriac liturgy includes an incense rite and priestly prayer that follows the introduction. Incense is then burned with the singing of a hymn followed by the prayer for acceptance of the incense.

The Maronite Rite grew out of the influence of the Syrian Monastery of Saint Maron. Followers of this tradition eventually migrated to Lebanon in the eighth century where they formed an autonomous church. The Maronite liturgy continued the usage of many ancient Syriac elements from both the East and West Syrian traditions. With the Crusades, the Maronites came under Latin influence

9

10

and entered full communion with Rome in the late twelfth century which led to a gradual Latinization of the liturgy in the thirteenth and even more so in the sixteenth. A revised edition of the Maronite Missal in the eighteenth century actually included a revised form of the Roman Canon, which served as the normative anaphora of the Maronite liturgy until recently. Today the eucharistic liturgy is largely celebrated in Arabic although the consecration and several other parts have remained in Syriac. Only two readings are proclaimed—a Pauline text and the Gospel—and six anaphoras are included in the latest edition of the Missal.

The Malankara Rite is used by the Malankara Orthodox and Catholic churches of South India. Thomas Christians who refused to submit to Western intervention eventually made contact with the patriarch of the Syrian Orthodox Church who agreed to provide them a bishop with the understanding that they would adhere to the theological and liturgical principles of his church. Thus was the Syro-Malankara Rite introduced in South India in the seventeenth and eighteenth centuries thanks to the Syrian Orthodox bishops sent there. The Malankara liturgy is based on the Syrian Rite with some local adaptations as we saw in the case of the Malabar Rite. As with the Malabar Rite, Malayalam now serves as the liturgical language within the Malankara liturgy.

The Armenian Family

The Armenian liturgy was originally based on a Syriac form of the Liturgy of Antioch, brought to Armenia in the second and third centuries by missionaries from northern Mesoptomia. But it was Gregory the Illuminator (+325)

11. Saint Gregory the Illuminator, 1658 synaxarion, Armenian Cilicia catolicos, Antlias, Lebanon.

11

12

13

who was linked with the church of Caesarea who carried the Cappadocian liturgy to Armenia which was propagated with the conversion of King Tiridates III and the entire Armenian nation in the year 301. The Armenian liturgy further developed in the fifth and sixth centuries with the incorporation of liturgical materials from Jerusalem that were translated and adapted for Armenian usage. Byzantine influence followed from the seventh through eleventh centuries. This blending of various liturgical traditions led to a certain duplication of rituals and multiplication of prayers. As Latin influence held sway in the twelfth to fourteenth centuries, the Armenian Rite came to include some Latin elements as well (e.g. a bishop's miter and use of the Latin *Confiteor* at the beginning of the Eucharist).

The Armenian Rite contains eight anaphoras with the Anaphora of Saint Basil (called The Anaphora of Saint Gregory the Illuminator) as the most ancient. Orthodox Armenians do not mix water with the wine and communion is given only under one form, unlike other Eastern traditions. Following the anamnesis within the Eucharistic Prayer there is a hymn to God the Father along with a hymn to the Holy Spirit after the epiclesis. The Nativity and Epiphany are celebrated as one feast on January 6 following ancient Eastern liturgical practice.

The Byzantine Rite

The Byzantine Rite grew out of the Patriarchate of Constantinople and was gradually adopted in the medieval period

14

15

16

12. Khor Virap ("deep pit") Monastery, built on the site where, according to tradition, Saint Gregory the Illuminator, the evangelizer of Armenia, was imprisoned. Mount Ararat is in the background.

13. Baptism of Christ, Edjmiazin Book of Gospels, seventh century, Matenadaran, Erevan, Armenia.

14. Exterior of Church of Hagia Sophia, Constantinople.

15. The large space in which Hagia Sophia's main nave is found. Constantinople.

16. Mosaic on Hagia Sophia's south door, Constantinople, 989 or 1019, symbolic commemoration of Theotokos, offered by Constantine's city and the Justinian church.

17. *Saints Cyril and Methodius, and five disciples, among whom are Saint Clement and Saint Naum, depicted on the Saint Naum fresco at Ocrida, 1806.*

18. *Interior of the Graničari Monastery, Serbia.*

19. *Church of the Virgin's Dormition, Moscow.*

20. *The Byzantine culture's main expansion routes, along which it spread the gospel.*

17

18

19

by the patriarchates of Alexandria, Antioch, and Jerusalem. This liturgy is known for its elegant and complex ceremony which drew largely from imperial court ceremony of Byzantium and also came to include a synthesis of Palestinian as well as Constantinopolitan rites. In the sixth century and especially with the construction of the great Hagia Sophia, the Byzantine Rite became imperial and became even more elaborate in ceremony and style especially in its frequent use of incense and the numerous processions accompanied by chants such as the Trisagion and the Cheroubikon. In fact, the rite contains two entrance processions. In the ninth century with the help of the "Apostles to the Slavs,"Cyril (+869) and Methodius (+885), the Byzantine Rite was diffused in the Balkan Peninsula and then in Romania and finally Russia in the late tenth century.

The cosmic symbolism and dimension of the rite is present in the numerous mosaics that adorn the church but also in the iconostasis also adorned with beautiful icons separating sanctuary from nave. Since the eleventh century, the Liturgy of Saint John Chrysostom has superseded the more elaborate Liturgy of Saint Basil. The Greek Liturgy of Saint James is also used by some communities on the Feast of Saint James (October 23). All of the anaphoras within the Byzantine tradition give special attention to the epiclesis—the calling down of the Holy Spirit upon the gifts and the liturgical assembly itself.

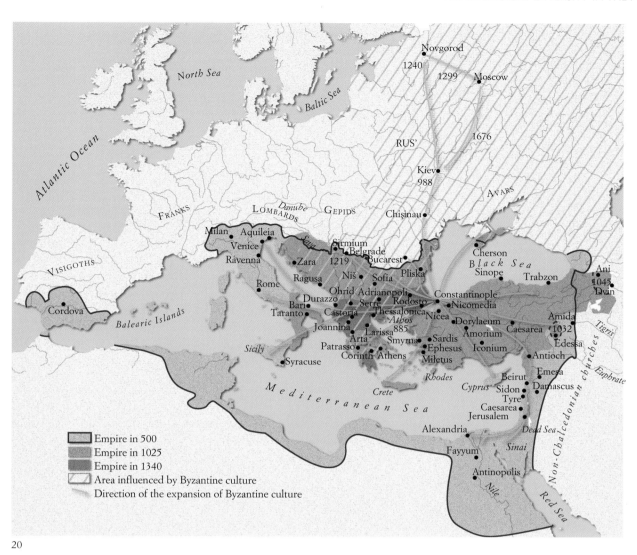

21. *Saint Sergius Trinity Cathedral, interior and iconostases, Moscow.*

22. *Illuminated page of Book of Gospels, Moscow, 1392. State Library, Saint Petersburg.*

20

22

21

13. THE STATIONAL LITURGY

The term *statio* dates back to the second century and was originally used more generally to describe public fasts as seen in the second-century work, *The Shepherd of Hermas*. It later came to signify assemblies convoked on specific days for specific purposes in predetermined venues. Tertullian referred to the weekly fasts of Wednesday and Friday as stational days, meaning days of fasting and prayer. At Rome and Carthage, those days also had a Eucharist but elsewhere, only prayers and readings. It was Tertullian's opinion that this meaning of *statio* derived from military usage where it meant standing on guard or at one's post. Isidore of Seville also referred to fasting as a *statio*.

Gradually, however, the term *statio* came to mean a place where one pauses and stays for a liturgical meeting and then simply referred to the liturgical meeting itself. Both Cyprian of Carthage and Cornelius, Bishop of Rome, spoke of a *statio* as a meeting of the bishop and people, for example, but not necessarily a liturgical meeting. But by the fifth century, the term came to refer to a special episcopal or patriarchal liturgy. Stational liturgies consisted of gatherings of the local church around its bishop on feast days and es-pecially during the Lenten season. On those occasions, Rome, Constantinople, and Jerusalem, but also cities like Hippo and Arles, were all transformed into sacred spaces as procession of the Christian faithful with their bishops or patriarchs filled the streets. In Constantinople, the stational liturgy contained a strong element of supplication and intercession as Christians there took to the streets, pleading for God's mercy in light of the numerous earthquakes endured along with droughts and other natural disasters. Heresies offered yet another cause for stational processions there where they served to counter the popular services of the Arians. John Chrysostom did much to promote what came to include elegant silver crosses illuminated with lighted tapers. The development of the liturgical calendar was clearly linked to the evolution of the "stational" liturgy as was the lectionary. On feast days, the *lectio continua* was interrupted so that more thematic readings could be chosen to correspond to the particular feast.

In addition to her numerous other contributions to understanding the enactment of liturgy in fourth-century Jerusalem, Egeria also offers precious information on the

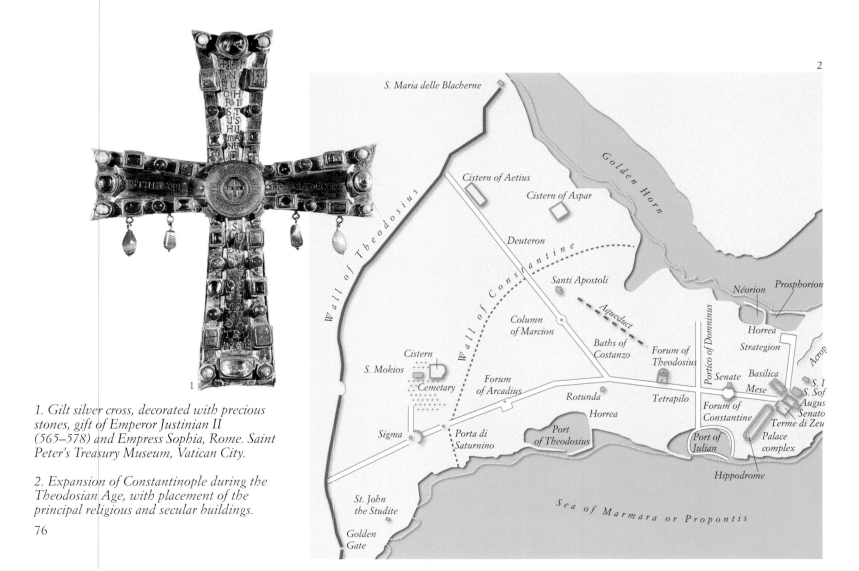

1. Gilt silver cross, decorated with precious stones, gift of Emperor Justinian II (565–578) and Empress Sophia, Rome. Saint Peter's Treasury Museum, Vatican City.

2. Expansion of Constantinople during the Theodosian Age, with placement of the principal religious and secular buildings.

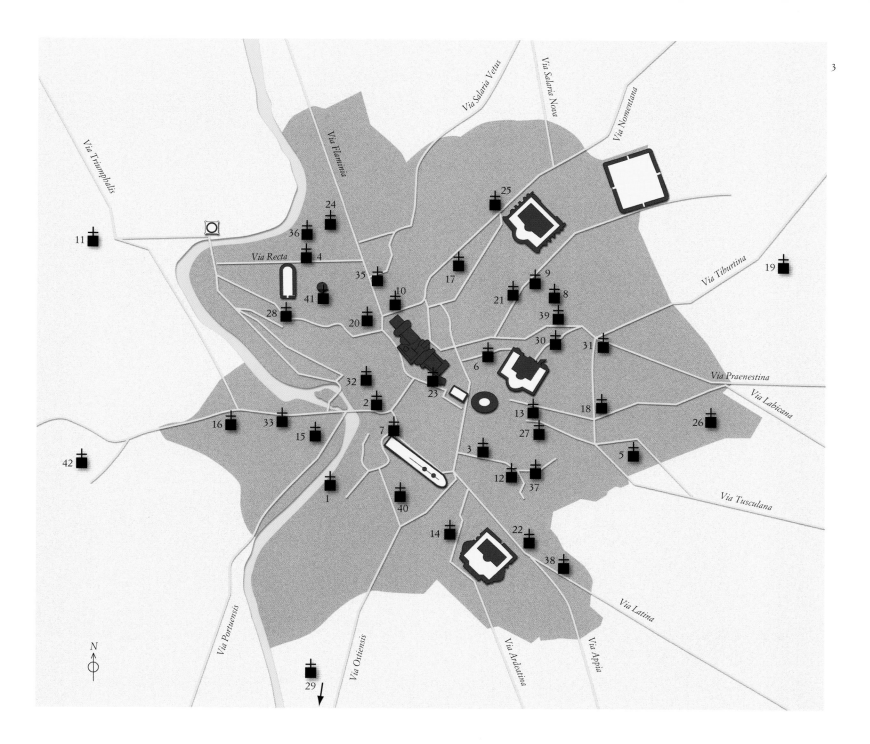

1	Ash Wednesday	*Santa Sabina all'Aventino*
2	Thursday	*San Giorgio al Velabro*
3	Friday	*Santi Giovanni e Paolo al Celio*
4	Saturday	*Sant'Agostino in Campo Marzio*
5	Sunday	*San Giovanni in Laterano*
6	Monday	*San Pietro in Vincoli al Colle Oppio*
7	Tuesday	*Sant'Anastasia (San Teodoro) al Palatino*
8	Wednesday	*Santa Maria Maggiore*
9	Thursday	*San Lorenzo in Panisperna*
10	Friday	*Santi XII Apostoli al Foro Traiano*
11	Saturday	*San Pietro in Vaticano*
12	Sunday	*Santa Maria in Domnica alla Navicella*
13	Monday	*San Clemente presso il Colosseo*
14	Tuesday	*Santa Balbina all'Aventino*
15	Wednesday	*Santa Cecilia in Trastevere*
16	Thursday	*Santa Maria in Trastevere*
17	Friday	*San Vitale in Fovea (via Nazionale)*
18	Saturday	*Santi Marcellino e Pietro al Laterano (via Merulana)*
19	Sunday	*San Lorenzo fuori le Mura*
20	Monday	*San Marco al Campidoglio*
21	Tuesday	*Santa Pudenziana al Viminale*
22	Wednesday	*San Sisto (Santi Nereo e Achilleo)*
23	Thursday	*Santi Cosma e Damiano in Via Sacra (Fori Imperiali)*
24	Friday	*San Lorenzo in Lucina*
25	Saturday	*Santa Susanna alle Terme di Diocleziano*
26	Sunday	*Santa Croce in Gerusalemme*
27	Monday	*Santi Quattro Coronati al Celio*
28	Tuesday	*San Lorenzo in Damaso*
29	Wednesday	*San Paolo fuori le Mura*
30	Thursday	*Santi Silvestro e Martino ai Monti*
31	Friday	*Sant'Eusebio all'Esquilino*
32	Saturday	*San Nicola in Carcere*
11	5th Sunday of Lent	*San Pietro in Vaticano*
33	Monday	*San Crisogono in Trastevere*
34	Tuesday	*San Ciriaco (Santa Maria in Via Lata al Corso)*
35	Wednesday	*San Marcello al Corso*
36	Thursday	*Sant'Apollinare in Campo Marzio*
37	Friday	*Santo Stefano al Celio*
38	Saturday	*San Giovanni a Porta Latina*
5	Palm Sunday	*San Giovanni in Laterano*
39	Monday	*Santa Prassede all'Esquilino*
40	Tuesday	*Santa Prisca all'Aventino*
8	Wednesday	*Santa Maria Maggiore*
5	Thursday	*San Giovanni in Laterano*
26	Friday	*Santa Croce in Gerusalemme*
5	Saturday	*San Giovanni in Laterano*
8	Easter Sunday	*Santa Maria Maggiore*
11	Monday	*San Pietro in Vaticano*
29	Tuesday	*San Paolo fuori le Mura*
19	Wednesday	*San Lorenzo fuori le Mura*
10	Thursday	*Santi XII Apostoli al Foro Traiano*
41	Friday	*Santa Maria ad Martyres in Campo Marzio (Pantheon)*
5	Saturday	*San Giovanni in Laterano*
42	2nd Sunday of Easter	*San Pancrazio*

4. Roman buildings underneath the Saint Anastasia Church, Rome (by P. Pietri, 1960).

5. Fifth-century clerestory and transept, most likely from the early Middle Ages, in Saint Anastasia Church, Rome.

4

5

stational system there. Here we see the Jerusalem liturgy fully celebrated as a movable feast where the entire body—both individual and collective—was used to express its praise of God. Present was a full complement of liturgical ministries and vesture, use of light and incense, along with numerous processions accompanied by the singing of litanies and hymns.

The Roman stational liturgy which grew from the fifth through the eighth centuries was very much a city liturgy—a liturgy celebrated by the Bishop of Rome with his presbyters, deacons, and faithful—taking place on Sundays and on other special days at a selection of specific churches—stations—in the city. It was organized in freedom and made use of the public space afforded it. Because of the laws that did not allow cemeteries within the walls, it was a liturgy celebrated both *In Urbe* and *Extra Muros*—both within and outside the walls. The liturgy was highly choreographed with great movement, transforming the entire city into sacred space on the festal day. Rome was the only city in the West with such a grand, imperial liturgy at the time, so it is not surprising that it came to be a source for imitation by others. Venues—called stations—were chosen for the various feast days depending on which basilicas contained the saint's relics. When the liturgical celebrations were not memorials of saints—during Lent, for example—other thematic connections between the liturgical day and the basilica were sought. Roman Christians gathered at the station for the major solemnities—Christmas with its eventual threefold celebration; Epiphany; Easter; and Pentecost—for the paschal cycle (from the start of Lent to the Saturday after Easter); the week after Pentecost; and the fasts of the seventh and tenth months.

There was no one basilica that occupied a central position in the city—not even the Lateran, despite its obvious importance. Rather, in the vast urban spread that was Rome in the fifth century, this movable form of worship was organized among the thirty or so places of worship that were often far from the city center. Thus, the concept of Saint John Lateran as Rome's cathedral would have been very foreign in that historical period. Indeed, when the pope referred to the Lateran, he preferred to speak of "*nostra ecclesia*"—our church. For example, outside the walls, the pope could convene the church of Rome for the celebration of the *natalacia*—birthdays—and the days of death of saints at the places where they were buried.

Since the pope or his delegate always presided, they were the most solemnly celebrated rites within the city. Whenever it was celebrated, representatives of the city church, of the *tituli* (named after the title owners of the house churches who had dedicated their property for church usage), and of the great basilicas, joined the pope for the liturgy. Ac-

6. Plan for Rome's Saint Anastasia Church (by Todini-Krautheimer).

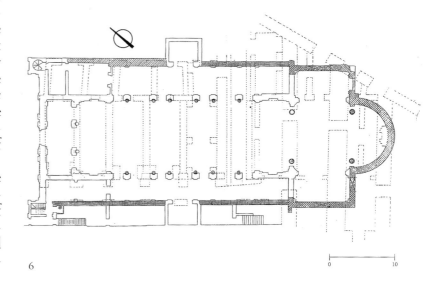

6

7

7. Mary and the Christ Child, fresco, left transept of Rome's Saint Anastasia Church, twelfth century. On Ash Wednesdays, a collection would be taken at Saint Anastasia's for the trip to Saint Sabina.

8

8. Detail of cypress wood door at Saint Sabina in Rome, dating back to the fifth century, with depictions of stories from the Old and New Testaments.

companied by his entourage, he processed from the first station (for example, the Lateran Palace where the Bishop of Rome resided) to the designated basilica (the second station) for that day's eucharist. He was either carried in procession on a chair or transported on a horse. A later development of the stational liturgy shows that on certain days of the year, as the Bishop of Rome departed from his residence with his assistants, the assembly was gathered in another church from which a solemn procession or litany was made to the stational church. In the Roman liturgy, this preliminary assembly was called the *collecta*. In its developed form, this preliminary assembly or *collecta* consisted of a prayer ad *collectam*, and then the procession moved to the designated station church. Thus, the seven major geographical regions of the city had their own processions designed to arrive at the basilica at more or less the same time. Those seven processions were each led by a processional cross—the stational cross of that region—carried by the deacon who oversaw the *diakonia* (outreach center) for the needy in those neighborhoods. During the procession,

psalms and litanies were chanted and the term *litania* was often applied to the procession itself.

When the pope or his delegate arrived at the station church with his entourage, he was greeted at the doors of the basilica by the clergy of that church along with a chorus of virgins. After each one paid the proper homage by kissing his feet, he was then accompanied to the sacristy to be vested in liturgical attire. This was the principal Eucharist of the day. It was customary to announce at a stational mass what was to be the date and place of the next stational liturgy, and of the *collecta*, if any. The archdeacon performed this function immediately after the pope's own communion at his *cathedra*. Despite its solemnity, however, the papal, stational liturgy maintained that noble simplicity typical of the classic Roman Rite.

The unity of the local church with its bishop was especially evident within the stational liturgy, and especially in the ancient practice called the *fermentum*, literally "leaven." This practice was peculiar to Rome. Although we cannot ascertain exactly how old the practice was, it was certainly

flourishing by the beginning of the fifth century and only disappeared sometime after the seventh. Afterwards, it was only retained within the liturgy of the Easter Vigil. When the pope presided at a stational liturgy, he sent to each of his clergy serving in the *tituli* within the city boundaries a particle of the bread that he had consecrated at that solemn Eucharist; this particle was called the *fermentum*. Acolytes carried it in linen bags, and the older theory suggests that when the presbyters in the different title churches received it, they placed it in the chalice before the distribution of communion. Thus, the different liturgies of the city were united with that of the bishop. Innocent I himself witnesses to this practice in his *Letter to Decentius*, Bishop of Gubbio, in the year 415. A more recent theory suggests that Roman presbyters might well have remained in the *tituli* for religious instruction with the catechumens on the morning of the papal stational liturgy, and the *fermentum* could have been carried back to them to be consumed so that they

9. *Medieval atrium at Saint Clement Church, Rome.*

10. *Saint Martin of Tours with palm branch, medieval decoration on the apse of the paleo-Christian Church of Saint Marcellus, Rome.*

11. *Medieval portico of the Church of Saint Cecilia in Trastevere, Rome.*

9

10

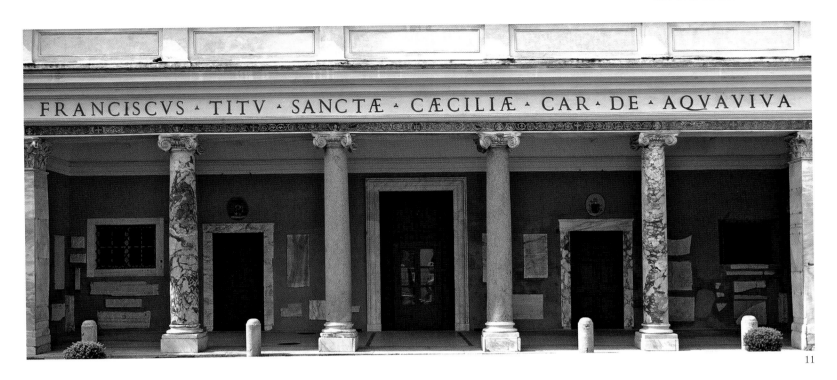

FRANCISCVS · TITV · SANCTÆ · CÆCILIÆ · CAR · DE · AQVAVIVA

11

would have had some share in the liturgy at which they were unable to be present.

Nevertheless, despite popular allegorical interpretations that have continued to the present day, the *fermentum* never symbolized the commingling of Christ's body and blood as some have suggested. The Eucharist celebrated by the presbyters in their churches constituted a second type of Roman liturgy of that era—obviously less solemn than the papal event, with corresponding books. Interestingly, the original intention of the *tituli* was for catechesis and penitential services (thus the more recent theory on the origins of the *fermentum*), while the basilicas were normative venues for baptism and eucharistic celebrations. This changed for practical reasons as the church continued to grow. We know of the existence of nine *tituli* prior to the fourth century—Tit. Clemente; Tit. Anastasia; Tit. Sabina, for example; and of three that were already in existence prior to the Peace of Constantine: Calisto; Cecilia; and Marcelo. Generally, these title churches were found in the most inhabited areas or neighborhoods. The number of *tituli* grew to twenty in the fourth century and twenty-five by the time of Leo the Great (440–461) in the fifth century. By the year 499, we hear of twenty-nine title churches. In the sixth century, the *tituli* received the name of a saint rather than that of the possessor or owner of the house. Of course, in some cases the name of the *titulus* remained as in the case of Santa Cecilia and Sabina. In other cases, however, the title church took on a different name as in the *titulus* of Byzantius which was renamed the Church of Ss. Giovanni e Paolo.

These smaller communities were not seen as parishes in the modern sense. The true parish was the diocese and the bishop was the pastor. Thus in its classic understanding, the *fermentum* symbolized the unity within the one parish with its pastor—the bishop. As the church grew and spread beyond the city walls, smaller churches were established in the countryside. Those communities were called "parishes" and their presbyters were called pastors. Innocent's letter to Decentius notes that the *fermentum* is not carried to those communities outside the walls but only to the *tituli*—clearly there is a different relationship. Thus in this liturgy celebrated outside the walls we have a third type of Roman liturgy. Because such communities were located in the countryside, they were deprived of the assistance of deacons, choirs, and other liturgical ministers, and thus the form that grew there tended to be simpler with less use of ceremonial and less music. Later, the Eucharist celebrated in specialized groups (celebrations during pilgrimages to the tombs of martyrs, votive Masses, private Masses celebrated in the pope's private chapel with his domestic staff) would find their origins in this third grouping. In this third type of Roman Eucharist, we can also locate the foundations for the ferial or weekday order of Mass and private celebrations without a congregation (except for one server) offered on behalf of the living or deceased.

During this classical epoch, the church of Rome developed its own appropriate liturgy that reflected the genius of the Roman people. That same liturgy, of course, that *romanità* also had its own limits and confines—the Roman cultural context of the fifth through the eighth centuries. Obviously, in Constantinople and Jerusalem that Roman liturgy would have appeared very much out of place. Nonetheless, the classic Roman liturgy of that period remains a model for other churches of the West in that it demonstrates the means of liturgical adaptation and inculturation proposed by the Second Vatican Council—a local liturgy for a local church that nonetheless always remains in communion with the Bishop of Rome and indeed, with the wider church of God throughout the world.

14. THE GENIUS OF THE ROMAN RITE

1. *On right section of the Arch of Constantine in Rome, Constantine is shown giving a speech to the Romans at the Forum. Example of a public ceremony.*

2. *The Hospitality of Abraham, detail of Santa Maria Maggiore's main nave, Rome. Abraham appears dressed in the clothing of a consul.*

On May 8, 1899, the British historian Edmund Bishop gave a conference for the Historical Research Society at Archbishop's House, Westminster, London, entitled "The Genius of the Roman Rite." That paper was later published in 1918 in his classic volume *Liturgica Storica: Papers on the Liturgy and Religious Life of the Western Church* and forever changed the way liturgical historians understand and describe the Roman Rite's unique characteristics. Bishop concluded that the genius of the Roman Rite could be summarized in two words: "soberness and sense."

The earliest composition of liturgical texts in Rome exhibited a dynamic not unlike what happened in other rites as we saw in the liturgical diversity within the ancient Eastern churches and in the non-Roman liturgical families of the West. A new type of liturgical improvisation emerged in Rome that was based on the faithful observance of certain canons, guidelines, or principles which were handed down within that local church from one generation to the next. Such improvisation and the eventual formulation of those liturgical texts was largely influenced by the Roman cultural genius which was quite different from what we saw in the fourth century Jerusalem or the imperial and solemn court ceremonial of the Byzantine liturgy celebrated at Hagia Sophia in Constantinople. Unlike the Christian East, the classical Roman genius was known by simplicity of form;

brevity; sobriety; and practicality, thus Bishop's description of the Roman liturgy as characteristically sober and sensible.

Popes like Damasus (+384), Innocent (+417); Celestine (+432); Leo the Great (+461); Gelasius (+496); Vigilius (+555); and Gregory the Great (+604) all made significant contributions to the formation of the Roman Rite and in the early composition of liturgical texts. For example, in the late fifth century Pope Gelasius introduced the Greek litany *Kyrie eleison* into the Roman Rite, which replaced the solemn prayers of intercession. That text was further emended and simplified by Pope Gregory the Great at the end of the sixth century, offering a shorter form of the *Kyrie* litany. Gregory also placed the Lord's Prayer immediately after the Eucharistic Prayer and before the *Fractio Panis*—the breaking of the bread—rather than between the *Fractio Panis* and Communion. The new position allowed the Bishop of Rome to say the prayers over the consecrated gifts at the altar rather than at the papal throne where he positioned himself for the fraction rite and received communion during papal stational liturgies. The *Gloria in Excelsis* first appeared in the Roman Rite during the pontificate of Pope Symmachus (+514) on Sundays and feasts during Masses at which bishops presided. The custom was eventually extended to liturgies at which pres-

3

4

byters presided, as well. The Syrian-born Pope Sergius (+701) introduced the Oriental litany *Agnus Dei* into the Roman liturgy, since he was well accustomed to it from his own cultural background.

The Roman liturgy of this period was not only classical in the sense that it embodied the Roman penchant for "soberness and sense"; it was also pure, indicating the fact that it had not yet come into contact with Gallican or Franco-Germanic elements that would arrive only in the eighth century. As the Roman Rite took shape, the "noble simplicity" of Roman culture (as the Second Vatican Council would also describe the Roman Rite) held sway. This was noted, for example, in the hymns sung at the Entrance, Preparation of the Gifts, and Communion, even during solemn papal, stational liturgies celebrated in Rome during this period. Only the pope approached the altar to proclaim the Eucharistic Prayer while the presbyters remained in their places. The bishop's pastoral staff was used in processions primarily as a walking stick—a physical support for the Bishop of Rome who often had need of it because of his age. The washing of the hands at the Preparation seems to be purely hygienic in this epoch with no symbolic reference to purification.

As the Roman Rite continued to evolve, the influence of the Roman imperial court would make for wordier and

3–5. Small nave on left (3), large nave (4), and floor plan (5) for Saint Sabina Church. Built under the orders of Pope Celestine I (422–432), Saint Sabina is perhaps the best preserved paleo-Christian church in Rome.

5

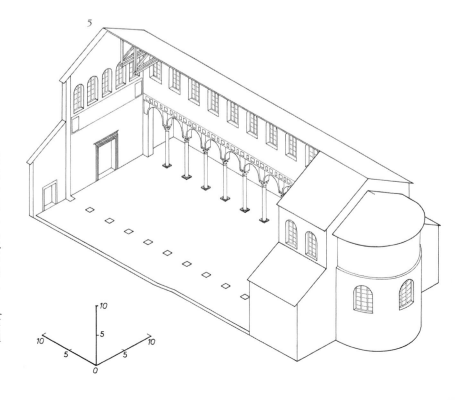

6

7

8

more elaborate prayers with court language employed. The Roman Canon (what is now Eucharistic Prayer I in the current Roman Missal) offers a perfect example of such elegant and formal language including the court gestures of beating the breast, bows, and genuflections. Even the length of that prayer as suggested with the other eucharistic prayers in the current Missal hints at something of the imperial influence inherently present in the Roman liturgy's development from the fifth through the eighth centuries.

The *Ordo Romanus Primus*—part of the collection of what came to be called the *Ordines romani*—is an important document for liturgical historians in trying to reconstruct the ways in which the church of Rome worshiped in the late seventh and eighth centuries, and the precise ways in which Roman court ceremonial gradually found its way into the Roman liturgy. Along with the medieval ordinals and ceremonials, the *Ordines romani* offer the foundation for

what we now call the *General Instruction on the Roman Missal*. The *Ordo Romanus Primus* is the oldest of the *ordines*, as the name suggests, and the first surviving *ordo* of a solemn papal Mass and, therefore, of the Eucharist celebrated in Rome during that period. Among other things, it provides a detailed description of the papal stational Mass at *Santa Maria Maggiore* on Easter morning. We are also provided with a description of the order of the papal procession on horseback from the papal residence at the Lateran, proceeding along the Via Merulana to the designated church for the celebration.

During the procession the pope's assistants carry candles; he is also accompanied by his councilors—presumably Roman presbyters. At a certain point in the procession, the district notary greeted the pope and informed him of how many were baptized the previous evening during the Easter Vigil: "In the name of our Lord Jesus Christ, last night

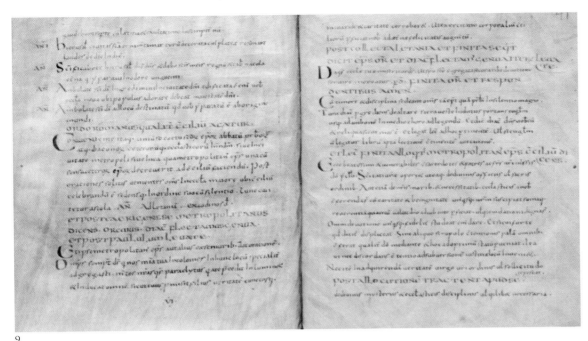

9

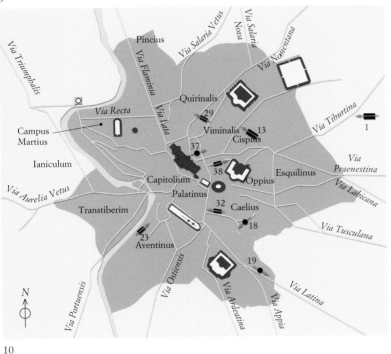

10

6–7. *Pope Damasus (366–384) and Pope Innocent (401–417), in paintings commissioned by Pope Leo the Great (440–461), which are found in the main nave of Saint Paul's Basilica Outside the Walls, Rome.*

8. *Sixth-century consular diptych, modified during the Carolingian period, with the following script added: "David rex, scs Gregor." Cathedral Treasury, Monza.*

9. *Roman Orders, mid-ninth century. Dombibliothek, Cologne.*

10. *Axial direction of Roman churches, 400–500:*
11 Saint Lawrence Outside the Walls.
13 Saint Mary Major.
18 Saint Stephen in the Round.
19 Saint John before the Latin Gate.
23 Saint Sabina.
29 Saint Vitale.
32 Saints John and Paul.
37 Sant'Agata dei Goti.
38 Saint Peter in Chains.

there were baptized in the Church of Saint Mary the Theotokos, nn. baby boys and nn. baby girls," to which the pope responded: "Thanks be to God." When the papal entourage arrived at *Santa Maria Maggiore*, the heads of that church were there waiting to greet the pope along with the choir and other church representatives who kissed his hands and feet. The original simplicity and soberness of the classical Roman Rite was slowly being influenced by the ceremonial of the Roman imperial court. And while this was not as elaborate a ceremonial as what was previously described during the Byzantine liturgy celebrated in the presence of the emperor at Hagia Sophia, nonetheless it would make for more elaborate prayers within the Roman Rite that employed imperial language.

We can note a similar simplicity and sobriety with regard to the eucharistic language employed in this period, which is more indirect than direct. In other words, we don't find much direct language that refers to the body and blood of Christ, for example. Rather we find terms like *cibus et potus* (food and drink); *sacramentum* (sacrament), etc. Saint Augustine's famous description of the Eucharist"—the gifts of God for the people of God—holy gifts for holy people"—makes this point explicit. Likewise, there is little evidence of what would later be called "Eucharistic adoration"—incensing the sacrament, etc. True enough, the late seventh- or early eighth-century *Ordo Romanus Primus* calls for the use of incense to be used in the Entrance procession, but unlike the extensive use of incense in the Byzantine Rite, for example, incense within the Roman Rite is used quite minimally in this period and that same *Ordo* makes no mention of any incensation of the eucharistic elements, as would come to be the case with the rise of scholastic philosophy and theology in the High Middle Ages.

15. LITURGICAL DIVERSITY IN THE WEST

1

Just as we saw in the wide array of liturgical diversity that was operative within the ancient Oriental churches, so too did the Christian West exhibit a diversity of liturgical families. Over the centuries, however, and largely due to political and ecclesiastical influence, the West would not enjoy the same degree of synodal structures of leadership and concomitant liturgical freedom and diversity, and the Roman Rite would eventually become the dominant liturgy of the West throughout the Middle Ages and then firmly established at the sixteenth-century Council of Trent (1545–1563). Today, while the Ambrosian Rite is alive and well and continues to be celebrated with its own proper liturgical calendar and books and its unique structure for the celebration of the Eucharist and Liturgy of the Hours, it is limited to the Archdiocese of Milan in northern Italy. The Hispanic (later called Mozarabic and then Visigothic) Rite has also survived, but to a much smaller degree: it is normally only celebrated in the Chapel of Corpus Christi in the cathedral of Toledo, and occasionally in several parishes in the city and surrounding area.

The other Western non-Roman liturgies—the Gallican and Celtic, for example—have all been suppressed. In our own day the Roman Rite is celebrated in all of the West and in Africa, Latin America, and the Far East, although since the Second Vatican Council there have been various attempts at inculturating the Roman Rite for local usage that more aptly reflects the cultural genius of the celebrating community. The "Roman Rite for the Dioceses of Zaire" (now the Democratic Republic of Congo), approved by the Holy See in 1988, offers a fine example of an inculturated form of the Roman Rite.

As these non-Roman Western liturgies evolved there were some other local liturgies or rites as well, greatly influenced by the cultural genius of those particular areas. There was, for example, the African liturgy, which grew largely in North Africa, as well as several local rites known in Italy: those of Benevento and Campana, as well as Ravenna and Aquileia. In Portugal, a unique rite grew in the city of Braga. Today those liturgies no longer exist and in some cases, information on those rites is either scarce or nonexistent, as

1. Early ninth-century panorama and chronology of African, Ambrosian, Roman, Mozarabic, Gallic, and Celtic rites.

2. Sixth-century baptismal basin from Sufetula (today known as Sheitla). Bardo Museum, Tunisia.

3. Baptistery ruins, with cruciform pool, from the grand Hippo Regius (Hippo) in the Christian quarter, Algeria.

4. Reconstruction of the Christian quarter of Hippo, around the grand basilica.

in the case of the African liturgy, and the Roman Rite is now celebrated in those places. Those obscure rites will briefly be discussed later but a word is in order now on the major Western non-Roman liturgies mentioned above.

The African Liturgy

It is probable that the Gallican and Hispanic rites have their foundations in the liturgy of northwest Africa and so it is appropriate that we begin there. Unlike Rome, which continued using Greek as a liturgical language until the time of Pope Damasus (+384), the liturgy in Africa was already employing Latin from the time of Cyprian (+258). In general, the African liturgy is divided in two periods: pre- Nicean, i.e., before the Council of Nicea in the year 325, and Post-Nicean. In the pre-Nicean period we have the testimony of Tertullian (+ after the year 220) and Cyprian of Carthage. That liturgy was reordered after Nicea as evidenced in the testimony of Augustine, Bishop of Hippo, whose writings extend from the years 380 to 430. There are also the writings of Ottato of Milevi (+ ca. 390), Victor of Vita (+ after the year 484), and Ferrand, Deacon of

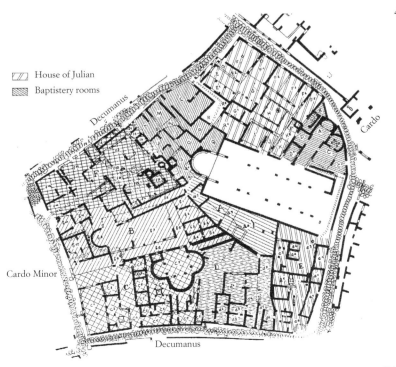

House of Julian
Baptistery rooms

Decumanus

Cardo

Cardo Minor

Decumanus

5. *Mosaic that illustrates the life and activities pursued by the wealthy in the ninth century. Bardo Museum, Tunisia.*

6. *Mosaic on the cover of a fifth-century tomb. The man, who is elegantly dressed, Victoria's praying posture, and the candle, roses, and Numidian roosters and doves lend a feeling of serenity to the entire scene. Bardo Museum, Tunis.*

5

6

Carthage (+ ca. 523). We also know that the African councils in the fourth and fifth centuries speak of liturgical texts—*libelli.* Unfortunately, those liturgical texts no longer exist today so the best we can do is to reconstruct the African liturgy according to the testimony of those mentioned above. As always, to understand the evolution of liturgy one needs to consider the wider socio-religious context and this is certainly the case here. The fact that Christianity in Roman Africa was restricted onto Romans or Afro-Romans without reaching the lower levels of society—the indigenous "African" levels—explains the disappearance of the church in Africa. In other words, once the Roman Empire disappeared, so did the church.

The African liturgy grew from the time that Christianity arrived in that area until the invasions of the Vandals and Muslims. In addition to a eucharistic liturgy in northwest Africa that was well developed, it also had a clearly structured liturgical celebration for the other sacraments, as well; a liturgical

year; and the Liturgy of the Hours. The earliest form of the African liturgy began with the Greeting, followed by the Liturgy of the Word, which included readings from the Old Testament; a New Testament Epistle and Responsorial Psalm; the Gospel followed and not preceded by an Alleluia sung only on Sundays and during the Easter Season; the Homily and Dismissal of the Catechumens. There was then the transitional rite to the sacramental action, which included the Prayer of the Faithful and Rite of Peace that concluded the Liturgy of the Word. The Eucharistic Prayer followed with the Anamnesis and Epiclesis coming after the Institution Narrative. The *Fractio Panis* or "Breaking of the Bread" preceded the Lord's Prayer and the blessing of the assembly preceded the reception of communion rather than at the end of the celebration where it is normally placed. By the time of Saint Augustine, the pre-Leonine Roman Canon was normative in the eucharistic liturgy and the Greeting of Peace had already been moved from the Liturgy of the Word to the

§ ANBRO SIVS

R TINI INTERITVM SACRIS OP

7

7. Saint Ambrose celebrating Mass in the Porziana (Saint Lawrence) Basilica, detail of apse mosaic, Milan.

Communion Rite as it was found in the Roman Rite, between the Lord's Prayer and the blessing of the assembly.

The Ambrosian Liturgy

Despite its name, the Ambrosian Rite should not suggest that Saint Ambrose began the rite nor was its major crafter although it is probable that he had some influence upon its development. Given his prominence as one of the foremost bishops of Milan, the rite adopted his name but, in essence, this rite is that of the church of Milan. There remains some question about the origins of the rite. For example, some scholars date the earliest collection of liturgical formulae in Milan to the middle of the fifth century during the episcopate of Eusebius, who was Bishop of Milan from 449 to 462 and a contemporary of Leo the Great. Others, however, contend that the earliest period of distinct Milanese texts would not come before the beginning of the sixth century, therefore coinciding with the papacy of Lorenzo I who reigned from 468 to 508.

There also remains the question of whether the Ambrosian Rite was influenced more by Eastern practice or Roman. On the one hand, it is no secret that for centuries, Bishops of Rome attempted to coerce or convince the Milanese church to abandon its own liturgical practice in favor of Roman tradition, and there was inevitably some Roman influence upon the shape of the rite. Indeed, Ambrose attests to a eucharistic prayer that bears a striking resemblance to the Roman Canon, which led some scholars to argue that the origins of the Roman Canon were actually not Roman at all, but Milanese. Attempts at Roman interference in the Ambrosian Rite were especially evident during the reign of Charlemagne, who desperately tried to Romanize the Milanese church, just as he labored to do throughout the Franco-Germanic Empire. Despite various Roman accretions, however, it also cannot be denied that Eastern elements

89

within the Ambrosian Rite are clearly present. Nor can we deny the probability of a certain contact with churches beyond the Alps and therefore of Gallican influence, as well. For example, just as in the Gallican baptismal rite, Christian Initiation in Milan included a foot washing of the newly baptized during the Easter Vigil. The Ambrosian Rite also had a relationship to the liturgy of other northern Italian cities such as Aquileia, Brescia, and Turin.

The medieval structure of the Ambrosian Mass began with a procession to the stational church but in the ninth and tenth centuries, that was replaced with the apologetic prayers of the celebrant at the foot of the altar followed by the Introit psalm as in the Roman Rite; the Gloria followed and was replaced in Lent by a litany of intercession. The introductory rites concluded with an *Oratio super populum* or "Prayer over the People" which corresponded to the collect prayer in the Roman Rite. The Liturgy of the Word contained readings from the prophets and the apostles, followed by a gradual psalm and Alleluia, the Gospel and Homily, dismissal of the catechumens; triple chanting of the *Kyrie eleison* and, after the twelfth century, a post-Gospel antiphon. The Exchange of Peace and General Intercessions with concluding prayer followed and then the offering of the gifts. Beginning in the ninth century the Creed was included (one century prior to its introduction into the Roman Rite) and was placed between the offering and prayer over the gifts followed by the Eucharistic Prayer, which contains a more elaborate doxology than what was found in the Roman Canon. As in the African

9

10

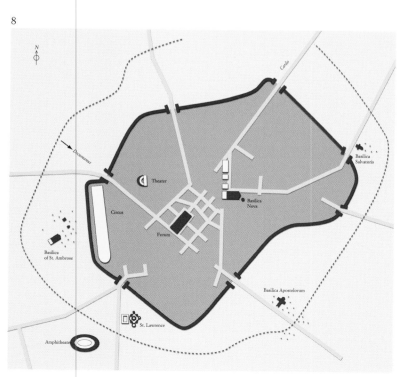

8

8. Milan churches and their axial direction, prior to the year 500.

9. Illumination that illustrates the eucharistic liturgy, from Gian Galeazzo Viscontis' fifteenth-century missal. Saint Ambrose Basilica's Capitular Archives, Milan.

10. Large window from the apse of the Milan Cathedral.

11

12

liturgy, the Breaking of the Bread is placed before the Lord's Prayer with Embolism, followed by the Prayer for Peace, Communion, final blessing, and dismissal.

The Hispanic Liturgy

Also called the Mozarabic or Visigothic Rite, the Hispanic liturgy was created and developed in the Iberian Peninsula from the arrival of Christianity until its eventual suppression by Pope Gregory VII in the year 1080. Taking his name from Gregory the Great, Gregory VII was bent on renewing the Roman liturgy and restoring the classic Roman genius to worship throughout the church. With such strong preferences for *Romanità* it was not surprising that he would suppress other rites in favor of universal Roman liturgical practice. Despite his best efforts, of course, he would succeed only in part. While his suppression of the Mozarabic Rite was eventually successful (except for the few places where it continues to be celebrated today), the bishops of Milan held on tenaciously to their ecclesial and liturgical principles despite Roman interference.

As mentioned earlier, the Hispanic liturgy had three different names corresponding to its unique evolution. While the more common and perhaps more accurate term for this liturgy is *Visigothic,* the term *Hispanic liturgy* is the older

11. San Juan de los Baños Church, Palencia, is possibly one of the first expressions of Visigoth art, since it has an inscription, from 669, of a dedication by King Recceswinth.

12–13. Bronze liturgical jug (12) and censer (13) from the Visigoth era, El Bovalar Basilica, Serós.

13

91

14. *Interior of the Mozarabic San Baudelio de Berlanga Church, Soria, Castille.*

15. *Frontispiece of the Gospel of Saint Matthew, from Juan de Albares' Bible, 921. Cathedral Archives, León.*

14

15

one, as it corresponds to the period in which the Roman liturgy evolved—*Visigothic* to the time of the Visigoth kingdom, and *Mozarabic* to the period of Muslim domination. Like the Ambrosian Rite, there is no common agreement among scholars regarding the exact origins and dating of this distinct rite. It is probable, however, that like the Gallican Rite, the Hispanic liturgy might well have been created from a shared liturgical patrimony that came from North Africa. Surely, the Iberian Peninsula's close geographical proximity to North Africa makes such a theory all the more plausible. What is known is that the euchological schools of Tarragon, Seville, and Toledo and the great church leaders there—Leander, Isidore, Eugenius, Ildefonse, and Julian—had significant influence upon the formation of the Hispanic liturgy. It is also possible that the schools of Cartagena and Mérida played some role in the shaping and structure of the Hispanic Rite.

The structure of the Hispanic liturgy is similar to what we shall see in the Gallican Rite but there are some differences. In the Introductory Rites, we find the *Gloria* as in the Roman Rite; by contrast, the Gallican Rite places a *Benedictus* in its place. On great solemnities the *Trisagion* (Holy God; Holy and Mighty; Holy and Immortal have mercy on us) was included after the *Gloria* and before the Opening Prayer. In the Liturgy of the Word, the celebrant kisses the altar and greets the assembly prior to the proclamation of the Word from the Old and New Testaments. The Alleluia comes after the Gospel; the liturgical assembly responds "Amen" after the words of consecration as in various Oriental traditions; the assembly also responds "Amen" to each petition in the Lord's Prayer. The Hispanic liturgy was the first to introduce the recitation of the Creed during the Eucharist—done each day at the Eucharist before the Lord's Prayer. Interestingly, the text read

16. *Saint-Pierre-aux-Nonnains presbytery enclosure, Metz. Musée d'Art et d'Histoire, Metz.*

17. *Gold paten, from the beginning of the sixth century. Cabinet de Medailles, Bibliothèque Nationale de France, Paris.*

lization, and the church played an important role in the entire process. Assimilation was set in motion by the conversion to Christianity of the Merovingian King Clovis in 496. He stimulated both the growth of the land and the cultural influence of the church. With the Merovingians who ruled primarily in the area of Paris and its environs, there began the process of stabilization and unification that would be completed under the Carolingians.

Thus, the Gallican Rite emerged within such a historical-cultural context; its greatest time of creativity was the sixth century with Caesarius, Bishop of Arles (+546) but would gradually wane with the adoption of the Roman rite through the Carolingian reforms. While the Gallican rite clearly contains Eastern elements that can be identified, it is less clear just how they got there. There appear to have been several contributing factors: Eastern bishops who governed important Western churches; Gallican pilgrims to the Holy Land who brought various Oriental traditions home with them; the Ostrogoth domination in the West, many of whom had been Arian; the influence of John Cassian (+435), disciple of John Chrysostom, who went to Marseilles in the years 415–416, bringing with him the liturgical and monastic traditions of the East which were gradually diffused through the efforts of the monastery at Lerins off the coast of modern-day Cannes, and also at Arles.

If the Roman liturgy was precise, simple, practical, and sober, the Gallican liturgy was just the opposite. Drawing upon Eastern influence and consistent with what we saw earlier in the ancient Oriental liturgies, the Gallican Rite was poetic and dramatic with a much greater use of incense than what we saw in the classic Roman Rite. While the Roman stational liturgy only used incense at the entrance of the clergy and the Gospel procession, the Gallican Rite gradually included the incensation of the assembly a number of times during the liturgy as well as the gospel book and altar. There was also much more variety in the choice of liturgical texts than was the case in the Roman Rite. This was especially evident in the Eucharistic Prayer in the Gallican Rite, which included many variations within the prayer in which single parts of the prayer changed each day. Only standard parts of the prayer such as the *Sanctus,* and the Institution Narrative ("Take and eat. . . . Take and drink. . . . ") remained fixed. Liturgical prayers in the Gallican Rite were often addressed to Christ because of the Arian heresy, which denied his divinity—a problem more acutely present north of the Alps than it was in Rome. In addition, since those prayers were more poetic and dramatic, they tended to be lengthier. After the liturgical reforms of Gregory the Great, the Roman Rite noted very few additions with the exception of the introduction of the *Agnus Dei* by Pope Sergius I (+701) as we have already seen, and also the eleventh-century introduction of the

Credimus—"We believe"—rather than *Credo*—I believe. Also typical of the Hispanic liturgy was the chanting of the acclamation *Sancta sanctis* with the showing of the chalice and paten to the assembly.

The Gallican Liturgy

The Gallican liturgy of the Franco-Germanic Empire was formed in the southern half of Gaul or medieval France, and is particularly important for its relationship to and eventual influence upon the Roman Rite, as we shall see. The Frankish kingdom came into existence after the arrival of the Franks who penetrated from the north and continued moving south into the cities and settlements along the Roman imperial highway. This resulted in the encounter between the old Roman culture and the "barbarian" culture—an encounter between barbarized Romans and christianized Germans which was the very seed of Western civi-

18

19

Nicene Creed on Sundays and feasts at the request of Emperor Henry II who asked that the Creed be sung at his coronation Mass as was customary in his own Gallican tradition. Unlike the Roman Rite, however, the Gallican Rite witnessed the multiplication of prayers and numerous other accretions. Processions were also more dramatic. The gospel book was not just carried to the ambo but borne in a triumphal procession through the midst of the liturgical assembly. Its announcement was greeted with enthusiastic acclamations: "*Laus tibi Domini*" and "*Laus tibi Christe*." The ambo was reserved for the reading of the gospel only; other biblical lessons were read from the steps of the altar, called the *gradus*. The *graduale* (gradual) and sequence thus developed as psalmodic and poetic texts between the epistle and the gospel to accompany elaborate gospel processions. As in the African and Hispanic rites, the Gallican rite also places the Rite of Peace as a bridge between the Liturgies of the Word and Eucharist before the offering of the gifts.

While in the Roman Rite there was only one collect prayer during the Introductory Rite, the Gallican liturgy had up to seven collect prayers. Prayers of a personal and devotional character (called *Apologetic Prayers*) were added into the Gallican Rite to be prayed privately by the priest or bishop celebrating the Mass. Prayers were also provided for the priest or bishop while vesting for Mass in the sacristy, as well as when approaching the altar at the beginning of

18. Partially reconstructed drum and cupola in the Fréjus baptistery. Started in the fifth century, after the one at Poitiers, it is perhaps the most beautiful and best preserved from the Christian Gaul era.

19. First page of the Sacramentary of Gellone, from the eighth century. Bibliothèque Nationale de France, Paris. Sacramentaries of this type were in use in Gaul during all of the eighth and part of the ninth century. They were later replaced by the Gregorian sacramentary.

Mass; at the Offertory; during the singing of the *Sanctus*; and before Communion. Those communion prayers were later ratified and accepted for the whole Western Church in the 1570 Missal of Pius V. Remembering those key Roman elements of simplicity, brevity, sobriety, and practicality, we can see how very different, indeed, the Gallican liturgy was expressed. This distinction between Gallican and Roman elements also helps us to better understand the contemporary Roman Rite, in order to better discern which components are truly Roman as opposed to those that are clearly accretions or additions from Gallican sources.

Interestingly, despite its creativity and insistence on the importance of cultural diversity and expression, the Gallican Rite was strong in retaining Latin as its liturgical language even as the Romance languages were beginning to develop. This was in sharp contrast to the Slavic lands where Cyril

20. *The route of Saint Columbanus across Europe, from Bangor to Bobbio.*

21. *Eighth-century goblet, Ardach, Ireland. National Museum of Ireland, Dublin.*

22. *Book of Durrow, opening page devoted to the Gospel of Saint Mark. Trinity College Library, Dublin.*

and Methodius made it their first task upon arriving in Moravia around the year 864 CE to translate the Bible and the Byzantine liturgy into Old Slavonic precisely for the credibility of the liturgy and of their evangelical mission itself.

The Celtic Liturgy

The mere name of this rite suggests its origin: the Celtic lands of Ireland, Great Britain, and Scotland, and in Brittany on the western coast of France. Thanks to the efforts of Saint Columba and the founding of Irish monasteries at Luxuil in France; Ratisbon in Germany; Saint Gall in Switzerland; and Bobbio in Italy, the Celtic liturgy spread there, as well. Some scholars actually speak of Celtic "liturgies" rather than "liturgy" as the rite took on a variety of forms as it was transplanted from one place to another. The fifth-century diffusion of Christianity in Ireland spread rapidly also because the Irish social constitution was based on that of the clan. Thus, the conversion of the head of the tribe meant that all his subjects went with him. The lack of large cities and

23. Illumination of a manuscript carried by Irish monks to the Saint Gall Monastery. Stiftsbibliothek, Saint Gall.

24. Illumination of the Book of Kells, one of the major Irish manuscripts. It is the oldest representation of Virgin Mary and Child found in a Western manuscript, Trinity College Library, Dublin.

23

24

the effect of the tribal regime made dependence upon a territorial hierarchy with the cathedral church at the center virtually impossible. So it was largely abbots and their monasteries that led the way and this monastic influence was also felt in the realm of liturgy. Those monks lived a monastic life of strict observance with frequent fasting and thus, their liturgical influence contained a strong penitential dimension. This was especially evident in the Celtic Liturgy of the Hours where, in some cases, the entire psalter of 150 psalms was chanted each day. The Celtic liturgical texts also focused more on the individual rather than the community, with a more privatized devotion rather than liturgical spirituality in evidence. When Augustine arrived on the British shores of Kent in the year 597 after his missionary voyage from his monastery of San Gregorio al Celio in Rome, he found liturgical practices quite dissimilar from those he knew in Rome. There are several extant sources of this rite dating back to the seventh through ninth centuries. The *Antiphonary of Bangor* was copied at the end of the seventh century (in the years 680 to 691) and is a collection of twelve hymns inserted between scriptural canticles: collect prayers, antiphons, and other liturgical passages related to the Divine Office. The

25. Seventh-century paten from Derrynafflan, County Tipperary, Ireland, National Museum of Ireland, Dublin.

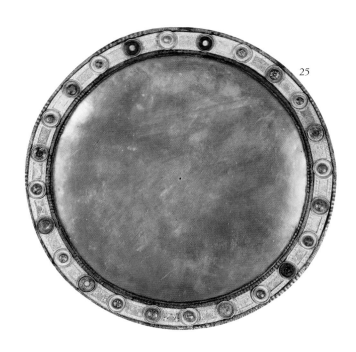

25

26. *Triumph of the Eucharist, floor mosaic in the Aquileia Basilica's Theodorian south hall.*

27. *Sacrifice of Abel and Melchizedek, Saint Vitale Basilica mosaic, Ravenna.*

26

27

text was composed at the Irish monastery of Bangor in Ulster, founded in the year 599. The structure of the monastic office as presented in this text is virtually identical to that of the Ambrosian Office, and as in the case of the Gallican tradition, the collect prayers are generally addressed to Christ. The *Missal of Stowe* is a manuscript dating from the end of the eighth century and takes its name from the castle of the Duke of Birmingham who owned the text. It contains a Roman liturgy prior to Gregory the Great with the Ordinary of the Mass including the canon but lacking variable texts. The three masses that follow the Ordinary reflect a different schema: that of the Gallican and Hispanic rites. The text is probably an itinerant text for missionaries. Interestingly, the name of Saint Patrick appears at least four times in the text. Some scholars also add the *Bobbio Missal* of the eighth century as one of the fonts of the Celtic Rite. It contains liturgical texts that are clearly Gallican in style, but also exhibits a certain Irish influence. Nonetheless, the Celtic Rite never reached its full development, as did the other rites discussed above. In general, the Celtic texts were composed in poor Latin, with a weak grammatical structure and a vocabulary that was greatly lacking.

Other Western Rites

Of the various rites in Italy mentioned above, the most important was the Liturgy of Aquileia, even as scholars fail to agree on the exact origin of the rite. Some contend that it came from Rome while others argue in favor of Alexandria or Constantinople. Be that as it may, it is probable that the rite dates from the late seventh or early eighth century. We know that Paulinus of Aquileia (+802) wrote liturgical hymns that were used in that liturgy. Centuries later in the sixteenth century, the Synods of Aquileia and Como attest to the existence of the Aquileian missal and breviary in the period mentioned above. Given the importance of Ravenna—both politically and ecclesiastically as an imperial capital in the fifth century and as the Byzantine provincial capital in the sixth and seventh—it is logical that it had its own distinct liturgy as well, but we lack the liturgical sources to know exactly what was done liturgically. The best liturgical source we have in Ravenna is that of architecture—churches and baptistries—whose architectural style and rich iconography offers much by way of understanding the liturgy as celebrated at Ravenna in that period.

16. The Evolution of Liturgical Books

1. *Calendar from the end of the eighth century, showing the celebration in honor of Saint Liborius. Bibiloteca Ambrosiana, Milan.*

2. *Deacon at an Ambo, Exultet from 1059–1071, Capua. Museo dell'Opera del Duomo, Pisa.*

3. *Gelasian sacramentary, mid-seventh century, Chelles, Vatican Apostolic Library.*

One of the essential tools for tracing the history of the liturgy and the tradition is a consideration of the liturgical books. It was during the period marked by the rule of the Carolingians and Ottonians that the first proper liturgical books were created. Among these we find liturgical books used for the Eucharist; the Liturgy of the Hours; the good ordering of the liturgy; and for the sacraments and other rites. Initially, the various books used for the Eucharist existed separately. There was a sacramentary for the presiding bishop or priest that possibly included the canon, as well; a lectionary for the reader; a book of the Gospels for the deacon; an antiphonary for the cantor; and a liturgical calendar for reference purposes. Obviously, such a variety of texts arose from the differentiation of liturgical ministries. Only in the thirteenth century were these books gathered into one book—the *Messale Plenum*. Similarly, there were various books related to the Liturgy of the Hours. There were books for the prayers; the readings which included scriptural and patristic readings as well as those from lives of the saints; all these were eventually combined into a single book—the breviary. It was also important to have liturgical texts that would offer the proper choreography about how the worship was to be carried out. This collection of texts describe in detail the liturgical celebrations of the church, including *ordines* (ordos); ordinals; and ceremonies. Finally, there was a group of books for use by bishops and presbyters in celebrating the sacraments and other rites: the *Pontifical* for the bishop and the *Ritual* for the presbyter. The study of liturgical books is both rich and complex as the texts are many and varied, each with a unique history and provenance.

As the Roman Church continued to take shape, its liturgical life also became more patterned and structured. A set of liturgical texts was prepared for a particular celebration and then placed in the archives of local churches as a record of the celebration. The one presiding collected the texts into booklets known as *libelli* (*missarum*). A *libellus* contained the presidential prayer texts for a particular Eucharist or a small collection of formulae for more than one Mass. They were originally composed by individuals for their own personal use in the churches where they served. Thus, the collections of written liturgical material came into existence, initially intended to serve as a model for other bishops and presbyters as they sought to compose their own liturgical texts.

Gradually, those private liturgical texts were diffused as they came to be copied and adapted. The more authoritative the original author, the more the texts were disseminated. As we saw in the Christian East, the fourth and fifth centuries witnessed a period of extraordinary liturgical cre-

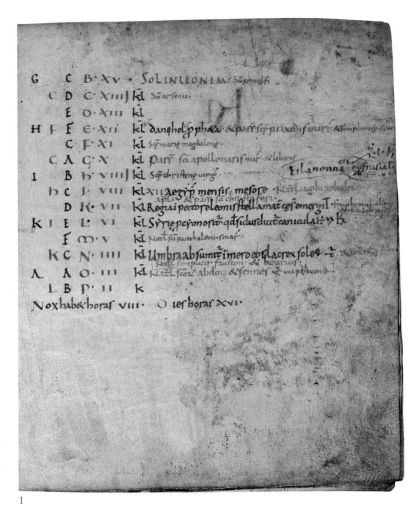

1

ativity in the Roman Church, as well, with numerous texts produced during that time. There were variable texts for the Eucharist; texts for the administration of the sacraments and for use in the Liturgy of the Hours. Those texts obviously reflected the Roman genius and cultural style.

The Gelasian Sacramentary

The *Gelasian* (or "Old Gelasian") *Sacramentary* was copied around the year 750 at the Monastery of Chelles near Paris, but the date of the original must be placed sometime after the pontificate of Gregory the Great (+604) since the Roman Canon that it includes contains additions made by Gregory. It must also be dated after the recovery of the relics of the Holy Cross by Emperor Herclitus in 628, since it contains texts for the Feast of the Exaltation of the Holy Cross. At the same time, we know that the text must have been composed prior to the reign of Gregory II (715–731) since it does not contain eucharistic formulae for the

4. Mixed Gelasian sacramentary, with miscellaneous holidays indicated. Universitas-und Landesbibliothek, Munster.

Thursdays during Lent—a practice introduced by that pope. The Gelasian is intended for presbyteral usage with three distinguishing characteristics. Firstly, it is divided into three parts: the liturgical year or temporal cycle; the sanctoral cycle including a common of martyrs and the Masses of Advent; and the Sundays of the year, including the Canon, Masses for various occasions (votive Masses), and other *varia liturgica*. Secondly, there is frequently an additional oration after the collect prayer and before the prayer over the gifts. It appears to have been a mixed book. Clearly, it is a Roman text with Gallican elements added, and thus it is not a pure Roman sacramentary. Thirdly, the Roman base itself is mixed: it is a combination of both papal and presbyteral elements. It is important to note that there were two liturgical traditions developing at the same time in Rome: one papal (Gregorian) and the other presbyteral (Gelasian). The Gelasian can be termed presbyteral because it contains everything needed by a presbyter in charge of a title church and nothing more.

5

The *Gelasian Sacramentary* was used in Rome during the seventh century and the first part of the eighth. Before the papacy of Gregory II, which began in 715, indeed, probably before the end of the seventh century, it was brought to Gaul by some pious pilgrim or visiting cleric who was enamored of the liturgy of Rome. In Gaul, the sacramentary exercised widespread influence and various Gallican elements were added to it to further assist its functionality in that particular cultural environment. Most notable was the insertion of five sections that are Gallican in origin concerning the rituals for ordinations; for the consecration of virgins; for the dedication of a church; for the blessing of water; and for funerals. It would seem that this sacramentary was instrumental in the romanization of the Gallican liturgy even before the eighth-century reforms of Pepin the Short but more as a private venture. It is therefore an important witness to the Roman-Frankish rite that was gradually developing north of the Alps.

The Gregorian Sacramentary

In the course of the seventh century, the Lateran Basilica developed its own distinctive collection of *libelli* and produced a sacramentary to be used exclusively by the pope not only at the Lateran but throughout the city, as well, as he celebrated the stational liturgy in designated churches throughout the

year. Although this book can no longer be attributed to Gregory the Great even as many orations are attributed to him, it was probably written in the first half of the seventh century during the pontificate of Honorius I (625–628) and was gradually augmented as new stational feasts and liturgies were added in the seventh and eighth centuries. In the second half of the seventh century, the papal sacramentary developed in different, distinct directions, each one leading to a different type of Gregorian sacramentary.

The Gregorian family of sacramentaries can be distinguished by those of the Gelasian tradition by two major characteristics. First, the fusion of the temporal and sanctoral cycles into one liturgical year and second, they normally had only three prayers for each Mass: the collect or opening prayer; the prayer over the gifts; and the concluding prayer or prayer after communion as is the case in the current Roman Missal. By contrast, the Gelasian books included many more prayers as we have already seen. Moreover, the number of prefaces in the Gregorian books was greatly reduced. The stational churches were clearly indicated and a special collect was included for the initial gathering when there was a procession. In the next section, we shall discuss the Gregorian Type I sacramentary or *Hadrianum*, which was sent by Pope Hadrian I to Charlemagne at the end of the eighth century, and its eventual supplement, the *Hucusque*.

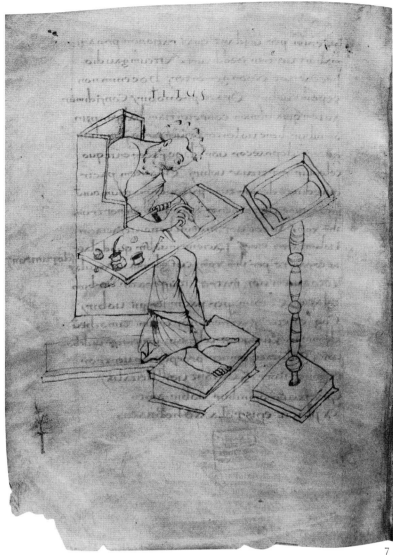

The Lectionary

As we have seen, the structure of the Liturgy of the Word is clearly attested to as early as the second century in Saint Justin's *First Apology*, but he states that the lector reads "as long as time permits" since there was not yet any fixed lectionary or ordo for what should be read at the Eucharist. In the early church there were two basic ways of reading the scriptures: a simple continuous reading of a biblical book or New Testament letter called *lectio continua*, or the thematic choosing of biblical passage according to particular feasts and seasons. In the earliest period the bishop or presbyter exercised considerable freedom in the selection of such biblical passages, but with the gradual development of the liturgical year and the stational liturgies, there was a parallel development of a system of fixed readings. The early existence of such a system—even before the compilation of the sacramentaries—can be deduced from homilies of the fathers and other historical evidence.

There were three different methods for indicating the liturgical readings: marginal notes, capitularies, and lectionaries. In the first system, notes were made in the margins of a codex of the Bible. This system presupposed that the Bible itself was a liturgical book, as it was used directly in the liturgy itself. In the second, scriptural selections were listed according to the initial and final words of the passage. Such

a list of pericopes could be appended to another liturgical book or could exist separately as a kind of companion booklet. As a liturgical book, it received all the honor it was due; the Book of the Gospels in particular was not only reverenced in the liturgical celebration, but was frequently illuminated and richly bound; the book of non-Gospel readings rarely received the same lavish attention. The third method was the lectionary proper in which all the required biblical readings were written in full with the passages arranged according to the established order of the cursus of readings. This system had the obvious advantage of practicality and ease of use, but with the normal growth and development of both the temporal and sanctoral cycles, such a lectionary could easily become outdated. These three methods did not follow each other consecutively, but rather existed side by side for many centuries until the lectionary came to dominate. The oldest Roman texts providing an organized system of liturgical readings are capitularies from the seventh and eighth centuries. When the Roman liturgy made its way over the Alps in the eighth century, the capitulary made the journey as well, but as two separate books: the epistolary and the evangeliary; there they were combined. Two principal families exist: one is the Roman foundation dating roughly to the beginning of the eighth century, and the other is the Franco-Roman synthesis slightly later— between the years 700 and 740.

8. Liber Pontificalis. Universiteits Bibliotheek, Leida.

*9. Bernward (960–1022), Bishop of Hildesheim's Book
of Gospels, 1011. Dom-und Diözesanmuseum, Hildesheim.*

Ordines Romani

We have already discussed the *Ordo Romanus Primus* and its importance for the reconstruction of the Roman stational liturgy. Those *ordines* were essential as companion volumes to the sacramentary since they contained the proper choreography for how the liturgy was to be executed. They also referred to the orations of a given liturgical action in various ways: either with a general remark such as "it is contained in the sacramentary" or with the *incipit* of the prayer ("here begins"), or with the entire prayer written out.

Like the other liturgical books, the *ordines* gradually made their way across the Alps into the Franco-Germanic Empire where they were gathered into collections that date from the eighth and ninth centuries. Those texts can now be distinguished between original Roman texts and those that contain Gallicanized adaptations. They treat a variety of liturgical rites: papal, episcopal, and presbyteral eucharists; baptisms; ordinations; funerals; the crowning of the emperor; dedication of churches; the liturgical year; the liturgy of the hours; particular feasts; rituals for the monastic refectory; liturgical vesture; etc. Through a careful study of the *ordines* one can distinguish between Roman and Franco-Germanic usage as well as note a gradual codification of orations, readings, and chants. They provide clues that cannot be found elsewhere about how the various liturgical actions were executed in that historical period of the eighth and ninth centuries.

The Roman-Germanic Pontifical of the Tenth Century

Initially, the liturgical texts that a bishop needed for the celebration of the sacraments and other non-eucharistic rites were found in the sacramentary with the rubrical directives for proper celebration contained in the *ordines*. With time, however, the bishop sought a more convenient source which would have both the episcopal orations and rubrics together in a single volume. The pontifical came to meet this need, blending together prayers from the sacramentary and the rubrics from the *ordo*. The first attempts to create a pontifical were made in the ninth century. In practice, however, the pontifical did not appear in a fully developed form all at once, rather a variety of different attempts and experiments were made over a considerable period of time.

The most important early representative of the pontifical is the *Roman-Germanic Pontifical* of the tenth century that was compiled at the Monastery of St. Alban in Mainz. Just as the eucharistic liturgy arrived at a point of synthesis in the Gregorian-Hadrian sacramentary with its Gallican supplement as we shall see, so also the non-eucharistic liturgy reached a new synthesis with the Roman-Germanic Pontifical.

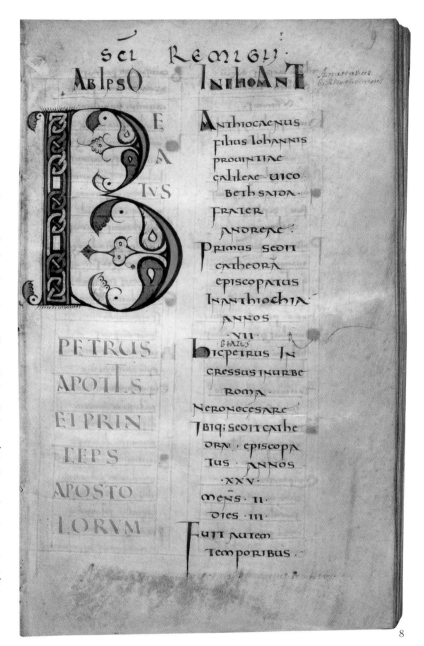

8

As the pre-eminence of the Gregorian sacramentary was the result of Charlemagne's desire to unify his kingdom both politically and religiously, so also a century or so later, the pontifical would serve a similar purpose. It is dated between 950 and 962 and attributed to a team of redactors at the monastery in Mainz under the leadership of the archbishop who was also the emperor's archchancellor; clearly its rapid spread of influence was due in no small part to the authority of the emperor and his chancellor—the archbishop—behind it. The migration of the Mainz Pontifical from the valley of the Rhine to the banks of the Tiber as Otto I along with his episcopal and monastic entourage made one of his many trips to Italy, inaugurated the second great stage of liturgical development in the Western Church. By the year 1150, the Ordinal of the Lateran Basilica cites this pontifical, giving it the name *Ordo Romanus*. By that period, the Roman-Germanic Pontifical was considered Roman, and it became the basis for all later pontificals.

17. Medieval Liturgical Centralization

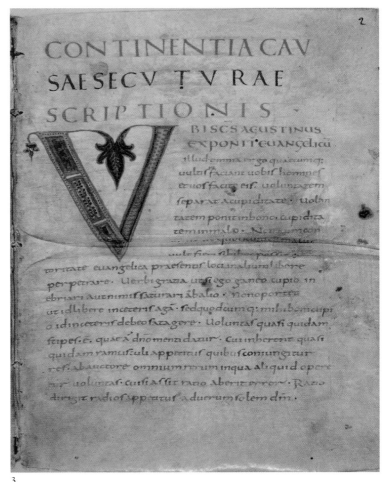

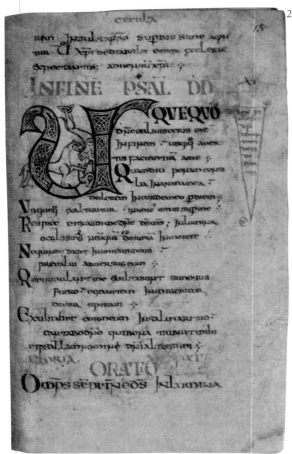

The Carolingians, who came from the area between the Rivers Meuse and Rhine, established a strong kingship by attracting and commanding the loyalties of their nobility. In such a way they succeeded step by step in taking over and consolidating power in larger areas of territory, and thus began the blossoming of the Frankish kingdom and the Carolingian renaissance which combined both reform and restoration. The succession of Pepin the Short, who was anointed king by Saint Boniface with the blessing of Pope Zacharias (+752), and reigned from 751 to 768, was himself the first sign of this renaissance. But the high point of that renaissance came in the year 800 when Pope Leo III (+816) crowned Pepin's son, Charlemagne, as the first emperor of the Holy Roman Empire; he ruled for the next twenty-eight years. Charlemagne's idea was that of a Christian culture within a church-state stimulated by competent bishops and monks under his personal leadership. Western Europe had become a reality and along with it came into existence a truly Western liturgy. Given his penchant for uniformity and a strong central government along with the standardization of laws and the encouragement of ecclesiastical reform, it was hardly surprising that Charlemagne would also work at suppressing the Gallican Rite in favor of a Latinized liturgy that would assist in unifying the em-

4. Bishop in front of pulpit during the Gloria, detail of the Carolingian Sacramentary of Dragon's (823–855) ivory binding, Bishop of Metz, circa 850, Bibliothèque Nationale de France, Paris.

5. Rabanus Maurus, guided by Alcuin, hands over his work to the Bishop of Mainz, Fulda, 840. Osterreichische Nationalbibliothek, Vienna.

pire both politically and ecclesiastically. To this end, Roman books and practices were imported into the Carolingian court and churches but were eventually adapted and inculturated so that they might more easily be received within the Franco-Germanic Empire.

In many respects, the Carolingian renaissance could be described as a liturgical renaissance as well, since the renewal of Christian liturgy was so much at the heart of those reforms: the profession of one faith was the ultimate goal for holding the Empire together. Prior to the Carolingian reforms there was in the Franco-Germanic Empire what some scholars called "liturgical anarchy." In other words, liturgies varied significantly from diocese to diocese as local bishops were able to control the shape of their own church's worship. As a result, those Gallican liturgies were never uniformly imposed on the Empire because they were too diverse and there was no central authority.

Pepin's dream, of course, was less realistic than he had imagined. It would prove impossible to give every local church in the empire an official copy of the Roman Rite because those texts just weren't available—at least not in so large a number. Nonetheless, Pepin prepared the way by encouraging the support of Roman liturgical books inasmuch as they were available, and by imposing the Roman

Rite in the empire but with a variety of local adaptations. In fact, the Gelasian sacramentaries of the eighth century bear testimony to this. Charlemagne, in his *Admonitio Generalis* of 789, wrote that his father Pepin had abolished the Gallican in favor of the Roman—or the recitation of the Roman orations—in order to show more visible unity with the Holy See. A century later, the last Carolingian emperor, Charles the Bald (+877), recalled that prior to the time of Pepin, the churches of Gaul and Spain celebrated the liturgy differently from the Roman Church. Such reforms, of course, would have been impossible without the support of bishops who also were engaged significantly in the process of Romanization north of the Alps. Bishop Chrodegang of Metz, for example, visited Rome in 753 and subsequently introduced Roman chant and the Roman Order of Mass to his diocese when he returned home. It was in this same period that the concept of the Roman stational liturgy was introduced at Metz, adopted for local usage.

The liturgical reforms initiated by Pepin were continued by his son Charlemagne. He had limited respect for the bishops of Rome and saw it as his task to direct the ecclesiastical authorities in his realm. The Rhineland became a stronghold for this administration with cities such as Aachen, Trier, Cologne, and Mainz serving as important

6. Illumination of the Book of Gospels, an Aquisgranum treasure, beginning of the ninth century. Domkapitel, Aquisgranum.

6

7

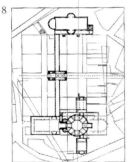

8

centers. The western part of the empire (France) would need decades before unity could be forged. Thus, in a reform begun by Pepin and continued by Charlemagne, the gradual suppression of the old indigenous Gallican liturgy would come to be supplanted by the pure Roman liturgy. Put simply, here we see a movement—even a sort of liturgical movement—but in reverse order: not from unity to diversity but rather from diversity to unity.

Having decided that a copy of the Roman sacramentary would serve as a key instrument in his reform, in the year 783 Charlemagne sent Paul the Deacon to ask Pope Hadrian (+795) for a pure Roman book without extraneous additions, with the intention of replacing the mixed Gelasian sacramentaries that existed in his empire. Two years later in 785, the pope sent a Gregorian sacramentary "in pure

7. Octagonal vault in the Palatine Chapel, Aquisgranum.

8. Reconstruction of the Carolingian complex at Aquisgranum. A long arcade connected the palace to the Palatine Chapel's atrium. In the center is the imposing door through which one could access the palace.

9. Interior of the Carolingian church, Saint Michaels', in Fulda.

10. Three plans for Benedictine monastic churches from the Carolingian period: a) Saint Salvator (A: initial phase; B: initial reconstructive phase; C) refurbishments and additions after 1656); b) Kornelimunster's Carolingian phase; c) Ratgar Basilica in Fulda.

9

11. Beginning of the Gospel of Saint Mark, Coronation Gospels, circa 800. Weltliche Schatzkammer, Kunsthistorisches Museum, Vienna.

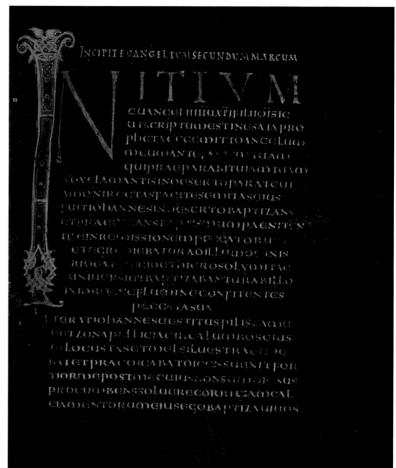

11

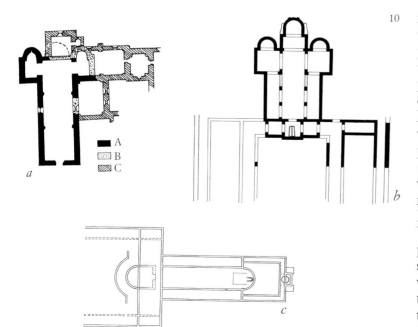

10

form." Unfortunately, when he sent a Gregorian sacramentary, the pope actually sent a papal text intended for use at papal, stational liturgies. The book would be of little help to Charlemagne, not only because it was a text limited to papal usage, but also because it lacked a significant number of texts: Sundays after Epiphany; the octaves of Easter and Pentecost; Funeral Masses; Votive Masses. A supplement would be needed. Known as the *Hucusque* (i.e., "Up to this point"), it was probably compiled by Benedict of Aniane (+821), who made a careful distinction between what texts were original and which ones were added in the supplement. Among other things, we find the inclusion of Votive Masses; Blessings; Different Prayers; Exorcisms; Lauds and Vespers. The eighth-century *Gelasian Sacramentary* was probably the source for the supplement, but there was also some material found in the Gallican books for Sundays that wouldn't have been included in the Roman book. Thanks to the *Hucusque*, elements of the mixed Gelasian sacramentaries once again entered into the Roman book: Roman and Gallican material became official in the Frankish church

12. Charlemagne's empire, showing monasteries that would receive imperial donations.

13. Fountain of Life, Godescalco's Book of Gospels, Charlemagne's school at his court, 781–783. Bibliothèque Nationale de France, Paris.

14–16. Fountain of Life (14), the evangelists John (17) and Mark (16), illumination of the Saint Médard of Soissons Book of Gospels, circa 820, Bibliothèque Nationale de France, Paris.

12

and were preserved in Western medieval material. Thus, ironically, the program of Romanization turned out to be a Gallicanization of the Roman liturgy.

Charlemagne was an interesting character: he never learned to write, nonetheless, he saw himself as God's instrument in the renewal of the empire. His emphasis on education and the proliferation of manuscripts with the help of monks led to the spread of the Roman liturgy as much as any legislation he enacted.

For its part, the Roman liturgy itself was undergoing its own change with a gradual waning of liturgical participation by the laity. Already in the eighth century the presidential prayers (including the Eucharistic Prayer) came to be prayed silently by the celebrant since having entered the sanctuary, he had entered the "holy of holies." In the ninth and tenth centuries, there was an increase in penitential prayers during Mass—the Penitential Rite itself as well as the Apologetic Prayers—largely due to Gallican influence. Likewise, we can observe the early stages of devotion to the passion of Christ and toward the real presence of Christ in the Eucharist—which will become Eucharistic

adoration. Thus, from the eighth century onward, we can note a definitive shift from a symbolic view of the liturgy to a more instrumental world view—from an understanding of "We are the body of Christ" to "There is the body of Christ and we are unworthy to consume it because of our sinfulness." In this period, then, we can observe an ever greater distancing of God within the liturgical context, symbolized by an ever greater distance between clergy and laity, and between the nave and the sanctuary.

In the practical order, this would come to be expressed in a waning of liturgical participation by the lay faithful. By the early twelfth century, for example, the laity was no longer invited to drink from the chalice at Communion, and a century later, the offertory procession in which members of laity brought forth the gifts of bread and wine for consecration also fell into disuse. Eucharistic devotion outside of Mass grew substantially in this period to the extent that the Feast of Corpus Christi was viewed popularly as a more important feast than Easter.

13

15

14

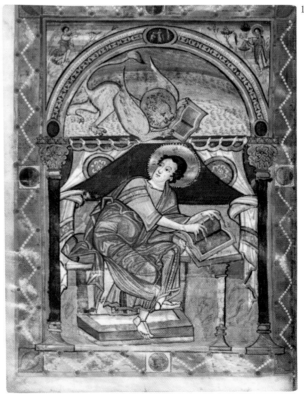

16

18. ROMANESQUE AND GOTHIC LITURGICAL ARCHITECTURE

1

2

3

1. Aerial view of the Civate complex: Saint Peter and the Saint Benedict/Saint John oratory.

2. Saint-Benoît-sur-Loire, north view from the abbey church's portico tower.

3. Wall and north lateral nave of the Saint Vincent (Galliano) Basilica.

The term *Romanesque architecture*, which evolved in the tenth and eleventh centuries, was chosen to indicate its emphasis on the Roman basilica that had originally developed under the patronage of the emperor Constantine. With a wide center aisle flanked by side aisles, this architectural style served well the needs of the Roman stational liturgy with its many processions. In the East, while the basilica plan was not unknown, more common was the central plan of a church in the form of a cross within a square, usually covered with a dome. Even today, this model is abundantly present throughout much of Greece and Turkey and elsewhere in the Christian East. The Romanesque model adapted the Roman stone arch as earlier Byzantine architecture had done, as well.

Prior to the emergence of Romanesque architecture, the Carolingian Renaissance of the ninth century made its own significant contribution. As Charlemagne was interested in promoting the Roman Rite in the Franco-Germanic Empire, it was not surprising that he would seek to promote the Roman architectural style, as well. He required his architects to study the churches and palaces of Rome and Ravenna, which was the last imperial capital in the West.

4. Presbytery (remodeled between the twelfth and thirteenth centuries), and frescoed apse-conch, in the Saint Vincent de Galliano Basilica.

5. Plan for the Saint Vincent de Galliano Basilica after its reconstruction under Aribert, around the year 1000.

6. Scenes of the Life of Christ, presbytery in Saint Martin's Church, Nohant-Vic.

7. Majestas Domini, sculpted headstone in Saint Sernin Church's ambulatory, Toulouse.

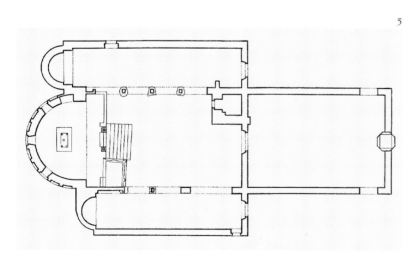

On the following pages:
8. Roman art centers.

9. Gothic art centers.

10. Majestic Virgin, detail of rose window found on Chartres Cathedral's north transept.

8

Centers of Romanesque art
■ Monastery
● Church

112

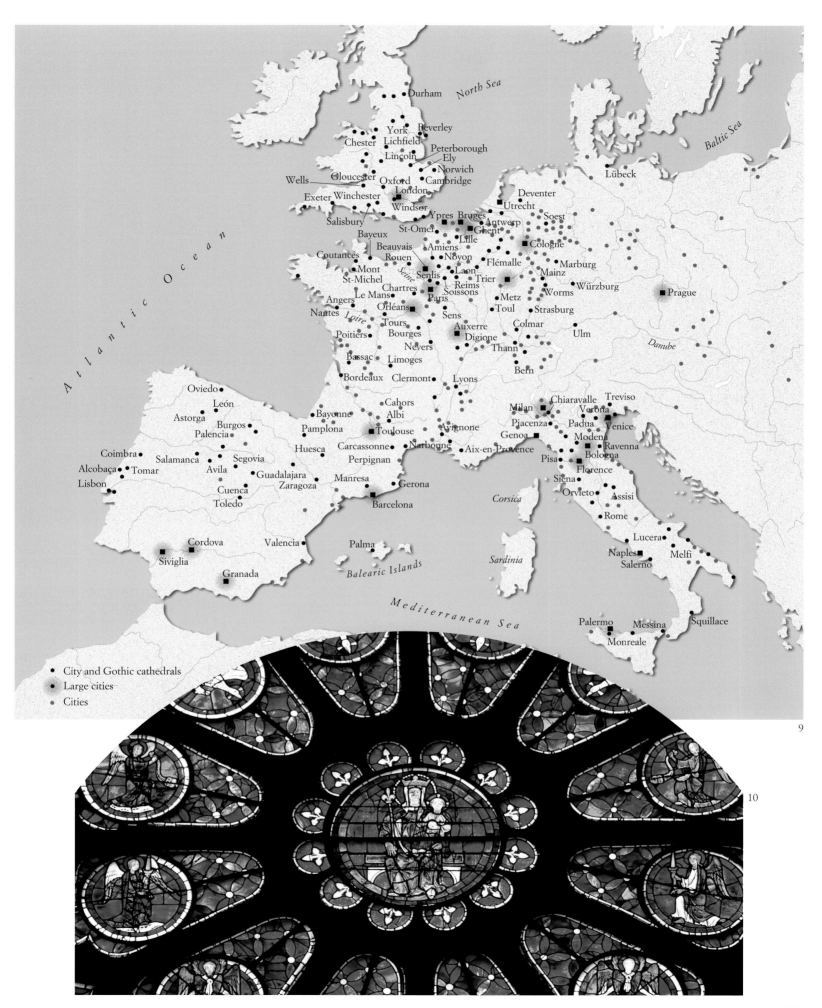

North Sea

Durham

York • Beverley
Chester • Lichfield
Lincoln
Peterborough
Ely
Gloucester • Norwich
Wells • Oxford • Cambridge
Exeter • Winchester • London
Windsor
Salisbury
Bayeux • St-Omer
Coutances • Beauvais
Mont • Rouen
St-Michel • Senlis
Angers • Chartres
Le Mans
Nantes • Orléans • Paris
Tours • Sens
Poitiers • Bourges
Bassac • Nevers
Bordeaux • Limoges
Clermont

Ypres • Bruges • Antwerp
Ghent • Lille
Amiens
Noyon • Flémalle
Laon
Reims • Trier
Soissons
Sens
Toul
Auxerre
Digione
Thann

Atlantic Ocean

Oviedo
León
Astorga
Burgos
Palencia
Coimbra
Salamanca • Segovia
Alcobaça • Tomar
Avila
Lisbon
Cuenca
Toledo

Bayonne
Pamplona
Huesca
Guadalajara
Zaragoza
Manresa
Barcelona

Cahors
Albi
Toulouse
Carcassonne
Perpignan
Narbonne

Avignone
Aix-en-Provence

Cordova
Siviglia
Granada

Valencia

Palma

Balearic Islands

Corsica

Sardinia

Mediterranean Sea

Deventer
Utrecht
Soest
Cologne
Marburg
Mainz • Würzburg
Worms
Metz
Strasburg
Colmar • Ulm
Bern

Lübeck
Prague
Danube

Chiaravalle • Treviso
Milan • Verona
Piacenza • Padua • Venice
Genoa • Modena
Pisa • Bologna • Ravenna
Florence
Siena
Orvieto • Assisi
Rome

Lucera
Naples • Melfi
Salerno

Palermo • Messina
Monreale • Squillace

Seine
Loire

Lyons

• City and Gothic cathedrals
• Large cities
• Cities

9

10

11

12

Thus, the new emperor's chapel at Aix-la-Chapelle copied those Roman designs.

Like those ancient Roman basilicas, the floor plans of early medieval church buildings were similar with a central nave leading to an apse or a choir, with aisles on either side. A major difference in the medieval Romanesque was that now that altar was pushed up much further into the apse and occasionally even against the east wall. This was to provide space for the choir of monks and canons who would gather in front of the apse to chant the Divine Office. This architectural style first appeared in northern Italy but gradually spread throughout Europe. Romanesque architecture typically had little decoration and very small windows, which was both consistent with the monastic tradition of simplicity and yet gave the impression of a medieval fortress with its huge supports and rounded stone arches. Stone roofs replaced those made of timber, which both protected these churches from fire and added to their grandeur. In France, Romanesque churches incorporated stone sculptures and poorer churches settled for paintings that depicted various biblical scenes.

Romanesque architecture, however, was soon replaced by the Gothic style, thanks to the newly constructed abbey church of Saint-Denis in northern France, where that architectural style was born in the twelfth century. After rebuilding the façade of the abbey church so that it was more imposing, architectural experimentation soon continued in the interior of the church as well. That experimentation yielded interesting results: thick walls and tiny windows were not necessary to build big buildings, but with the proper balancing of weight within the arches, the rest of the building could be constructed of light stonework and larger jewel-toned, stained-glass windows. By using pointed instead of round arches, greater height was made possible. Flying buttresses on the outside of the building would allow for further support, all of which made heavy stone pillars unnecessary. By filling those large windows with stained glass, biblical stories could be told much in the way as was done in Romanesque wall paintings. And so, the Gothic epoch of church architecture was born and lifted the spirit to soaring heights with twin-spired facades. Salisbury Cathedral in England, begun in the thirteenth century, offers a classic example of such Gothic architecture. While the Gothic style continued to grow in northern Europe as late as the sixteenth century, Italy saw the birth of a new architectural style in the late fifteenth century that would gradually give way to the Baroque in the sixteenth and seventeenth centuries.

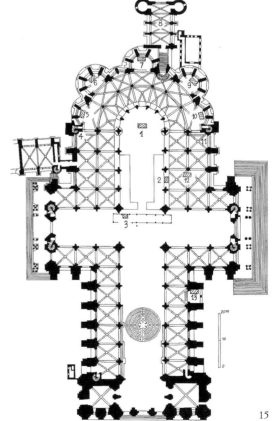

13. Main nave in the Gothic Saint Denis Abbey church.

14. View of Chartres Cathedral's façade.

15. Plan for Chartres' Gothic cathedral.

19. The Hybrid Roman Rite and the Reforms of Pope Gregory VII

1. *Pope John XII, at Otto I's Door, before Pope Leon VIII, who has prevailed over his rival, detail of an illumination from Giovanni Villani's* Nuova Cronica, *fourteenth century.*

2. *Announcement to Shepherds, Henry II's (1014–1024) Book of Gospels, Richenau, 1022. Bayerische Staatsbibliothek, Munich.*

3. *Main nave of Saint George (Oberzell) Church, Reichenau.*

4–5. *Coronation of Henry II (4), Henry II On the Throne (5), and Book of Gospels, Ratisbone, 1002–1014. Bayerische Staatsbibliothek, Munich.*

The Roman-Franco-Germanic liturgy found its way to Rome at the beginning of the tenth century, thanks to the political scheming of Emperor Otto I along with a succession of Ottomon emperors and German popes. Without giving it much thought, those popes celebrated the Gallicanized Roman liturgy that they had known back in their own dioceses. Even prior to their arrival, the Franco-Germanic liturgy was regularly celebrated in the Lateran Basilica, thanks to the gift of Gallican liturgical books given by the monks of Reichenau. Thus, the Roman liturgical influence in the Franco-Germanic Empire began to reverse itself, and the "pure and classic" Roman Rite became the "hybrid" Roman Rite. The singing of the Nicene Creed on Sundays and feasts, for example, was never a Roman tradition. But when the Emperor Henry II travelled to Rome in the eleventh century for his coronation, he asked permission to have the Creed sung during his coronation Mass as was the custom in his native land. The permission was granted and the Creed became a part of the Roman Rite in 1014, but never as a fixed element. Charlemagne had already introduced it into the Gallican Rite in 794. The Church of Milan, which followed the Ambrosian Rite (and still does), adopted the Eastern practice of placing the

3

4

5

117

6. North view of the Cluny abbey church's surviving bell tower.

6

Creed immediately before the Eucharistic Prayer in the ninth century. The apologetic prayers (such as "O Lord, I am not worthy to receive you . . . ") are also typical of the Gallican Rite, but they, too, entered into the Roman Missal in great abundance. Thus, what we now call the "Roman Rite" is actually an amalgamation of various rites in hybrid form, even as the Second Vatican Council (1962–65) attempted to restore the Roman liturgy to its classical and pristine form.

The tenth and eleventh centuries were especially challenging for the church and her worship, beginning with a serious decline in the quality of the popes elected in that period and their lack of moral credibility because of their lifestyles, and wielding of political power. This made the entrance of Gallican elements into the Roman liturgy easier. One sign of hope in that period was the contribution made by monasteries such as Cluny, which led an important monastic reform that included a return to a more simplified and sober liturgical life. It was only with the election of Pope Gregory VII in the year 1073, that the church's moral authority would be restored. Deliberately choosing his name after Gregory the Great, the new pope desired to emulate his example of papal service exercised in humility. His accession to the papal throne had profound consequences for the liturgy of Rome. He challenged abuses in the church such as the acquisition and sale of holy orders, and ecclesiastical appointments and clerical concubinage. He forbade the laity from taking part in a Mass celebrated by a married priest. To counteract the civil control of church offices, he built up and consolidated the image and authority of the pope. Feasts of the popes were to be kept in every local church and were inserted into the liturgical calendar; bishops had to make an oath of allegiance to the pope before their ordination; the naming of the pope in the Roman Canon was to be observed everywhere. Part of Gregory's strategy in the reform of the clergy was to reestablish the traditional liturgical usages of the church of Rome before the Germans took over its government. Gregory began the tradition of metropolitan archbishops coming to Rome to receive the pallium as a sign of unity with the See of Rome and successor of St. Peter. Thanks to Gregory's various initiatives, the popes again took the lead in the liturgical reforms for the next three hundred years.

This was especially evident in the reigns of Pope Innocent III (1198–1216) and Pope Honorius III (1216–1227), which witnessed further development in the shape of the Roman liturgy. Indeed, from the time of Gregory VII onward, the popes attributed to themselves liturgical authority for all the churches. It was under the leadership of Innocent III that the Fourth Lateran Council was convened in 1215, which required clergy to study theology, to pray the Liturgy of the Hours every day, and to be responsible for the upkeep of church buildings. It also made stipulations regarding the obligation of annual confession and Easter communion, and made the first official use of the term *transubstantiation* for the changing of bread and wine into the body and blood of Christ. However, Innocent was most associated with one particular liturgical novelty: a type of liturgy that would respond to the particular situation of the Roman Curia, which at that time functioned as an itinerant administrative body. For their travels, the Pope and other members of the Curia needed portable liturgical books with a simplified format. For this purpose, a missal, a pontifical, and a breviary were composed. Clearly, the intention of Innocent II was neither a codification nor unification of liturgical usages. Nevertheless, due to circumstances, this type of liturgy was adopted by the Friars Minor who, besides being closely linked to the Roman Curia, were often itinerant. In addition to having ties with the Curia, the Franciscans were also pastoral workers and consequently were responsible for the adaptation of the curial liturgical books to the needs of parishes. Thus, the liturgy of the Roman Curia spread beyond the small group of ecclesiastics for whom Innocent III had originally intended it.

7

9

7. Encounter Between Saint Benedict and Totila, detail of the Codex Bendictus, Vat. Lat., 1201, executed in 1070 under the direction of Abbot Desiderio, in Montecassino. The story of the encounter explicitly refers, above all, to what happened in 1077 between Henry IV and Gregory VII in the imperial circle at Canossa. Montecassino was one of the main meeting places during the time of the Gregorian Reform.

8. Giotto, Pope Innocent III's (1295–1300) Dream, longitudinal section of the upper basilica, Assisi.

9. Political map of Europe, end of the eighth century.

8

20. Popular Medieval Piety and the Growth of Eucharistic Devotion

Despite various papal liturgical reforms such as those just discussed, the pastoral reality on the local level was quite different, and there was a widening of the gap between liturgy and life. The liturgy had become increasingly clericalized and was celebrated almost exclusively as the property of the clergy, and the laity were merely passive observers. The offertory procession during which the laity brought forth the bread and wine had ceased; the chalice was no longer offered to the people at the moment of holy communion; and the various liturgical ministries that had been exercised by different members of the liturgical assembly were now performed solely by the priest celebrant. Even when there was a choir singing the various parts of the Mass, the priest was obliged to recite all the words of those liturgical texts under his breath—*sotto voce*—as the choir sang them. It was not surprising, then, that the *Messale Plenum* of the Roman Curia in which all liturgical texts were combined into one book for itinerant usage became normative for the whole church. This was because it was no longer necessary to have distinct books for the various liturgical ministries since the priest celebrant had subsumed all the ministries into his own. The sanctuary had become the *sancta sanctorum* in which only the clergy entered, and the Mass came to be whispered as the priest, celebrating

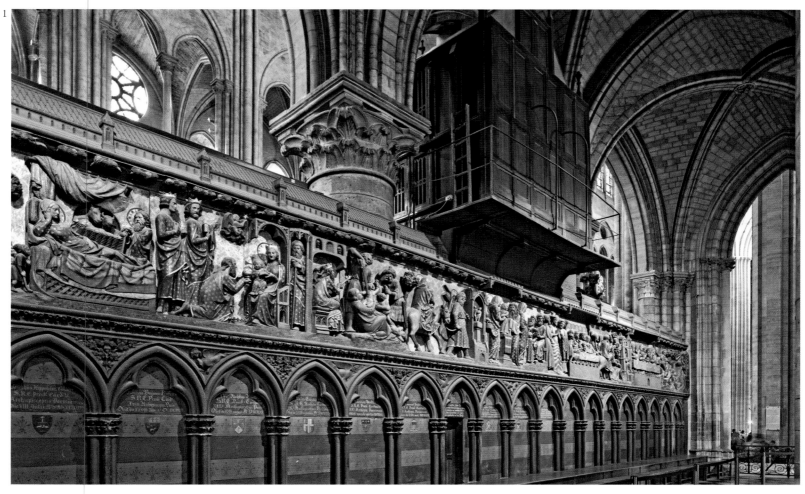

1. Left side (in relation to the entrance) of the choir loft enclosure in Notre Dame Cathedral, Paris. On one side, the choir loft is shielded from the faithful because, at this point, there is a widespread tendency to separate the clergy's space from that of the people; on the other side, its perimeter is embellished to the point that it truly becomes a new construction inside the cathedral.

2. Rogier van der Weyden, Triptych of the Seven Sacraments, 1440–1445, Kroninklijk Museum voor Schone Kunsten, Anversa. The sacraments are described as if they are a private matter that only involves the one who administers them and the one who receives them in so many of the Gothic chapels. In this depiction, the Eucharist, experienced exclusively by the worshipper and sacristan, does not even stand out.

2

toward the East with his back to the people, offered the holy sacrifice.

It is within such a context that Eucharistic adoration grew, along with miracles related to the Eucharist, private Masses, and an overall privatized and individualistic spirituality. In some cases, chapels within European cathedrals and monasteries were endowed for the perpetual celebration of Masses, whose fruits were applied to the deceased with monetary offerings given for each liturgical celebration. These chapels known as *chantries* had priests assigned to them to celebrate Mass continuously throughout the day, perhaps twenty or thirty times each day. Some of these priests (called *altarists*) had no other duty than to celebrate those Masses. And there was great need since as many as one thousand Masses could be requested for a deceased person. Such occurrences made it necessary to forbid priests to celebrate more than thirty masses per day. Of course, wealthier members of the church had a certain advantage here, as they were able to afford to have more Masses celebrated for the benefit of deceased family members. The poor and underprivileged had no recourse but to rely upon the mercy of God since the celebration of such Masses in memory of their loved ones was impossible. As we shall see, it was this sort of pastoral reality that Martin Luther strongly criticized at the advent of the sixteenth-century Reformation.

Even though Masses were being celebrated at virtually every hour of the day, the faithful were no longer receiving communion. Various ascetical practices, such as fasting and abstinence, and the unworthiness of the communicants (requiring confession and absolution), had so discouraged the faithful from receiving communion that the Fourth Lateran Council (1215) had to insist on at least an annual Easter communion, as we have seen. The Council of Trent (1545–63) did little to improve the situation. Indeed, the rubrics in the 1570 Missal of Pius V imply that communion of the lay faithful is more the exception than the norm, with phrases such as "If there are any members of the laity who will receive Communion then. . . . " Not surprisingly, then, eucharistic devotion grew in the late Middle Ages and the Renaissance, offering at least the possibility of "spiritual communion."

With the introduction of the elevation of the bread and wine during the Eucharistic Prayer at the beginning of the thirteenth century, the people were now invited to gaze at the elements at the moment of their consecration into the body and blood of Christ. This became quite popular and church leaders often complained that people dashed from church to church just to see the elements elevated, in an effort to witness the miracle of transubstantiation several times each day. Of course, it wasn't just the fault of the people, since priests received larger stipends for holding the host up longer. Sometimes the faithful would even cheer their clergy on as in thirteenth-century England: "Higher, Sir John! Higher!" In Cologne from about the thirteenth century, a bell was rung to signal the people's attention that

3

the consecration was taking place; this practice gradually spread throughout the rest of Europe. Thus, the stage was set for further exposition of the sacrament. The Feast of Corpus Christi grew within such a milieu, along with Corpus Christi processions in which the Blessed Sacrament was carried in a monstrance. Before long, Corpus Christi surpassed even Easter as the most popular and, indeed, the most important, feast of the liturgical year. Eucharistic adoration and Benediction with the Blessed Sacrament grew as well, along with pious practices such as the Forty-Hours Devotion, in which members of the lay faithful kept watch in parish churches and chapels day and night during eucharistic exposition.

This period also witnessed a significant growth in popular piety helped by the Franciscans and their propagation of such things as the Christmas crèche or crib in which the humanity of Christ was highlighted and reverenced. Devotion to the Blessed Virgin Mary and the saints grew as well, and prayers such as the rosary, novenas, and other devotions came to be prayed in the vernacular during Mass. Those devotions served as a sort of substitute for the liturgical participation they could access no longer, since the Mass was now celebrated exclusively in Latin and largely in silence. Also during this time,

4

5

6

3. Saint Mang's ciborium, mid-fourteenth century, Harburg Castle, Donauworth.

4. Raphael, Miracles at the Bolsena Mass, *Eliodore's Room, Vatican Palaces.*

5. Attavante degli Attavanti (1452–1517), Corpus Christi Procession, *Biblioteca Medicea Laurenziana, Florence.*

6. Giovanni Francesco Barbieri, also known as Il Guercino, Saint Thomas Aquinas Carrying Out the Office of Corpus Christi, *Saint Dominic Basilica, Bologna.*

7

8

9

7. The Franciscans will contribute to the spreading of popular practices of piety, like the manger scene, which is on a fourteenth-century fresco in the Saint Francis Convent chapter house at Pistoia.

8. Banchi's brotherhood, in Giovanni Sercambi's Chronicles, beginning of the fifteenth century. State Archives, Lucca

9. Activities of the Archconfraternity, Rome's Holy Spirit Hospital, in Liber Hospitalis S. Spiritus, mid-fourteenth century. State Archives, Rome.

10–11. Piero della Francesca, Polyptych of the Misericordia, 1445–1460, and detail. Museo Civico, Sansepolcro.

10

11

lay confraternities grew throughout Europe with their own regular meetings, processions, and penitential practices, along with direct service of the poor and disenfranchised in cities like Seville, Florence, Rome, and Naples, to name just a few. Spiritual movements like the mystical piety of Meister Eckhart (+1327) and the *Devotio Moderna* movement of Thomas à Kempis (+1471) gave rise to a private rather than corporate spirituality and offered further challenges to the sort of liturgical piety and participation constitutive of the church's corporate identity as the mystical body of Christ head and members. Rather, the liturgical piety that ruled the day was one preoccupied with gaining fruits of the Mass along with a certain competition among the lay faithful to gain as many as possible.

Thus, such medieval piety offered some interesting contrasts: growth in religious fervor, Catholic piety, and the living out of the Catholic faith, but without the eucharistic celebration and the reception of holy communion as that indispensable source—the "source and summit of the Christian life" as the Second Vatican Council (1962–65) would state many centuries later.

21. The Sixteenth-Century Reformation

1

At the beginning of the sixteenth century, the desire to reform the church and society was already present. Almost everyone wanted a reformation but the question was "what type of reformation?" People had become profoundly disillusioned with both institutions. They looked back to better, purer times—to the pristine beauty and simplicity of the early church which offered a model but failed to remain intact: the holiness, purity, poverty, and strong faith of those earlier centuries had all disappeared. The Humanists viewed the medieval period negatively as barbaric. Indeed, Humanism—especially within the Italian Renaissance—had little interest in religion but preferred philosophy and literature, with the exception of the North which tended to look more kindly on religion. In general, however, the Humanists believed that the church was a scandal created by the pope and his court, by bishops, and by the Dominican and Franciscan friars. They argued that what was lacking was belief and understanding: too many popes, bishops, and priests were dishonest. Too often, the clergy lived very well, while the laity suffered, often living without adequate food. Popes, cardinals, and bishops were ignorant preachers and teachers, they contended. In fact, it was often the case that clergy received little or no theological training prior to their ordination. Moreover, papal power had lost much of its influence. For example, in Spain, the state took control of the church in its famous inquisition; in England, the church was also controlled by the government. In France, the pope agreed to a treaty giving the state the power to nominate bishops ("The Treaty of Bologna") while in Germany, princes took their own directions. Theology had lost its privileged place in the academic world and was now replaced with philosphy.

Liturgically, the situation was no better. Liturgy had become ever more distant from the people, and gazing at the host actually became more important than eating and

2

drinking the Lord's body and blood. It was no longer possible for the laity to touch the host and take communion in the hand. People now went to church to "hear Mass" and it wasn't surprising that they began to ask about when one needed to arrive at Mass so as not to miss or lose the "fruits" that were being offered. This new language of the "fruits of the Mass" emerged gradually, first stating that three spiritual fruits could be gained by those who "heard" Mass (i.e., were present). That number soon increased to eight and then ten, with one of the fathers of the church cited for each fruit that was transmitted from the holy

1. The Ideal City. Galeria Nazionale delle Marche, Urbino. Rosario Assunto has written, in La città di Anfione e la città di Prometeo (Jaca Book, Milan, 1997), in relation to this work attributed to Francesco di Giorgio Martini (1439–1501), about how the latter summarized "the dying fifteenth century."

2. Mass for the Dead, miniature by Jan van Eyck (circa 1390–1441), The Hours of Turin-Milan, fifteenth-century manuscript. Museo Civico d'Arte Antica, Turin.

3. Hartmann Schedel, View of Rome, *from De Temporibus Mundi, Nuremburg, 1493.*

4. Portrait of Martin Luther, *from Lucas Cranach the Elder's studio, 1529. Galleria Nazionale degli Uffizi, Florence.*

5. Ulrich Zwingli in a portrait from the period.

4

5

sacrifice at the altar. In this way, people were encouraged to attend Mass but also encouraged to believe in a false security, that they could save their own souls—almost mathematically calculated—by their presence at Mass and receiving of the assigned fruits. Masses were also multiplied in this period, especially for the deceased: more Masses, more fruits. Indeed, it was not uncommon to have as many as a thousand Masses celebrated for a deceased person to assist that soul's movement from purgatory to heaven. It was within such an atmosphere that the Reformation was born. While there are many reformers who could be mentioned,

Martin Luther (+1546), Ulrich Zwingli (+1531), and John Calvin (+1564) are certainly three of the most important; Luther and Zwingli represent the first generation of reformers, and Calvin represents a second generation. The Lutheran reform was far more conservative when compared with the others, and therefore closer to Catholic sacramental thinking and practice. Luther was an Augustinian, after all, and his own liturgical reforms closely follow much of what Saint Augustine advocated regarding the Eucharist in relationship to the community, for example, and eucharistic participation flowing into the gospel service of the poor and needy. Luther criticized the excessive practice of indulgences, the exaggerated cult of the saints, the preoccupation with pompous forms of cult, and private Masses with their accompanying stipends. Although Luther introduced his liturgical reforms in 1523, he launched his general reform in 1520 with his classic text "The Babylonian Captivity" in which he exposed what he called the "three slaveries of the Catholic Church": the refusal to give the chalice to the laity; the doctrine of transubstantiation; and the doctrine of the Mass as sacrifice. Regarding the consecration of the eucharistic elements, Luther preferred something closer to what is often called *consubstantiation*, in which the elements are transformed into the body and blood of Christ even as they remain bread and wine. This was in sharp contrast to Catholic doctrine, which states that once the elements are consecrated into the Lord's body and blood they cease to be bread and wine. Regarding the sacrificial character of the Mass, Luther was happy to accept the Mass as sacrifice in the Augustinian, patristic understanding of the term—a sacrifice of praise and thanksgiving—but not in the medieval, scholastic sense of the Mass as "the unbloody sacrifice of Calvary." He accepted the primacy of only two sacraments: baptism and Eucharist, since they were the only two sacraments founded directly in the Christian scriptures. Nonetheless, he maintained ritual structures for Christian marriage, ordination, confirmation, penance, and even anointing of the sick.

Luther's reform was fundamentally pastoral in scope. He strove to recover the centrality of Sunday as the Lord's Day and advocated weekly rather than yearly communion, which should be received in the hand, with the chalice offered as well. The Eucharist was to be celebrated in the vernacular rather than Latin with serious attention to the importance of preaching. He also encouraged the praying of the Liturgy of the Hours in parishes.

Like his German counterpart, Ulrich Zwingli began his own liturgical reforms in the same year—1523. Whereas Luther was an Augustinian, Zwingli was a diocesan priest in Switzerland who was scandalized by the abuses he observed on the pilgrimage route to the great Benedictine monastery of Einsiedeln. Unlike Luther's liturgical reforms, which largely left intact much of the Catholic liturgy, Zwingli opted for a much more radical renovation of worship: he changed the forms of liturgy; abolished holy days and much of the liturgical year; and abandoned the lectionary system that often corresponded thematically to various feasts and seasons of the church year in favor of a continued reading of an entire book of the Bible. In general, Zwingli retained as little ceremony as possible. Like Luther, Zwingli launched his reform with a sort of

treatise that specified the use of scripture reading in the vernacular and provided a eucharistic canon consisting of four prayers: a thanksgiving; an epiclesis or calling down of the Holy Spirit to petition the benefits of communion; a memorial or anamnesis; and a prayer for worthy reception of the communion when it was received. Two years later in 1525, he replaced the Latin liturgy with one completely in German, which specified that the Eucharist only be celebrated four times a year. Ministers were not to wear any liturgical vesture, only a cassock or academic robe. The altar was replaced with a communion table from which bread and wine were administered to the people in their seats using wooden trays and very small cups for each communicant. Thus, the normative Sunday worship in Zwinglian churches was a Liturgy of the Word with a sermon.

John Calvin was French, had been a student of theology at the University of Paris from 1523 to 1528, where he met Ignatius of Loyola, among others. While a seminarian, he began to doubt his priestly vocation and left. In 1533, he left the Catholic Church altogether, believing that he had a mission to restore the church to its original purity. At the heart of Calvin's eucharistic theology is the Holy Spirit, who raises us up to eat and drink with Christ. Indeed, Calvin offers one of the few examples in the Christian West of a very high epicletic theology or theology of the Holy Spirit in relation to the Eucharist—something that is much more abundantly present in the Christian East. Calvin affirmed the doctrine of the real presence but raised questions about exactly what type of presence is intended, noting that the Last Supper was not about adoration of the host. Ecclesiologically, he had problems with the language that spoke of the Pope as head of the church, arguing that since Christ is head of the church, the Eucharist is always an act of the church. Essentially, Calvin tried to work out a *via media* between Luther and the more Protestant Swiss theology of Zwingli. Calvin greatly admired Luther's works and read almost all of them. Nonetheless, he developed a very different eucharistic theology from that of Luther, and actually wrote more against the Lutheran doctrine of the Eucharist than he did against the Roman Church!

The English Reformation, unlike its counterparts on the continent, never exhibited the sort of doctrinal protestation as seen in the writings of the German, French, and Swiss reformers. Rather, it was the issue of Henry VIII's divorce that led to the establishment of the Church of England—which remained fundamentally Catholic both in its theology and practice. At its heart was the *Book of Common Prayer*, first composed by Archbishop Thomas Cranmer (+1556) in 1552. Unlike other books of the Reformation, this Anglican text relied heavily on Catholic

6. John Calvin, in a sixteenth-century portrait produced by an anonymous artist. Bibliothèque Publique et Universitaire, Geneva.

7. Pulpit in "Calvin's auditorium" in Geneva, where he usually taught. The auditorium welcomed exiled Protestants from all over Europe.

8. View of Geneva Cathedral, where Calvin preached.

9. Calvinist community gathering in Leone, in the building known as the Paradise Temple, around 1565.

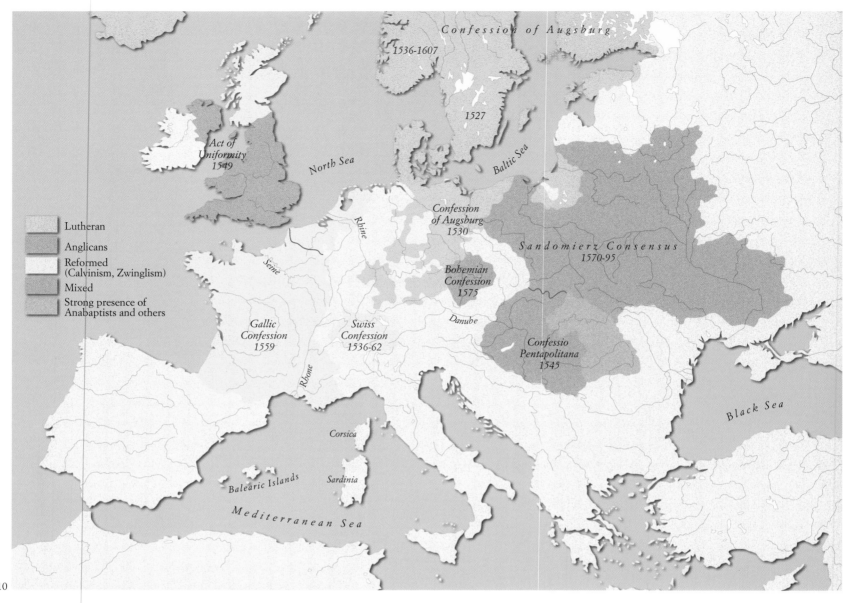

10

Lutheran

Anglicans

Reformed
(Calvinism, Zwinglism)

Mixed

Strong presence of
Anabaptists and others

Confession of Augsburg
1536-1607

1527

Act of
Uniformity
1549

North Sea

Baltic Sea

Confession
of Augsburg
1530

Sandomierz Consensus
1570-95

Rhine

Bohemian
Confession
1575

Gallic
Confession
1559

Seine

Swiss
Confession
1536-62

Danube

Confessio
Pentapolitana
1545

Rhone

Black Sea

Corsica

Balearic Islands

Sardinia

Mediterranean Sea

liturgical books—pontificals, missals, and breviaries, for example. The Spanish or Mozarabic Rite served as the source for the baptismal ritual found in the *Book of Common Prayer*, which also contained daily offices for the communal celebration of Morning and Evening Prayer in English churches and chapels. In large part, this was because of the strong Benedictine influence in England, which Anglicanism had inherited and sought to maintain. Even today, Roman Catholic churches would be hard-pressed to match the beauty of Anglican Evensong as chanted each day at Westminster Abbey and Saint Paul's Cathedral in London, or in the colleges of Cambridge and Oxford.

11

ANNO · ETATIS · SVÆ · XLIX ·

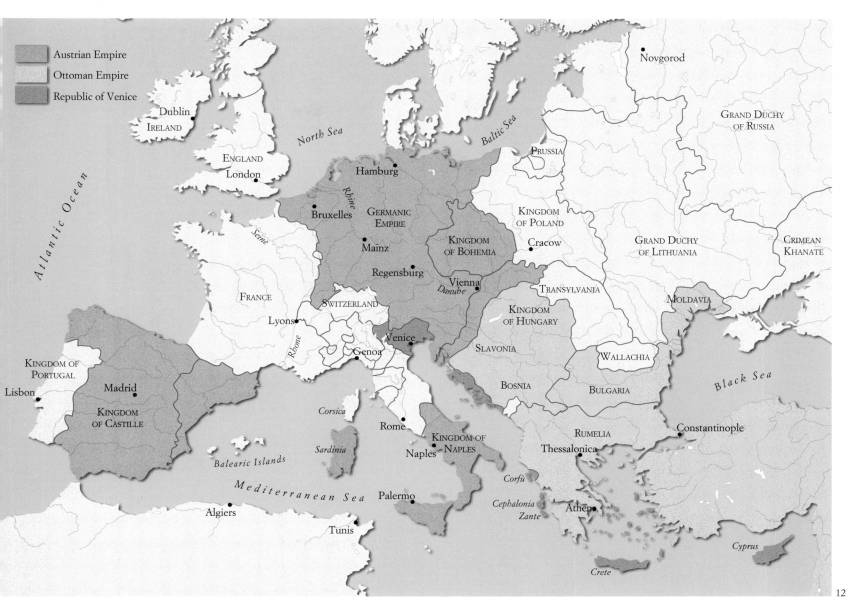

Novgorod

GRAND DUCHY OF RUSSIA

IRELAND
Dublin

North Sea

Baltic Sea

PRUSSIA

KINGDOM OF POLAND

GRAND DUCHY OF LITHUANIA

CRIMEAN KHANATE

ENGLAND
London

Hamburg

Rhine

GERMANIC EMPIRE

Bruxelles

Seine

Mainz

KINGDOM OF BOHEMIA

Cracow

Atlantic Ocean

Regensburg

Vienna
Danube

TRANSYLVANIA

MOLDAVIA

FRANCE

SWITZERLAND

Lyons

Rhone

Venice

KINGDOM OF HUNGARY

SLAVONIA

WALLACHIA

Black Sea

Genoa

KINGDOM OF PORTUGAL

Lisbon

Madrid

KINGDOM OF CASTILLE

BOSNIA

BULGARIA

Corsica

Rome

RUMELIA

Constantinople

Sardinia

Naples

KINGDOM OF NAPLES

Thessalonica

Balearic Islands

Mediterranean Sea

Palermo

Corfù

Cephalonia
Zante

Athens

Algiers

Tunis

Crete

Cyprus

12

13

14

10. The religious situation in Europe during the fourteenth century.

11. Hans Holbein the Younger (1498–1543), Henry VIII, 1541. Galleria Nazionale, Rome.

12 Europe's political situation during the first half of the fourteenth century.

13. Gerlach Flicke, Thomas Cranmer (1489–1556), 1545. National Portrait Gallery, London.

14. Monks' choir in Westminster Abbey.

22. THE COUNCIL OF TRENT (1545–1563)

1. The Fourth Lateran Council, drawing from William of Tudela's and an anonymous successor's Ballad of the Albigensian Crusade, 1215–1230.

2. View of the northwest corner of the courtyard at the Pope's palace in Avignon, and sections of Benedict XII's Old Palace (1334–1342).

3. Giovanni di Paolo, Saint Catherine before the Pope at Avignon, *circa 1461. Museo Thyssen-Bornemisza, Madrid. The pope in the painting might be Gregory XI (1370–1378)—in which case, the supplication is for the return of the popes at Avignon to Rome—or Pope Urban VI, who was invited to confide in Divine Providence in order to overcome the difficulties that resulted from the Anagni schism.*

4. Sweden's Holy Brigade, Marshal Boucicaut's illumination from the Hours, 1408–1411. Musée Jacquemart-André, Paris.

1

2

The late eleventh-century reforms of Pope Gregory VII set in motion a series of changes in Western culture that would set the stage, to some degree, for the sixteenth century Council of Trent. First, the Gregorian reforms established an ecclesial system in which canon law would achieve a rank within church life that it had not enjoyed prior to that period. Second, the concept of reform (or reformation) would be intrinsically linked with a restoration of the church's ancient traditions and disciplines, best articulated in the canons themselves. While the Fourth Lateran Council of 1215 made its own significant contribution in declaring transubstantiation an article of faith and the requirement of an annual confession and communion, recognition of the church's need for reform grew even more in the fourteenth and fifteenth centuries given the urgency brought on by the Great Western Schism.

While the papacy was at Avignon from 1309 to 1377, all of the popes were French and the majority of the cardinals held French episcopal sees. Most of these popes were men of good character, and did their best to tend to their administrative tasks without abuse of the system, although none was able to break away from the "benefice system," which treated church offices (*beneficia*) as pieces of property to be bought or sold, exchanged, granted as rewards, and, especially, taxed. This system was essentially a moneymaking operation that had little to do with the pastoral life or mission of the church. Moreover, papal centralization increa-

3

4

5

singly impinged upon the authority of local bishops and thereby challenged the ancient tradition of local church governance and synodal structures of leadership that had remained intact in the Christian East. Soon, the church would suffer even greater challenges in three-competing papacies in which three men simultaneously claimed to be pope.

At the urging of Catherine of Siena (+1380) and Bridget of Sweden (+1377), Pope Gregory XI (+1378) transferred the papacy from Avignon back to Rome in January 1377, just a year before his death. Thus, when he died in March 1378, most of the cardinals were already in Rome. The French majority among them would have gladly returned the papacy to Avignon but the clergy and people of Rome intervened and demanded an Italian pope. Amidst significant conflict, the cardinals chose Bartolomeo Prignano, the Archbishop of Bari, who took the name Urban VI (+1378). Urban VI was not skilled in diplomacy and sought to terminate French dominance over the papacy once and for all, and to introduce various reforms in the papal court, much to the annoyance of the largely French College of Cardinals. Four months after his election, twelve of the sixteen cardinals assembled at Anagni south of Rome declared their previous choice void because they claimed it had been dictated by mob violence, and elected Cardinal Robert of Geneva as Pope Clement VII (1378–1394), inaugurating the great schism of the West in which he was the first antipope.

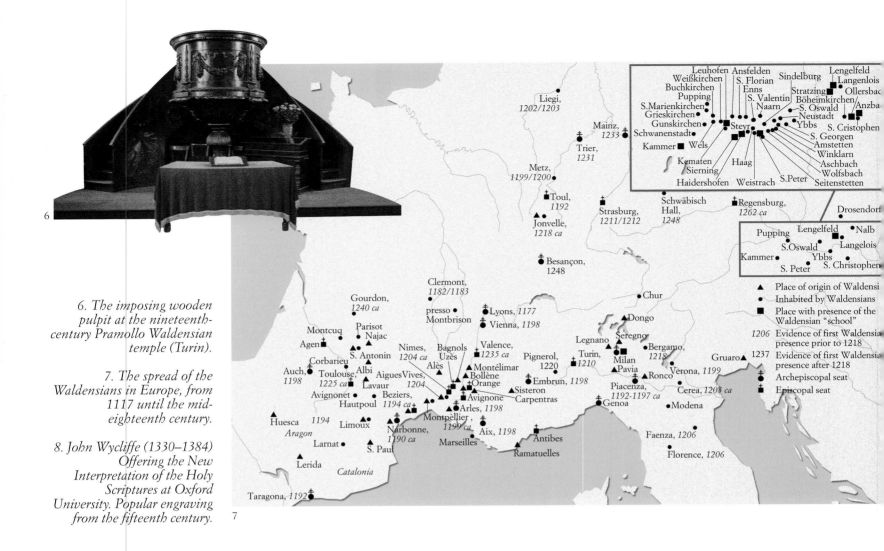

Liegi, 1202/1203

Mainz, 1233

Trier, 1231

Metz, 1199/1200

Toul, 1192

Jonvelle, 1218 ca

Besançon, 1248

Strasburg, 1211/1212

Schwäbisch Hall, 1248

Regensburg, 1262 ca

Drosendorf

Leuhofen Ansfelden
Weißkirchen   S. Florian   Sindelburg   Lengelfeld
Buchkirchen   Enns   Stratzing   Langenlois
Pupping   S. Valentin   Böheimkirchen   Ollersbac
S.Marienkirchen   Naarn   S. Oswald   Anzba
Grieskirchen   Steyr   Neustadt
Gunskirchen   Ybbs   S. Cristophen
Schwanenstadt   S. Georgen
Kammer   Wels   Amstetten
Kematen   Winklarn
Sierning   Haag   Aschbach
Haidershofen   Weistrach   S.Peter   Wolfsbach
Seitenstetten

Pupping   Lengelfeld   Nalb
S.Oswald   Langelois
Kammer   Ybbs
S. Peter   S. Christophen

Chur

Clermont, 1182/1183

Gourdon, 1240 ca

presso
Montbrison

Lyons, 1177

Vienna, 1198

Dongo

Legnano   Seregno

Bergamo, 1218

Gruaro   1237

Montcuq

Parisot
Najac

Agen

S. Antonin

Nimes, 1204 ca   Bagnols
Uzès

Valence, 1235 ca

Pignerol, 1220   Turin, 1210   Milan

Verona, 1199

Corbarieu

Auch, 1198   Toulouse, 1225 ca   Albi   AiguesVives, 1204

Alès

Montélimar
Bollène
Orange

Embrun, 1198

Pavia   Ronco

Piacenza, 1192-1197 ca   Cerea, 1203 ca

Avignonet   Beziers   Lavaur

Sisteron
Carpentras

Avignone

Genoa

Modena

Hautpoul   1194 ca

Arles, 1198

Montpellier, 1199 ca

Huesca   1194
Aragon   Limoux

Narbonne, 1190 ca

Aix, 1198

Faenza, 1206

Larnat

S. Paul

Antibes

Marseilles

Lerida   Catalonia

Ramatuelles

Florence, 1206

Taragona, 1192

Legend

▲ Place of origin of Waldensi
● Inhabited by Waldensians
■ Place with presence of the Waldensian "school"
1206 Evidence of first Waldensia presence prior to 1218
1237 Evidence of first Waldensia presence after 1218
‡ Archepiscopal seat
⊕ Episcopal seat

6. The imposing wooden pulpit at the nineteenth-century Pramollo Waldensian temple (Turin).

7. The spread of the Waldensians in Europe, from 1117 until the mid-eighteenth century.

8. John Wycliffe (1330–1384) Offering the New Interpretation of the Holy Scriptures at Oxford University. Popular engraving from the fifteenth century.

9. In the presence of the Princess of Saxony's (she was the protector of the Reform Movement) family, Jan Hus (1372–1415) and Martin Luther administer the bread and wine communion. Wood engraving by Lucas Cranach.

With such a schism brought on by the papacy itself, reform was more urgent than ever and now extended beyond church practice in relation to canon law to include the issue of belief itself in light of the more ancient church tradition. By the beginning of the fifteenth century, the two great reform movements that operated within the medieval church—Catharism and the Waldensian movement—had been fairly well contained. Catharism had been essentially dismantled, while the Waldensians had been isolated and driven underground. Yet at this very time between the years 1375 and 1425, two new movements of significant proportions grew—one in England led by John Wycliffe, and the other in Bohemia led by Jan Hus. In 1380, Wycliffe published his treatise *On the Eucharist*, in which he rejected the dogma of transubstantiation as illogical, unscriptural, and unfaithful to the teaching of the early church. For his part, Hus became a zealous advocate of the reform of the clergy, and was appointed preacher at the Bethlehem Chapel of Prague in 1402, the center of the Czech reform movement within the church where he soon gained a large following. Wycliffe and Hus have often been seen as forerunners of the Protestant Reformation, which is true in part regarding their protest against ecclesial abuses and overall call for church reform. However, the fundamental doctrines of the Protestant reformers owed little of their substance to the agenda of Wycliffe and Hus. At the Council of Constance (1414–1418) emer-

10. *Antonio Baldana,* De Magno Scismate, *circa 1420. Biblioteca Palatina, Parma. This illumination depicts the Council of Constance (1414–1418) and the flight of Pope John XXIII (1410–1415).*

11. *Execution of Girolamo Savonarola and His Two Dominican Brethren at Florence's Piazza della Signoria, on May 2, 1498. Painting by anonymous artist.*

ged the slogan that would be the Magna Carta within the church for the next century: "reform in faith and practice, in head and members."

Even after the settlement of the great schism, the call to reform within the church remained strong especially with regard to the reform of abuses within the papal curia itself. This would continue up to the Council of Trent, in which half of the Tridentine decrees were about reform (*de reformatione*). Both at the Council of Constance and the Council of Basel (1431–1449), there was a certain level of anti-papalism already present, but a widespread anti-clericalism became rampant at the beginning of the sixteenth century in an unprecedented way. The Dominican reformer Girolamo Savanorola (+1498), for example, led the people in Florence in a revolt against the pope and his clique—the members of the Roman Curia and, indeed, of the pope's own family. He was a passionate preacher who denounced the immorality of the Florentines and the contemporary clergy and prophesied on the future of the church until his excommunication by Pope Alexander VI in 1497. He was eventually hanged as a schismatic and heretic in the marketplace in Florence.

From the outset, then, it is important to state that the Council of Trent was not only interested in responding to the critique of the Reformers, but also to acknowledge that the Catholic Church was itself in need of reform, and that there was at least some truth in what the Reformers had

been complaining about. In the end, the council didn't succeed in unifying the churches of the West as it had hoped, but it strengthened Catholicism especially in regard to liturgical uniformity. Having explored the fundamental elements of the Protestant Reformation in the previous chapter, this historical background of rather complicated developments within the Catholic Church itself and various calls to reform in the centuries leading up to Trent is important, in order to properly situate the Council of Trent and understand the sorts of challenges it was facing when it opened on December 13, 1545. At the beginning, it was a rather small assembly, composed of just three legates, one cardinal, four archbishops, twenty-one bishops, and five superiors general of religious orders.

We can distinguish three fundamental characteristics of the Tridentine liturgical reforms. First was the centralization of liturgical authority organized under the pope and the Roman Curia. The centralization was a response to the Reformers, thus eliminating all innovations introduced by individuals and correcting liturgical abuses that were rampant in this period. To this end, the Congregation for Sacred Rites was founded in 1588, twenty-five years after the conclusion of the council. A second characteristic, which flows from the first, was a strong emphasis on rubrics in order to maintain liturgical uniformity throughout the universal church. This led, however, to a new mentality: rubricism had moral and juridical consequences

12. Titian (?), Session of the Council of Trent, *Louvre Museum, Paris.*

13. Frontispiece of the collection of canons and decrees from the Council of Trent sessions, held under Popes Paul III (1534–1559), Julius III (1550–1555), and Pius IV (1559–1565).

regarding issues such as the validity of the Mass. Rubrics that were once descriptive guidelines became obligatory norms. Thirdly, there was the pastoral dimension to the council, evidenced by significant discussion on topics such as communion under both species for the laity and greater use of the vernacular in Mass. A well-kept secret is that those two items were not flatly rejected at Trent. In fact, not a few bishops spoke out positively in favor of both subjects. In the end, however, the bishops opted for prudence, judging that it was inopportune to make such changes at that time since more catechesis would be needed. Nevertheless, Trent did encourage vernacular preaching on Sundays and feast days, and as had already been the case in Bavaria, vernacular hymnody during low Masses when there was no choir increased significantly after the council. Certain concessions for the giving of the chalice during distribution of holy communion were granted, as well: Pius IV allowed permission for communion under both forms in Germany in 1564, just one year after the council closed. The Archbishop of Prague granted a similar concession for his own archdiocese in 1573 in response to a request that came from the Jesuit college there.

At the heart of the Tridentine liturgical reform was a desire to return to the classic Roman Rite in order to show the Protestants its great value. The project of classic reform, however, ultimately proved impossible. For one thing, it was too difficult to delineate and separate the original norms, but the bishops also sensed the need to avoid liturgical archaeology. Thus, liturgical texts were not changed, and the medieval liturgy rather than the patristic was chosen as the basis for that conciliar reform. The twenty-second session in 1562 was especially important for the liturgical reform, since it treated the widespread problem of liturgical abuses: Mass should be celebrated only in consecrated places; magical treatment of the host was to cease; disrespectful and inappropriate liturgical music was to cease; bishops were to control their priests regarding Mass stipends; superstition around the number of fixed Masses was to stop. Positively, that same session expressed the desire that members of the liturgical assembly should receive communion at every Mass; liturgical preaching in the vernacular was advocated; and the sacrificial nature of the Mass was upheld and proclaimed free of error. Clergy were reminded that water should be added to the wine for the offering—something that the Reformers had suggested was unimportant.

It was, however, the twenty-fifth and final session of the council that ultimately dealt with the reform of the Mass and the Divine Office (Liturgy of the Hours), but time had run out and the desired liturgical reforms could not be accomplished. So the council fathers gave Pope Pius IV the task of reforming the liturgical books—a task which he

took up immediately by appointing a liturgical commission to carry out the council's wishes. This project was continued by his successor, Pius V, which resulted in the promulgation of the Tridentine Roman Breviary in 1568, and the Roman Missal two years later in 1570. The bre-

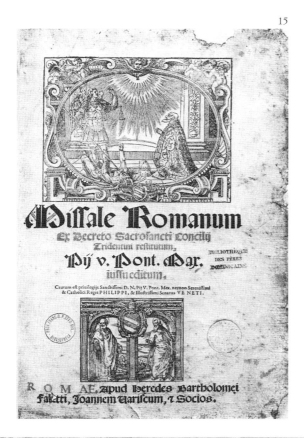

15

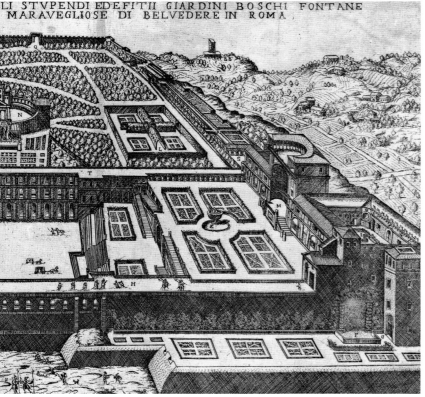

CLI STVPENDI EDEFITII GIARDINI BOSCHI FONTANE
MARAVEGLIOSE DI BELVEDERE IN ROMA

14. *Mario Cartaro, true-to-life drawing of the beautifully constructed woods and garden fountains, and precious items from the Belvedere in Rome, 1574 engraving. At the top and in the middle of the garden is the pavilion of Pope Pius IV.*

15. *Frontispiece of Pope Pius V's (1566–1572) missal, Rome, 1571. Bibliothèque du Saulchoir, Paris.*

published the Roman calendar, more than three hundred saints had been added to the calendar. Thus, the reduction of the sanctoral cycle left one hundred and fifty seven free (ferial) days, especially in Lent, in order to respect the penitential season rather than celebrate a saint's feast or memorial on those penitential days. The missal was based primarily on the earlier missal of the Roman Curia. Rubrics were added that had been taken from the 1502 *Ordo Missae* of John Buchard of Strasbourg, the papal master of ceremonies. However, since Buchard's rubrics were intended for Mass with a congregation, they needed to be altered for the Tridentine Missal, since the private Mass now had become normative, even when a congregation of lay faithful was present.

After the publication of the new breviary and missal, there were still other liturgical books to be reformed. Once the Congregation of Rites was firmly established, this task became much easier. In less than fifty years, all the liturgical books were revised and promulgated. The liturgical calendar was revised in 1582 under the leadership of Pope Gregory XII; and the Roman martyrology was revised in 1586 and again in 1589. Use of the Tridentine liturgical books was made obligatory for the whole Western Church, except in provinces or dioceses that could demonstrate a two-hundred year history of their own usage. Exceptions to the rule of Rome, therefore, included certain medieval religious orders (the Dominican Rite, for example), and the Dioceses of Milan (the Ambrosian Rite), Toledo (the Mozarabic Rite), Trier, Cologne, Liege, Braga, and Lyons. However, we must not be naïve in thinking that the implementation of Tridentine liturgical books was uniformly established. France, for example, refused to accept the Tridentine liturgical norms of Roman centralization well into the nineteenth century. In addition, in neighboring Germany, the Diocese of Muenster waited until 1890 to implement the Missal of Pius V—three hundred and twenty years after its promulgation! Nevertheless, the Roman liturgy established at Trent lasted for the next four hundred years until the Second Vatican Council (1962–1965); it perdured even as the externals around that liturgy changed in the realm of architecture, music, and popular piety. Thus, we cannot speak of a "Baroque" liturgy as we speak of a "Medieval" liturgy, despite the fact that we can easily identify Baroque elements within the Roman Rite, as we shall see in the next chapter. Those changes, however, were largely cosmetic or superficial rather than organic in terms of the effect that they had on the execution and celebration of the Roman liturgy itself.

viary was a return to the traditional Roman office, albeit shortened and simplified. Choral elements were restored for praying the Divine Office in common, and the sanctoral cycle was simplified with a preference for the Roman martyrs. Between the years 800 to 1568, when Pius V

23. LITURGY, ART, AND ARCHITECTURE IN THE BAROQUE ERA

1. Saint Peter's Vatican Basilica, intersection of the transept with the cupola, and Gian Lorenzo Bernini's baldachino.

2. Andrea Sacchi's (1599–1661) canvas depicts the Church of the Gesù, prior to the use of decorative paintings. Galleria Nazionale d'Arte Antica, Palazzo Barberini, Rome.

1

2

With the founding of new religious orders in the sixteenth century, such as the Jesuits and the Theatines, a new religious architecture was needed since those orders were not bound to pray the Divine Office in common, and therefore the "choir" (choir stalls) that often divided the nave from the altar in medieval churches was no longer needed. Those new orders were directed to apostolic service and they recognized that spending a significant amount of time each day in church chanting the Liturgy of the Hours would mean less time for the service of the poor and needy. Thus, a new architectural style unfolded. In Baroque archi-

tecture, the church design was opened up to create one single, unified space allowing for clear sightlines to view the altar, with a special emphasis on visibility and audibility. Its style was flamboyant and intended as a feast for the eyes. This is especially visible in Gianlorenzo Bernini's (+1680) baldachino in St. Peter's Basilica.

Those new religious orders born in the wake of the Counter Reformation had a newfound emphasis on preaching and catechesis, thus the ambo or pulpit became prominent and placed in the center of the church for better audibility. This led to the accusation that Jesuits were really "Protestants in

3

6

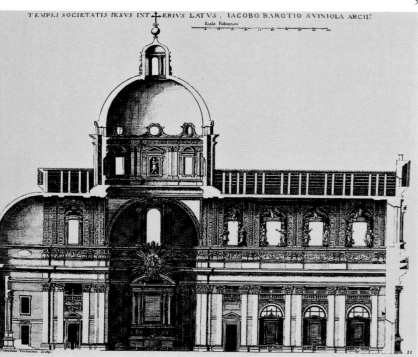

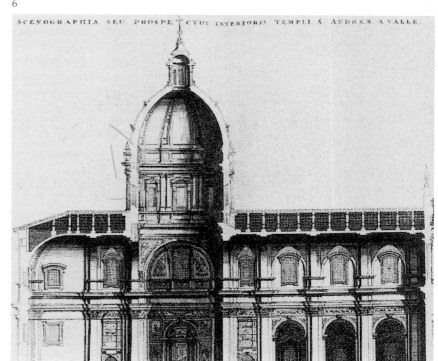

4

7

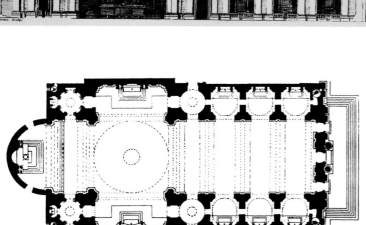

5

3. *Church of the Gesù, Rome, Vignola (1507–1573) façade (1573–1577).*

4. *Longitudinal section (by D. de Rossi) in Rome's Church of the Gesù.*

5. *Plan for Rome's Church of the Gesù.*

6. *Façade (1655–1665) of Rome's Sant'Andrea della Valle Church, the work of Carlo Rainaldi (1611–1691).*

7. *Longitudinal section (by D. de Rossi) in Rome's Sant'Andrea della Valle Church.*

8. *Andrea Commodi (1560–1648), The Pilgrim Ignatius Sees the Baby Jesus in the Consecrated Host, beginning of the seventeenth century, Farnesian Chapel in Rome's Church of the Gesù. The scene, which is set in the Gesù's presbytery, depicts elements of liturgical worship of that time, from the presence of musicians to the raising of the altar.*

9. *Interior of Munich's Saint Michael Church.*

10. *Interior of Rome's Church of the Gesù and its hall.*

disguise" since they gave so much attention to the importance of biblical preaching. Undaunted, they continued their "ministries of the Word" and insisted that young Jesuits practice their preaching skills publically in the churches and piazzas of Rome, and be critiqued with regular evaluations. This new apostolic thrust, which also exhibited a new liturgical mentality, is best seen in the Church of the Gesù in Rome's historical center, the mother church of the Jesuits built between 1568 and 1575 and considered the prototype of all Baroque architecture. Thanks to the missionary efforts of the Jesuits, the Gesù style was copied again and again throughout the world. When Jesuit missionaries wrote back to Rome asking superiors for permission to build a church, it was precisely the architectural plans of the Gesù that were sent. Its ornate design was not what the Jesuits had in mind, of course. Indeed, they preferred a barreled ceiling made of wood that would help project sound to the back of the church, especially as they preached their sermons. However, the Cardinal Protector (Farnese) who was financing the operation wouldn't hear of it and insisted on a much more ornate, gold-gilt ceiling, which is exactly what the Gesù received.

In this same period, Charles Borromeo made his own contribution to Baroque liturgical architecture as Archbishop of Milan. In 1576, an archdiocesan synod in Milan called for the installation of communion rails to assist the faithful

11. *Daniele Crespi (1598–1630), detail of* Saint Charles Borromeo's Fast, *Church of Saint Mary of the Passion, Milan.*

12. *Ciborium from Milan Cathedral. Conspicuous elements of the images that follow relate to the architectural instructions and the furnishings for Saint Charles Borromeo's churches.*

13. *The partition wall in Milan's Church of Saint Maurice, with openings for viewing the elevation of the host on the left, and for the monarchs' communion on the right, when they would participate in Mass from the choir loft in the rear.*

14. *Milan Cathedral's main nave with high altar, its development made necessary by the underground construction of Saint Charles' crypt.*

15. *Milan Cathedral's crypt, used for winter choir by canons, and for relics.*

11

12

13

in kneeling to receive the sacrament, thereby creating a new barrier between the nave and chancel. This custom gradually spread throughout the world. In the following year, 1577, he published "Instructions on the Architecture and Furnishing of Churches" with extraordinary attention to detail and a certain scrupulosity in evidence. For example, he recommended that a wooden partition run down the middle of churches in his archdiocese, separating men from women and avoiding any potential occasion for temptation during Mass and celebration of other sacraments. He likewise called for the construction of wooden confessionals in that same document, insisting that there be separate confessionals for men and women in separate parts of the church lest there be distractions. He insisted that tabernacles be placed on the main altar where Mass was celebrated—an unfortunate development that caught on because of the Reformation.

In such an architectural setting, the celebration of the Mass came to resemble the great cultural creation of the Baroque era and its most popular one: opera. The first opera was composed in the year 1600, and it gradually influenced the growth of nonparticipation in Catholic liturgy. Masses were

14

15

16

17

18

composed for orchestra by such great masters as Mozart and Beethoven. The lay faithful in this period came to expect in the liturgy the religious equivalent of the opera, with all its pomp and seriousness. Thus were various Baroque elements added—music, drama, processions, for example, but those elements remained at the periphery of the liturgy itself. The liturgical assembly would be seated to hear and enjoy the choir and orchestra perform the *Gloria*, for example, but it was more ornamentation than integrally linked to the community's prayer. In some respects, this type of Baroque music gave the impression that the liturgy was actually a concert accompanied by Mass. It was also in this period that the choir was moved from the front of the church in the chancel and placed upstairs to a gallery often near the rear of the nave, where the pipe organ was now installed. In 1657, Pope Alexander VII decreed the church musicians should take an oath to sing only those things prescribed in the breviary or missal, and stated that music imitating dance or things profane should be abolished.

Occasionally, there were congregational hymns sung at Mass. Already in 1592, for example, the Synod of Breslau decreed that vernacular hymns should be inserted at the gradual (before the Gospel) and after the consecration wherever Latin singing was not the custom. The *Cantual of Mainz* (1605) encouraged the incorporation of German hymns in the Mass, both during a sung Latin Mass (with the option of replacing Latin chants of the gradual, offertory, and communion with a German hymn). At low Mass,

however, singing simply continued throughout the Mass except that the *Cantual* provided for singing to stop during the reading of the Gospel, the consecration, and at the final blessing. In 1623, the Jesuits working in Cologne published their *Spiritual Psalter* for local usage, replete with vernacular hymns and psalms to be sung together. These practices continued throughout the Baroque period—a historical epoch marked by fanfare and Catholic piety, theater, and feast.

As the Baroque penchant for drama and the flamboyant spread throughout Europe, a very different dynamic was taking place on the other side of the world in Asia—a dispute that came to be known as the Chinese Rites

19

20

Controversy and demonstrated the tension between the Catholic and classical culture of Europe and its encounter with the non-Christian cultures of Asia through the experience of Catholic missionaries. Those missionaries exhibited a plurality of styles and evangelical strategies; some were more open and imaginative than others. Jesuits like Matteo Ricci, who arrived in Beijing in 1601, took on the dress and customs of the Mandarin Chinese, gaining their acceptance and respect. Ricci and his colleagues argued that newly baptized Christians should be allowed to continue the ancient practice of venerating the memory of their deceased parents and relatives, along with other rituals associated with the Confucian tradition.

These symbolic practices were admitted because there was no divinity worshipped within those acts that were largely cultural. Above all, the Confucian cult was linked to civil government and life, and to scholarship. It included bodily gestures such as the *kowtow* and the offering of incense and money, food, and wine at home shrines. All went reasonably well for some years until Dominican and Franciscan missionaries arrived in the 1630s. Once their own missionary centers were established, they sharply rebuked the Jesuits for an improper blending of religious traditions and appealed to the Holy Office in Rome. In 1645, and after significant debate, Pope Innocent X issued a decree, which forbade Chinese Catholics from continuing to practice the veneration of ancestors and the cult of Confucius. The controversy raged on for over a century until in 1742 Pope Benedict XIV decreed that all Christian missionaries were obliged to take an oath against the Chinese rites and those non-Christian rites were to be definitively abolished. Two hundred years later, in 1939, the oath was rescinded but it was too late. Christianity had long since proven itself to be a foreign enterprise, incapable of adapting itself to Chinese life and culture.

24. CATHOLIC WORSHIP IN THE ENLIGHTENMENT

1. Cornelius Jansen (or Jansenius, d. 1638), engraving from the period.

2. Confusion of Jansenism, etching released in France by the Jesuits during 1653.

The Enlightenment was an eighteenth-century philosophic movement characterized by belief in the power of human reason and by innovation in political, religious, and educational doctrine. And like many other aspects of church life, liturgy was not immune from its effects. But in order to understand how Catholic worship evolved during the Enlightenment, we need to look back briefly at the seventeenth century and the advent of the Jansenist movement, named after the Augustinian scholar Cornelius Jansen (+1638), a professor at the University of Louvain and Bishop of Ypres at his death. The movement represented a reaction to the external religiosity of Baroque Catholicism in the middle of the seventeenth century but continued to be alive and well throughout the eighteenth century and even into the nineteenth. As a reform movement of deep piety and ethical earnestness, Jansenism appealed especially to the rising middle class, intellectuals, the Dominicans, and the Augustinians.

Jansenists shared with Lutherans an aversion to externality and a desire for more participation in lay worship. To that end, Jansenists urged the church to restrain the cult of the Blessed Sacrament in favor of greater attention to the eucharistic celebration itself. In France, Jansenist influence led to the production of the so-called "neo-Gallican rites" in which various French dioceses developed their own liturgical books as a response to the Tridentine emphasis on liturgical centralization and rigid uniformity. Those French texts contained rubrics in the vernacular and exhibited notable variety from one diocese to another. Indeed, by the eighteenth century, 90 out of 139 dioceses in France had their own distinct liturgies.

An even more interesting liturgical example within Jansenism came not from France but from Tuscany toward the end of the eighteenth century. In 1786, Scipione de Ricci (+1810), Bishop of Pistoia-Prato, convoked a synod in which he called for a restoration of the pure liturgy of the early church. As was the case in the patristic era, the synod recognized the leadership of diocesan bishops in the governance of their own dioceses always in consultation with and with the approval of the diocesan clergy council. The Synod of Pistoia promoted active participation of the laity in the liturgical action, and criticized devotion to the Sacred Heart, processions carrying saints' relics, and other popular devotions. Such pious exercises only detracted from the centrality of Christ in the liturgical celebration. Vernacular worship was to be introduced;

3. *Europe's political situation at the middle of the eighteenth century.*

4. *Scipione Ricci (d. 1638).*

Masses were to be combined and unnecessary Masses eliminated so that the communal dimension of the Eucharist could be enhanced. Masses celebrated simultaneously at side altars were to be abolished. The centrality of Sunday was to be restored and parishes were to have a principal Eucharist with the pastor as president. The one presiding was to pray the Eucharistic Prayer and other presidential prayers in a loud, clear voice. Communion distributed to the assembly was to be consecrated at that particular Eucharist and not taken from the tabernacle as if it were a dispensary of "leftovers" saved from earlier Eucharists. The normative time for celebrating the sacraments of Christian initiation (baptism, confirmation, Eucharist) was during the Easter Vigil on Holy Saturday night. The Jansenist insistence on serious sacramental preparation reveals itself here as the synod insisted on baptismal preparation for parents and godparents along with the preparation for couples preparing for marriage.

Interestingly, as we compare the liturgical reforms of Vatican II and those proposed at the Synod of Pistoia, there does not appear to be a significant difference. However, unlike the reforms proposed at Pistoia, the groundwork for the reforms of the Second Vatican Council was laid in more

147

5. *Marie Ellenrieder (1791–1863),* Ignaz Heinrich von Wessenberg (1774–1860), *1819. Wessenberggaleria, Konstanz.*

6. *William Hamilton (1751–1801),* John Wesley, 1788. *National Portrait Gallery, London. John Wesley (1703–1791) was the Methodist Revival's biggest exponent.*

5

6

than fifty years of preparation, evidenced in the biblical, ecclesiological, ecumenical, liturgical, and patristic movements that breathed new life into the church and provided the necessary theological foundations for the reforms. The Synod of Pistoia had no such preparation, and was done in a largely non-consultative manner, crafted essentially by the local bishop, who was eventually deposed in 1790 and died in exile in 1810. The synod was condemned in 1794 by Pope Pius VI.

The church in Germany held its own congress in the same year as Pistoia, 1786. Unlike Pistoia, however, the Congress of Ems succeeded in producing a liturgical reform that enjoyed better longevity in encouraging vernacular worship, one principal Mass each Sunday, and preaching during the Mass rather than beforehand as a sort of prelude to the liturgical act. This was so despite the fact that the convocation of bishops addressed the delicate question of papal primacy and German independence from Rome; the issue had been a major concern of some of the

more prominent bishops attending the meeting. The Diocese of Constance became the center of the German reforms that emphasized liturgical participation, congregational singing, and liturgical preaching. Under the leadership of the diocese's vicar general, Ignaz Heinrich von Wessenberg, a decree was issued in 1803 requiring all Sunday and feast day Masses to be celebrated before noon and that a sermon be preached. Six years later in 1809, a further decree stated that every parish should have one principal Mass on Sunday morning with both the singing of vernacular hymns and preaching during the Mass—it had become customary to preach before Mass as a sort of prelude to the liturgical act. Further attempts at increased liturgical participation continued for a number of years, but Rome was less than pleased and by 1855, the German liturgical innovations had essentially been discontinued.

The liturgical situation at the time was more hopeful outside of Roman Catholicism. In the eighteenth century, John

7. Engraving of a sermon in a public park, by an anonymous artist of the period. Meetings with people were one aspect of the Methodist Revival.

8. Frontispiece of the first Methodist hymnal by John Wesley, from 1741.

9. Credulity, Superstition, and Fanaticism, William Hogarth (1697–1764), engraving released in 1762. The artist viciously attacked certain fanatic excesses carried out by Methodist preachers, which ended up in the creation of monsters that entrapped the faithful. Reference is made to William Romaine with the chandelier's Globe of Hell, and Wesley and Whitefield are two of the Reform Movement actors who stand out in the work.

7

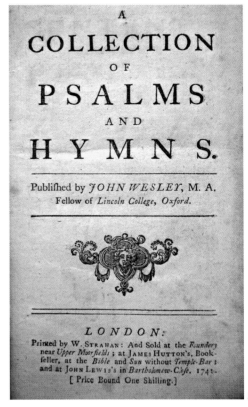

8

Wesley inaugurated the Methodist revival within the Church of England with a focus on more personalized vernacular preaching and the centrality of baptism and Eucharist. His brother Charles offered his own contribution in the rich composition of English hymns that were at once poetic and theologically profound. The first Anglican hymnal, *Collection of Psalms and Hymns*, was published in 1737. Those Wesleyan hymns continue to be sung today throughout Christendom, including in English-speaking Catholic churches. Early Methodists developed what was called the "Preaching Service," which included a series of general intercessions following the sermon, along with extemporaneous prayer and hymn singing. John Wesley produced his own simplified version of the *Book of Common Prayer* in 1784, just two years before the Synod of Pistoia and the Congress of Ems.

9

25. THE NINETEENTH CENTURY

1. Engraving at the Musée Carnavalet in Paris. It is an illustration of the massacre of priests in September of 1792 during the Reign of Terror in France.

2. Jean-Auguste Dominique Ingres (1780–1867), Napoleon on the Imperial Throne, *1806. Musée de l'Armée, Paris.*

The French Revolution wreaked significant havoc on church life throughout Europe and the nineteenth-century church was very much on the defensive especially in the years 1815 to 1880. Such a posture is hardly ideal for providing a good climate of renewal, and the liberal bourgeois culture and Romanticism which are features of this period could contribute little to any development in Catholic liturgy. So in the nineteenth century, the church appeared as an institution on the defensive, ever ready to issue condemnations of all novelties. This century was still prevalently marked by the Baroque. With the restoration of the church after the the French Revolution and Napoleon, there was an attempt to reconstruct what had been destroyed. In opposition to the Enlightenment, the first decades of the nineteenth century emerged with an accent on sentiment. Romantic religiosity was not interested in liturgy. At best, it regarded it as a historical piece of aesthetic value but not much more. Gradually, there emerged a certain appreciation of the Christian tradition, and thus of the liturgy itself: a revival of Gregorian chant and a rediscovery of ancient liturgical texts, missals, and pontificals. Slowly, the situation would improve. Bishops, religious orders, and clergy committed themselves to an action of spiritual renewal aimed at the formation and education of the people, with the goal of raising the quality of their piety.

3. Popular 1840 drawing that illustrates the renewal of religious fervor during the first half of the nineteenth century among all social classes: the Jesuits and other religious congregations organized missions to Christianize France, once again.

4

5

4. Eugène Delacroix (1798–1863), *Liberty* Leading the People, 1830. Louvre Museum, Paris. The painting was mostly based on mythical and patriotic themes.

5. Eugène Delacroix, Pietà, 1844. Louvre Museum, Paris. The work was commissioned for a chapel dedicated to the Virgin Mary.

6. *Don Prosper Guéranger (1805–1875), who restored the Benedictine Order in France by re-establishing the monastery at Solesmes in 1833. Engraving by Ferdinand Gaillard. Bibliothèque Nationale de France, Paris.*

7. *The imposing Abbey of Saint Peter of Solesmes, built in 1896 by Guéranger's successor, Paul Delatte.*

8. *The Saint Maurus (Beuron) Chapel (1868–1870) in Württemburg, a project carried out by Peter Lenz (1832–1928).*

9. *Peter Lenz,* Pietà, *sketch for a fresco, 1865, Beuron Abbey. Beuron was one of the centers where Benedictine art was revived, and home to an art school. Because of the Kulturkampf, its monks transferred to Czechoslovakia and Austria.*

6

7

The refounding of the Benedictine monastery of Solesmes offers a clear example of such efforts at restoration and renewal. In 1833, Prosper Guéranger (+1875) refounded that abbey, which had been suppressed during the French Revolution, and became its abbot. His desire was that the new Solesmes respond to the needs of the contemporary church while remaining faithful both to the monastic rule and to church teaching. It would also assist in essentially bringing France back to Rome: bringing about ecclesial unity and uniformity in France rather than the local liturgical innovations, which he considered either too Protestant or Jansenist. Thus, unlike the rest of France, the Eucharist and the Liturgy of the Hours were celebrated strictly according to the Roman Rite. To this end, Guéranger advocated a return to Gregorian chant as the official music of the church's worship.

In the 1870s, the monks of Solesmes embarked on a study of chant manuscripts by returning to medieval sources and purifying texts of accretions, as was seen in the form of chant used at Regensburg that had spread throughout Europe. In rediscovering the purity of Gregorian chant, the monks made a valuable contribution. In fact, the chant research done at Solesmes attracted so much attention that when Pope Pius X issued his first motu proprio in 1903 (*Tra le sollecitudini*) on the subject of sacred music, it was precisely the chant of Solesmes that he endorsed as the

church's only official chant. While Guéranger made a very significant contribution to the renewal of the Catholic Church in France, it must also be said that he was more of a restorationist than reformer. Interestingly, some of the local French liturgies he opposed were later accepted by the Second Vatican Council and incorporated into the Missal of Paul VI. Guéranger believed that every change—especially through a liturgy celebrated in the local language of the people—was considered an attack against the church and a lack of the Catholic spirit. His research led him only as far back as the medieval period, which also explains why he came up with different results than the Jansenists, whose research was much more patristic-based. For Guéranger, liturgy was not about "full, active, and conscious participation" as would be articulated at Vatican II, but rather about contemplation; liturgy was veiled in mystery.

Two important movements emerged within nineteenth-century England that had a serious role to play within Anglican liturgical renewal: the Anglo-Catholic Oxford Movement founded in 1833, and the Camden Society (later Ecclesiological Society) founded at Cambridge in 1839. These two movements will be discussed in greater detail later in this text.

8

9

26. Theological Foundations of the Liturgical Movement

Later in the nineteenth century, Catholic theologians associated with the German university at Tübingen recovered the ecclesiological understanding of the church as the Mystical Body of Christ, which would have significant implications for the renewal of the church's worship in the twentieth century. Johann Adam Möhler was born in 1796 in Wuetemberg, the son of a local baker. In 1815 at the age of nineteen he began theological study at the newly opened seminary of Ellwangen. But that seminary proved too distant from intellectual centers and two years later was moved to Tübingen and incorporated into the university. This was particularly astonishing since Tübingen already had a well-established Protestant theological faculty and hardly needed a second school of theology.

Nonetheless, the Catholic faculty of theology established itself and registered growing interest in new trends in both German Romanticism and idealist philosophy. This moved Catholic theological study at Tübingen away from the sort of classical scholastic and rationalistic theology, and toward a more integrated scientific and historically conscious approach that would greatly influence Möhler's own theological inquiry. At the heart of German Romanticism, and consequently central to the theological agenda at Tübingen, was a rediscovery of the organic model of the church, and the role of the Holy Spirit within the Christian community and its worship. Given such concerns, it is not surprising that the Pauline and patristic model of the church as the Mystical Body of Christ would be rediscovered there.

Möhler was ordained priest in 1819 and three years later he began his tenure as professor of church history at Tübingen. As preparation for his new position, he took a seven-month sabbatical visiting both Catholic and Protestant theological faculties around Germany, meeting with professors and students, and auditing various lectures. In Berlin, he heard lectures by Schleiermacher and was deeply impressed by the vision and approach of the Jewish-Lutheran church historian Johann August Wilhelm Neander. Those encounters had a profound impact on both his teaching and writing.

As professor at Tübingen, Möhler initially focused his interests around patristics, which offered a new vision of the church in relation to nineteenth-century German society. This led to the publication of his first book in 1825: *Die Einheit in der Kirche* ("Unity in the Church"), basing much of his research on the work of Schleiermacher and Neander. This book was not without its difficulties, however, and Möhler would later attempt to re-state some of the propositions and convictions exhibited in that text. Nor was the book uncontroversial: it both inspired numerous young Catholic intellectuals and at the same time alarmed

1

a number of church leaders, as it seemed to call into question the hierarchical nature of the church itself. His second book, *Symbolik,* was published in 1832 and was his magisterial work, in which he explored Protestant doctrinal positions in relation to Catholic tradition.

Thanks to Möhler's openness and scientific curiosity along with that of his colleagues, what evolved was what came to be known as the "Tübingen School," which stood out in sharp contrast to the sort of Catholic theology being done on the rest of the continent in the nineteenth century. Not surprisingly, the Tübingen theologians were considered suspect: Catholic theology of that epoch tended to be ahistorical and did not look kindly on modern philosophy. Even at the dawn of the twentieth century, some conservative critics blamed the Tübingen School for the evolution of Modernism. Nevertheless, Mystical Body theology provided the necessary theological foundation for the liturgical movement itself. Möhler and his colleagues at Tübingen argued that worship had the responsibility to assimilate in an interior manner the doctrine or theology that the church had exemplified or witnessed internally. Möhler chose the image of the church as a community, which offered a vision of the baptized that was quite different from a view of the church as institution where the laity remained passively in the background. The divine life was communicated by the apostles not to individuals but to a community of sisters and brothers who were incorporated into that same body of Christ.

In Möhler's image of the church, it was important that the community speak to God in the language it was given—the vernacular—just as it used that same language on a daily

1. Bell tower at Saint George Collegiate Church in Tübingen, home of the university, which was founded in 1477, and which became one of the most important in Germany, so much so that one could say that Tübingen stands for the university.

2. Gustave Coubert, Funeral at Orans, *1849. Louvre Museum, Paris. In this painting, the religious event is emphasized by its social and community dimensions.*

3. Jean-François Millet, detail of The Angelus, *1858. Louvre Museum, Paris. The communitarian aspect of the religious activity clearly emerges from this work, with its two peasants who, at a standstill, are gathered together.*

basis in ordinary life. Thus, God would be honored by being addressed in one's mother tongue, which was a divine gift in the first place. Other nineteenth-century theologians joined Möhler in promoting a similar ecclesiology. Their research laid the foundations for the First Vatican Council's *Dogmatic Constitution on the Church of Christ* in which the proposed draft began: "The Church is the Mystical Body of Christ." Had that council not been interrupted, it is quite probable that this doctrine would have become part of the church's regular vocabulary significantly earlier, rather than when it did with the papal encyclical *Mystici Corporis* Christi issued by Pius XII in 1943. Nonetheless, the work done at Tübingen provided the theological foundations for the twentieth-century liturgical movement.

27. The Twentieth-Century Liturgical Movement

1. *Pope Leo XIII.*

2. *Pope Pius X.*

3. *Emil Nolde, at the beginning of the last century, tackled religious and Christian themes, using forms that were strongly Impressionist, as in* The Last Supper, *produced in 1909, which underlines awareness of everyone around the table with the chalice. Statens Museum for Kunst, Copenhagen.*

4. *Main nave in the Maria Laach Abbey Church, the Rheinland.*

Thanks to the inspiration offered by the Tübingen School, Vatican I (1869–1870) had already made some proposals to reform the Divine Office (omitting hagiographic legends, obscure hymns, unknown saints, etc.), but the council had no time to address the question of liturgical reform. Meanwhile, it was clear to church leaders that the liturgy did not influence the life of the faithful, because they did not understand it and hence did not actively participate in it. At the turn of the twentieth century, however, that situation began to change. In 1902, at the very end of his pontificate, Leo XIII issued an encyclical on the holy Eucharist *Mirae Caritatis* in which he offered a rich vision of liturgy intrinsically linked to the life of the church. The Pope spoke of the Eucharist as the antidote to a world in which individuals were selfishly concerned about their own gains and personal advances, seduced into competing in a "race for wealth, to a struggle for possession of commodities which minister to the love of comfort and display." But those individuals, like the rest of human society, "have their being from God, so they can do nothing good except in God through Jesus Christ, through whom every best and choicest gift has ever proceeded and proceeds." Pope Leo then continued: "But the source and chief of all these gifts is the venerable Eucharist, which not only nourishes and sustains that life the desire whereof demands our most strenuous efforts, but also enhances beyond measure that dignity of man of which in these days we hear so much."

Leo XIII's social concern was well expressed in his 1891 encyclical *Rerum novarum*, so it wasn't surprising that he dedicated a significant part of *Mirae Caritatis* to the relationship between the Eucharist and charity. We read: " . . . Men have forgotten that they are children of God and brethren in Jesus Christ; they care for nothing except their own individual interests; the interests and the rights of others they not only make light of, but often attack and invade. Hence frequent disturbances and strife between class and class: arrogance, oppression, fraud on the part of the more powerful; misery, envy, and turbulence among the poor. . . . Our chief care and endeavor ought to be . . . to secure the union of classes in a mutual interchange . . . which, having its union in God, shall issue in deeds that reflect the true spirit of Jesus Christ and a genuine charity. . . . This then is what Christ intended when he instituted the Venerable Sacrament, namely, by awakening charity towards God to promote mutual charity among men."

With the election of Pius X in 1903, the new pope carried forth his predecessor's vision of liturgy as the source of the church's life and mission as well evidenced in his motu proprio *Tra le sollecitudini*, already mentioned, issued in the first year of his papacy. While the principal subject was sacred music, it also encouraged active participation in the liturgy, describing it as the church's most important and indispensable source: "Since we have very much at heart that the true Christian spirit be revived in all possible ways

3

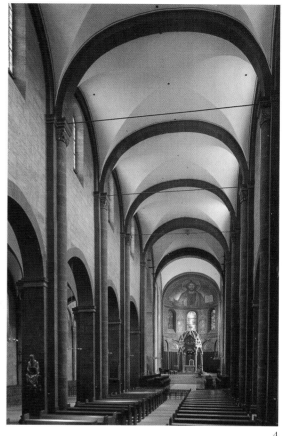

4

and that it be maintained among the faithful, it is above all necessary to provide for the holiness and dignity of the sacred places where precisely the faithful gather to draw this spirit at its primary and indispensable source, that is, active participation in the sacred mysteries and in the public and solemn prayer of the Church." The decree encouraging frequent communion *Sacra Tridentina* followed in 1905, stating that "frequent and daily communion . . . must be open to all the faithful of whatever class or condition." Five years later in 1910, the age at which children received first communion was lowered to the age of seven. Some years later, in 1928, Pope Pius XI issued a papal bull *Divini Cultus* in which he proclaimed: "It is most important that when the faithful assist at the sacred ceremonies . . . they should not be merely detached and silent spectators."

The European liturgical movement began in Belgium in 1909 at a Catholic labor conference held at Malines. A Benedictine monk of the Abbey of Mont César, Lambert Beauduin, was invited to address the conference on the topic *La vraie prière de l'église* ("The True Prayer of the Church"). During his lecture, he advocated full and active participation of the laity, not only in the area of liturgy but also in all aspects of church life and ministry. At that meeting, Beauduin encountered the lay historian Godfrey Kurth, and the two began to strategize on how best to make their dream of more participative worship a reality in Belgium. Beauduin used Pius X's motu proprio as the basis

for his talk and eventual founding of the liturgical movement in Belgium, calling that papal text the Magna Carta of the movement itself. Only two months later, the monks of Mont César began a monthly publication called *Liturgical Life* with the number of subscriptions soon exceeding 70,000. The first liturgical conference was held at the monastery in 1910—a one-day congress that drew more than 250 participants. Two years later in 1912, the Mont César began hosting annual liturgical weeks, which further communicated the message of the liturgical movement—a message that was further assisted by Beauduin's numerous publications.

As the liturgical movement gained strength in Belgium, it soon caught on in Germany, with a more scientific emphasis thanks to the scholarly contribution of the monks of Maria Laach in the Rhineland. The German movement emerged through contact in 1913 between the Benedictine Ildefons Herwegen (+1946) and several university students who expressed interest in a deeper living out of the liturgy in daily life. Herwegen invited the students to join the monastic community during Holy Week, 1914, where they would participate in the liturgical offices and join the monks in their daily life and work. During the visit, Herwegen and his guests explored various possibilities for promoting liturgical renewal in Germany and the ways in which those students might become protagonists of that renewal among their peers at the university. Once

Herwegen became abbot of the monastery, he had an even greater platform for promoting the renewal of worship in the German church, and was diligent in encouraging younger monks to pursue liturgical study and research.

One such monk was Odo Casel (+1948) who had been an early disciple of Herwegen's at the University of Bonn, where Casel was a student and Herwegen served as chaplain. Casel flourished in the discipline of liturgical scholarship and became a prolific writer in the area of liturgical theology, writing hundreds of articles and books with significance far beyond the confines of Germany. Most famous was his text *Das cristliche Kultmysterium* in which he argued that the Christian sacraments had their foundations in the early Mediterranean religions such as the cult of Mithra. Despite the limits of Casel's research, his interpretation opened up the richness of the liturgical life as it symbolically expresses the church's self-identity as the mystical body of Christ. In addition to Casel, other protagonists of the German liturgical movement included fellow Benedictine Cunibert Mohlberg, as well as the diocesan priest Romano Guardini (+1968), Franz Doelger, and Anton Baumstark. In 1923, Guardini published his text *Vom Geist der Liturgie*, which soon became a classic in liturgical spirituality.

The Benedictine women of Herstelle made their own significant contribution to liturgical research. Casel had lived for a time at Herstelle and managed to transmit his own passion for the liturgy to the nuns there whom he served as chaplain and teacher. Aemiliana Löhr (+1972), for example, whom Casel described as his best student, wrote more than three hundred articles, liturgical poems, and books in her lifetime.

While the German liturgical movement is largely known for its scientific contribution in the realm of research and publications, it was not without its pastoral dimension. At Maria Laach, for example, the first *Missa recitata* facing the liturgical assembly rather than oriented toward the East was celebrated in the crypt of the monastic church on August 6, 1921. Abbot Herwegen gave permission for the celebration of the Mass *ad experimentum* but chose not to be present himself. Rather, he delegated the prior, Albert Hammenstede, to be the celebrant, and determined that the Mass would be celebrated at 6:00 AM. The Mass included the praying of the ordinary parts of the Mass in common, albeit in Latin, and the assembly's participation in the offertory procession, each one placing his or her host on the paten when entering the crypt for Mass, and then presenting those gifts at the altar. Word quickly spread among neighboring clergy in the Diocese of Trier that the monks had "become Protestant," and the monastic experimentation was reported to the bishop. When the bishop made his own quiet visitation to observe the reported liturgical abuses, he was moved to tears, and celebrated Mass facing people the following year at the diocesan Eucharistic congress using a portable altar, much to the consternation of the monastery's opponents. Elsewhere in Germany,

5

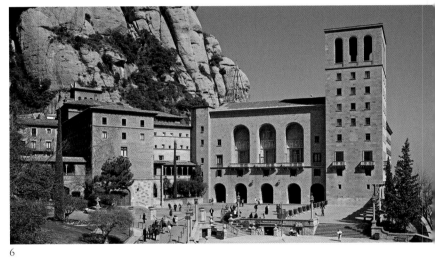

6

Johannes Pinsk (+1957), who served as chaplain at the University of Berlin, and another diocesan priest, Hans Anscar Reinhold, were strong advocates of social activism whose foundation was located in the sacred liturgy. Both spoke out forcefully against the Third Reich in their preaching and Reinhold was forced to flee Germany as a result, emigrating to the United States where he continued to promote a socially conscious view of worship that challenged racism and injustice in all its forms.

Under the leadership of Romano Guardini, a close relationship grew between German theologians and architects, which led to the publication of an impressive document on liturgical architecture issued by the German bishops in 1938. In other parts of the world where such a relationship was lacking—in the United States, for example—liturgical architecture failed to advance and the preference for the neo-Gothic architectural style continued to hold sway. By contrast, the German document clearly reflected a mutual trust between architects and clergy, and was ahead of its time in suggesting the use of poured concrete and new,

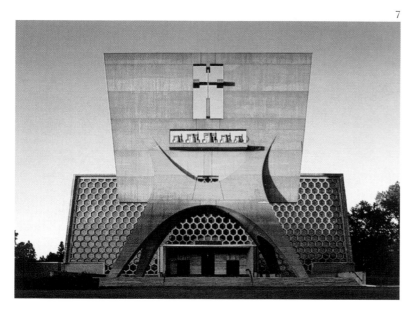

7

5. View of Finalpia Monastery, Savona, where the abbot Bonifacio Bolognini founded the Rivista Liturgica in 1914.

6. Our Lady of Montserrat Basilica and Monastery, Catalonia.

7. Façade of Saint John's Abbey Church in Collegeville, Minnesota.

innovative models with freestanding square altars facing the people—models which more appropriately corresponded to the agenda of the liturgical movement. Less than ten years later in 1946–47, Johannes Wagner founded the Liturgical Institute at the University of Trier and his colleague Balthasar Fischer held the first chair in liturgical studies established within Trier's theological faculty. In neighboring France, the *Centre de pastorale liturgique* was founded in Paris in 1943 by two Dominicans, A. M. Roguet and Pie Duploye, with its well-known periodical *La Maison-Dieu* begun in 1945. The *Institut Supérieur de Liturgie* opened its doors the following year in 1946 with the great French Dominican Pierre-Marie Gy as one of its cornerstones.

In Austria, it was Augustinians, rather than Benedictines or Dominicans, who pioneered the liturgical movement in that country centered at the Augustinian monastery of Klosterneuburg near Vienna. The chief protagonist was Augustinian canon Pius Parsch (+1945) who used his nearby parish, St. Gertrude, as a sort of laboratory for liturgical experimentation. Parsch made it his aim to combine his academic interests with the pastoral in a common goal of biblical and liturgical renewal. He did this principally through two important publications: *Das Jahr des Heiles* (which appeared in English as *The Church's Year of Grace*) published in 1923 as a pastoral commentary on the church year; and *Bibel und Liturgie* founded three years later in 1926 to foster the integral relationship between the sacred Scriptures and liturgy, in the hope of recovering the Bible's rich treasures for Catholics who were not accustomed to reading it. Some years later and from a more scientific perspective, the Jesuit liturgical historian Josef Andreas Jungmann (+1975) made an extraordinary contribution to the field in his monumental two-volume work *Missarum Sollemnia: The Mass of the Roman Rite*. Jungmann spent a number of years working on that text as university professor at Innsbruck, and it was finally published in 1948.

The French liturgical movement drew inspiration from contacts with the Russian Orthodox emigrants who had taken refuge in France in the aftermath of the Bolshevik Revolution of 1917. Unlike the West, the Orthodox liturgical spirit had remained faithful to its patristic foundations and to tradition in general, offering a steady ritual style with repetitive ritual behavior. Liturgical pioneers in France found much merit in the Eastern liturgical approach and relied upon its example as they continued to shape their own agenda of liturgical reform. One can find similar developments elsewhere in Europe—in the Netherlands where the first liturgical week was held at Breda in 1911; in Catalonia at the Benedictine monastery of Montserrat; in the Czech Republic at the Benedictine monastery of Emmaus in Prague; and in Croatia and Poland. The liturgical movement in northern Italy centered around the Benedictine monastery of Finalpia in Savona, and in Milan and Bergamo, with figures such as Benedictine Abbot Emanuele Caronti and the Abbot Ildefonso Schuster who later became Cardinal Archbishop of Milan, as well as the Bishop of Bergamo Adriano Bernareggi (+1953) who founded the *Centro di Azione Liturgica* (CAL).

From Europe, the movement spread to the Americas: the United States and Brazil. In 1925, the German-American monk, Virgil Michel (+1938), founded the movement in the United States at his monastery of Saint John's Abbey, Collegeville, Minnesota, and the Brazilian movement was founded by Benedictine Martinho Michler at Rio de Janeiro in 1933. Both in Brazil and the United States, the movement enjoyed a strong pastoral emphasis with particular attention to worship's social dimension. In 1925, Virgil Michel founded both a publishing house—the Liturgical Press—and a monthly periodical, *Orate Fratres* (later *Worship*), to serve as the primary instrument of communicating the message of liturgical renewal in North America.

8

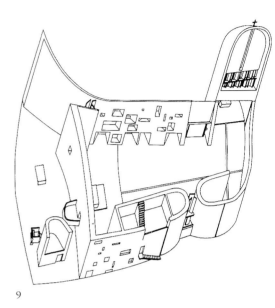

9

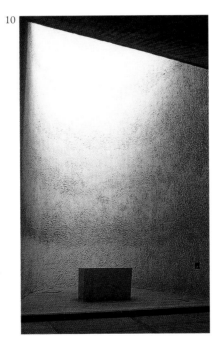

10

8–10. Le Corbusier, exterior (8), axonometry (9) and side chapel (10), Notre-Dame-du-Haut, Ronchamp, 1954.

11

11. Le Corbusier, La Tourette Convent, Éveux-sur-l'Abresle, interior of the hypogean chapel, 1957.

12. Le Corbusier, Notre-Dame-du-Haut, Ronchamp, openings on the side wall.

13

13. *Capuchin Sisters Chapel, altar and retable, Tlapan, Mexico.*

14–15. *Eero Saarinen, exterior and apse interior of the Kresge Chapel at the Massachusetts Institute of Technology (MIT), Cambridge, Massachusetts, 1950–1955.*

16–17. *Henri Matisse, interior and exterior of the Chapelle du Rosaire, convent of the Vence Dominican nuns, Provence, 1951. The altar is laid out at an oblique angle that stretches out toward the nuns' high-backed chairs and the seating area for the faithful.*

18. *Henri Matisse. On the left,* Madonna and Child, *and in the background,* Via crucis, *Chapelle du Rosaire.*

14

15

28. THE LITURGICAL MOVEMENT IN ANGLICAN AND PROTESTANT CHURCHES

1

2

The United Kingdom had its own share of liturgical pioneers especially among Anglicans. The Oxford Movement, founded in the nineteenth century under the leadership of such figures as E. B. Pusey, John Henry Newman, and John Keble, and the Tractarian Movement—so-called because of the series of tracts it issued which called the Church of England back to its Catholic traditions and ceremonials of the past—had a revolutionary impact. Anglo-Catholicism grew out of Tractarianism with the adapting of Roman liturgical rubrics for Anglican usage, enlightened by the reliance on Roman liturgical sources, as well. The nineteenth-century Christian Socialist movement was foundational for what became the Parish Communion Movement in the early twentieth century, which encouraged a greater frequency of the sacrament with emphasis on worship's social responsibility. It must be acknowledged, however, that within Anglicanism there was and remains a certain variation of style and practice. The Evangelical wing of the Church of England, for example, showed greater interest in more informal styles of worship with a particular mission to the unchurched. Evangelical Anglicanism generally appeared more Protestant than Anglo-Catholic churches, with less frequently celebrated Eucharist and less ceremonial.

Anglican liturgical pioneers Henry de Candole (+1897) and A. Gabriel Hebert (+1963) were deeply influenced by Catholic liturgical pioneers like Lambert Beauduin, Ildefons Herwegen, and Odo Casel. De Candole pub-

lished two important works in 1935: *The Church's Offering: A Brief Study of Eucharistic Worship,* and *The Sacraments and the Church: A Study of the Corporate Nature of the Church.* The following year he published a small booklet, *The Parish Communion,* in which he contended that the Eucharist should be the main liturgical rite of the Church of England and it should be celebrated as a corporate act with the involvement of the entire parish community. He was also instrumental in founding the group "Parish and People" which attempted to communicate the ideas of the Roman Catholic liturgical movement as they grew in continental Europe. In the same year as De Candole's two publications, 1935, Gabriel Hebert published an important book *Liturgy and Society*, on the relationship between liturgy and issues of justice. The book was his own attempt to disseminate the principal themes of the European liturgical movement among Anglicans in the United Kingdom. Interestingly, Hebert attributed his own liturgical vision to his association with the Benedictine monks of Maria Laach.

Another protagonist in the British liturgical movement was Anglican Benedictine of Nashdom Abbey, Gregory Dix (+1951) whose seminal work *The Shape of the Liturgy* (1945) remains a classic even today. In that text, Dix delineated the four-fold action within the Eucharist of taking, blessing, breaking, and giving, imitating Jesus' actions at the Last Supper. All of these efforts were ratified in 1955 with the establishment of the Church of England's

3. Dom Gregory Dix, Anglican Benedictine monk and priest of Nashdom Abbey.

4. Religious service in the Cathedral Church of Saint John the Divine, New York City.

3

published *The Book of Common Order*, which was largely based on the Scottish liturgical text.

By and large, for Protestants both in Europe and North America, collaboration in the wider task of liturgical renewal offered the opportunity to claim the theological and liturgical foundations of the early Church, which were the patrimony of all Christians, and to reaffirm the Catholic dimension of their Reformation roots. The Methodist Church's Brotherhood of Saint Luke (renamed the Order of Saint Luke in 1948) was founded in 1946 to promote such renewal of worship. In that same year, liturgical pioneers in the U.S. Episcopal Church founded the Associated Parishes for Liturgy and Mission as a means of encouraging a return to the centrality of the Eucharist within Anglican worship and to foster a greater corporate and social awareness that was necessarily connected to authentic liturgical participation. The various projects of liturgical renewal within individual Anglican and Protestant churches was ultimately affirmed internationally in 1951, when the World Council of Church's Commission on Faith and Order issued a report which stated: "There is a growing sense that worship is not to be thought of as a gathering of individual pious Christians, but as a corporate act in direct relation to the Lord of the Church."

Liturgical Commission. Three years later at the Lambeth Conference of 1958, the Commission made two significant reports: one on the fundamental role of the *Book of Common Prayer* within the Anglican Communion and another on the role of saints within Anglicanism.

The Presbyterian Church of Scotland registered its own nineteenth-century foundations for liturgical renewal. As early as 1849, the church's General Assembly had appointed a committee to prepare forms of service for parishes and individuals without ministers. In 1856, the General Assembly of the Church of Scotland required the clergy to read two Scripture readings on Sundays from the Old and New Testaments, and admonished them to be more diligent in observing liturgical rubrics found in the *Directory of Worship*. Two years later in 1858, the church issued a book entitled *Prayers for Social and Family Worship*, and founded the Church Service Society in 1863, which set itself to raise the standards of its worship and encouraging proper liturgical formation for its ministers. By the early years of the twentieth century, the Church of Scotland had reclaimed much of its liturgical heritage that had been lost because of the Puritans who had little interest in liturgical ceremonial. Scottish Presbyterian liturgical renewal bore fruit in the publication of *The Book of Common Order* in 1940, which combined the best of the Catholic liturgical tradition with a genuine Protestant and Reformation faithfulness. Six years later, the Presbyterian Church in the United States

4

29. The Vernacular Movement

1

2

1–2. *Saints Cyril and Methodius, depicted by a modern icon (1), private collection. The two saints used the language of the people and translated the Bible and the liturgy for the Slav population. Detail (2) of Kiev's Slavic-language psalm book. State Library, Saint Petersburg.*

One of the hallmarks of the sixteenth-century Reformation was its insistence on the vernacular. Even aside from vernacular usage within liturgical prayer, Martin Luther published his major treatises in German precisely to assure a wider readership among the masses. Ulrich Zwingli, Luther's contemporary, insisted that his own works be published in Swiss-German, while second generation reformer John Calvin was published in his native French. The results of such a paradigmatic shift to the vernacular had significant effects far beyond the borders of Reformation Germany, Switzerland, or France. A fundamental shift occurred in 1520 when Luther made the decision to leave his platform as an academician, where he would argue in Latin to the academic elite, in favor of a new role as pastoral reformer arguing and promoting his cause in German to a much wider public. The advantage of vernacular usage was seen even more clearly in Switzerland, where vernacular public debates between

Reformers and Catholics were followed immediately by a plenary vote where assembled citizens would decide on whether or not to accept the Reformation. Not surprisingly, vernacular usage was a non-negotiable when it came to preaching and liturgical reforms.

Luther is often viewed as the leader of vernacular reform in the sixteenth century, perhaps because his liturgical reforms are the best known. However, he was hardly the first. Indeed, at the time Luther was engaged in his own liturgical revisions of the Roman Rite, there was already vernacular experimentation taking place elsewhere in Germany and Switzerland. In 1522, Wolfgang Wissenburger introduced German liturgies at Basel, joined by Johann Schwebel who produced a similar vernacular translation at Pforzheim. Kaspar Kantz prepared his own German Mass in that same year at Nördlingen to be used by the Carmelite community where he served as prior. In 1523, Thomas Müntzer arrived in Alstedt as pastor of the main Church of Saint John in the New Town and almost immediately published his Evangelical German Mass, Matins, and Vespers set to plainsong, which he completed the following year. Even as he recognized Müntzer's good intentions, Luther criticized the pastor's vernacular efforts for having been done in haste, as reflected in the final product.

Despite Luther's concerns about moving too quickly with makeshift vernacular translations, liturgical texts in German continued to be produced. In 1524, Diobald Schwartz prepared the Strasbourg German Mass, a conservative revision of the Roman Rite, and Martin Bucer produced his own vernacular liturgical rite called *Grund und Ursach*. Bucer began guiding the revision of the Strasbourg liturgy in 1525, which underwent eighteen

3. *Frontispiece of Martin Luther's German-language catechism, published in 1529, xylograph, from Lucas Cranach the Elder's workshop.*

4. *Thomas Müntzer engraving.*

5. *Martin Bucer etching.*

revisions over a period of fourteen years until 1539 when the definitive Strasbourg German Mass was published. And as the Strasbourg liturgy continued to be revised, other vernacular worship continued to emerge. In 1534, a German Mass that included a revision of the Roman Canon was prepared at Worms while vernacular liturgies were introduced in Ruetlingen, Wertheim, Königsberg, and Strasbourg.

It is plausible that the Bucerian liturgical structure had some influence on Luther's own reforms. Luther was less quick to respond than others with a rapidly composed vernacular worship, but rather pondered the pastoral situation carefully before making changes. He was above all dedicated to the promotion of "evangelical freedom," and a key element in that "freedom" was language with special attention to the ordinary and uneducated layperson. Thus, in Luther's liturgical reforms we see a fundamentally pastoral approach. Well ahead of his time, he also realized that producing quality liturgical texts required more than a literal translation from Latin into German. Some of his Reformation colleagues had done just that, and Luther recognized the limits of such an approach. He finally published his vernacular version of the mass—the *Deutsche Messe*—in 1526, and it conservatively followed the structure and form of the Roman Rite, although he continued to allow for Mass to be celebrated in schools where those in the congregation would be able to grasp that which was being said.

Vernacular promotion played a major role within the English Reformation, as well. The architect of the Anglican *Book of Common Prayer*, Archbishop Thomas Cranmer, provided the Church of England with a fundamentally Catholic liturgical book. In its composition, he relied on ancient liturgical sources such as missals, pontificals, and church offices, along with sound liturgical principles such as vernacular worship and active participation of the faithful. It was at Nuremberg in Lent of 1532 that Cranmer had his first experience of Lutheran worship in the vernacular. While it is not clear whether his thoughts turned immediately to the creation of a similar liturgical book in English, what is clear is that his Lutheran experience during the Nuremberg sojourn had a significant effect on his own desires for vernacular worship in England. Two years earlier, George Joye had already published a vernacular edition of the psalter from Martin Bucer's Latin version published in 1529. In that same year as Joye's vernacular publication, 1530, he published a second text, *Hortulus Animae*, which bore a common title used for devotional primers of the period. The difference was that unlike other primers of the day, Joye's text included vernacular versions of the liturgical hours, penitential psalms, and some prayers taken from Luther's *Short Catechism* published in 1529. Joye's two books were quickly condemned in England, but a certain fascination with things Lutheran remained, helped largely by Henry VIII's determined break with Roman Catholicism in the years 1532–34.

It was not surprising, then, that the Council of Trent (1545–63) needed to take up the vernacular question as we saw earlier, precisely because it was an issue already widely disseminated among the Protestant Reformers. Nor was it surprising that within the Catholic Church, a number of vernacular concessions were granted in the four centuries between Trent and Vatican II. For example, Pope Paul V gave permission for the use of Mandarin Chinese in the celebration of Mass and the Divine Office at the Jesuit

6. *A mandarin and a Jesuit holding up a letter from China. Frontispiece by Athanasius Kircher, China Monumentis qua sacris qua profanes, Amsterdam, 1667.*

7. *Engraving by an anonymous artist depicting the arrival of Jesuit missionaries in North America.*

6

7

Mission in Peking. In 1631, full vernacular privileges were granted to missionaries in Georgia for the celebration of Mass in either Georgian or Armenian. On the other side of the Atlantic in the region around modern-day Montreal, Jesuit missionaries received permission from the Holy See for use of the Iroquois language in the liturgy. At the first Diocesan Synod of Baltimore held in November 1791, Bishop John Carroll (+1815), allowed some use of English within liturgical celebrations: the Gospel was to be read in the vernacular on Sundays and feast days, followed by a sermon in English, and vernacular hymns and prayers were recommended, as well. In 1822, Bishop John England of Charleston, South Carolina, edited the first American edition of the Roman Missal in English. In 1850, the Catholic Press in England chronicled its own vernacular debates. This is well exhibited in a "Letter to the Editor" by the now Blessed John Henry Newman published in the *Tablet*, in which he defended the use of the vernacular in liturgical celebrations at Brompton Oratory, London, in response to another writer who was strongly critical of the practice.

As late as 1851 and again in 1857, the Holy See refused to allow liturgical translations in the vernacular, even as a tool for the laity in greater appreciation of the Mass. All of that changed exactly twenty years later when, in 1877, the same Pope Pius IX (1846–78), who forbade vernacular translations, completely reversed his decision, allowing any bishop to authorize a translation and the use of vernacular missals by the laity. Pope Leo XIII (+1903) later put such missals on the ordinary *imprimatur* basis according to the judgment of each bishop.

At the dawn of the twentieth century, further vernacular advances around the world were registered. In 1906, Pope Pius X granted permission to certain regions of Yugoslavia to use the classic Paleoslav language in liturgical celebrations. Fourteen years later in 1920, Benedict XV granted a similar permission for the use of Croatian and Slovenian and for the vernacular singing of the epistle and Gospel in solemn masses; he also allowed the use of Czech in those parts of Bohemia were it had been customary since the fifteenth century. Pius XI was elected Pope in 1922, and his interest in and support of the missions was reflected in his openness toward greater use of the vernacular, especially in mission lands. Soon after his election, Pope Pius remarked that "the question of the vernacular is a grave one, but there can be no objection to its being discussed." Subsequent years found a series of permissions granted for bilingual liturgical books. A bilingual Ritual was approved for Bavaria in 1929 and a Vienna edition in 1935, which was used throughout Austria.

In 1945, the International Vernacular Society was founded to promote worship in local languages on the grounds that the continued use of Latin in the liturgy challenged intelligibility and ultimately impeded evangelization. The organization drew up to 10,000 members worldwide with a large constituency coming from the United Kingdom and North America, including a number of bishops. The vernacular agenda was further promoted by the Society's journal

8. John Carroll, first bishop of Baltimore.

*9. German-language missal, edited by Anselm Schott,
monk of Beuron, at the end of the nineteenth century.*

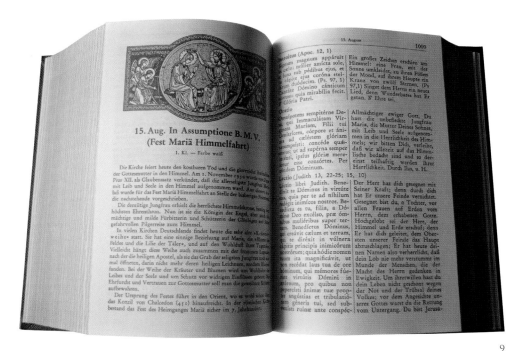

8

9

Amen. Some of the pioneers within the wider liturgical movement, however, had serious reservations about the "vernacularists'" rather aggressive approach, and were concerned that their own efforts at promoting the liturgical renewal might be discredited by too close an association with the Vernacular Society, thus they kept their distance. Indeed, many protagonists within the liturgical movement were skeptical that Latin would ever be abandoned in favor of the vernacular, and they felt that it would be counterproductive to waste their energies on fighting a battle that would never be won.

The vernacularists did win some victories. In 1941 and 1942, permission was granted to translate the Roman Ritual and create bilingual editions in Africa, China, India, Indo-China, Indonesia, Japan, and New Guinea. Such translations would obviously be of great help to the task of evangelization in those far-flung corners of the globe. In 1948, a bilingual Ritual was approved for France for the celebrations of Baptism, Marriage, and Anointing of the Sick. The following year in 1949, a translation of the Missal of Pius V in Mandarin Chinese was approved with the exception of the Roman Canon, which remained in Latin. In those parts of India were Hindi was spoken, permission was granted in 1950 for the use of that vernacular in the celebration of the sacraments. A German-Latin edition of the *Collectio Rituum I* was published in 1951 which contained even more vernacular than what had been produced in France.

Nevertheless, the vernacular debate among the bishops at Vatican II was quite heated. After many long, and at times tense, discussions, helped by the lobbying and gentle persuasion of some pro-vernacular bishops present at the council, consensus was finally reached on December 7, 1962, during the thirty-sixth General Congregation when the bishops approved the first chapter of the liturgy schema—the document that would eventually become the council's Constitution on the Sacred Liturgy. That first chapter included approval for the use of national languages within Catholic worship. Among the 2,118 bishops present, 1,922 voted in favor, 180 voted favorably but with some reservations, 11 were opposed, and 5 votes were held. There were still some rough edges to be worked out, for example, regarding the different usage of Spanish in Spain and in Latin America, and the ways in which Latin liturgical texts should be translated: either literally or more interpretively so that they captured the meaning of the word or phrase in a dynamic way. Such tensions would ultimately need to be dealt with after the council ended, and were eventually treated by the International *Consilium* charged with the task of implementing the liturgical reforms around the world.

30. POPE PIUS XII AND THE LITURGICAL RENEWAL

1. *Peter Paul Rubens, Jesus consecrating the bread and wine, detail of* The Last Supper, *1632. Pincoteca di Brera, Milan. The day after the Council of Trent concluded, the Church solicited contributions from artists to support eucharistic worship.*

2. *Illumination from Hildegarde of Bingen's Scivias; the Church, as a mystical body, radiates from the Holy Spirit.*

3. *Pope Pius XII.*

4. *Cardinal Joseph Ratzinger presiding over the Easter vigil mass at Saint Peter's Basilica on March 26, 2005.*

We have already discussed Pope Pius X's motu proprio of 1903 *Tra le sollecitudini* which spoke of the liturgy as the "true and indispensible source for the Christian life"—a principle which became the liturgical movement's magna carta. This theme was further developed in Pius XII's 1947 encyclical *Mediator Dei*—the first papal encyclical on the Sacred Liturgy. *Mediator Dei,* of course, was not exactly a carte blanche approval of the liturgical movement's agenda. On the contrary, even as the Pope allowed for certain adaptations and concessions (e.g., the use of the vernacular in certain rites), he was also quite critical of some aspects of the liturgical movement and advised caution in proceeding. Nonetheless, that encyclical officially recognized the liturgical movement and inaugurated a series of liturgical changes that would lead to the reforms of the Second Vatican Council. For example, in that same year Belgium received permission for the celebration of evening Mass on Sundays and holy days. For their part, the pioneers of the liturgical movement interpreted *Mediator Dei* positively as a certain ratification of their efforts, and continued to promote the Sacred Liturgy as that "true and indispensible source" for Christian living—a concept that would remain foundational for Vatican II's Constitution on the Sacred Liturgy. The founder of the European liturgical movement, Lambert

Beauduin, acclaimed the document, for example, stating that Pius XII's encyclical had rehabilitated the liturgy and returned it to its proper primacy of place within the church's life and mission.

In many respects, the encyclical *Mystici corporis*, which Pius XII had promulgated four years prior in 1943, provided the needed theological foundation for understanding the church's worship and its need for renewal. Speaking of the church as the Mystical Body of Christ together with the liturgy as the church's "true and indispensable source," implied and indeed demanded an intimate link between worship and social concern. That Mystical Body theology had been recovered at Tübingen in the second half of the nineteenth century as we have already seen. The liturgical pioneers of the twentieth century wisely adopted that theology in shaping its own agenda of liturgical renewal. When read together, Pius XII's two encyclicals of 1943 and 1947 affirm the fundamental truth of Christ—head of the church and chief liturgist as center of the liturgical action, and members of Christ's church hierarchically ordered as participants within that liturgical action. Clearly, the publication of the encyclical *Mediator Dei* revived interest in the liturgy throughout the church.

As a response to *Mediator Dei*, Pius XII established a secret commission for liturgical reform on May 28, 1948, chaired by the Prefect of the Congregation of Sacred Rites, Cardinal Clement Micara, which continued its work for

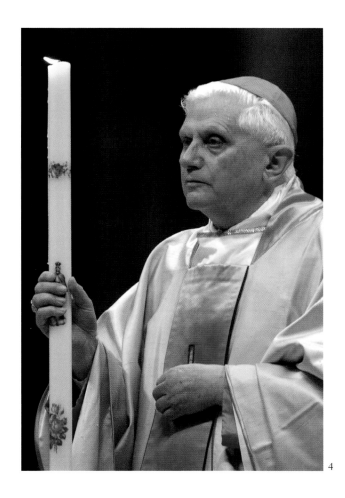

4

3

twelve years until it was dissolved in 1960. Known as the "Pian Commission," its contribution was quite significant and pastoral in scope. Very soon, its efforts bore fruit in concrete results. For example, the Holy See granted permission for an abbreviation of the required Eucharistic fast from the midnight before receiving Communion to just one hour prior. This led to the possibility of celebrating Mass in the evening, as well, since prior to the shortened fast, it would have proven very difficult to fast from the midnight prior until Mass on the following evening. The Commission was also responsible for the restoration of the Easter Vigil in 1951, followed by the reform of the Holy Week liturgies in 1955. While the work of the Pian Commission is largely unknown, it offers an important historical piece as we attempt to understand the liturgical reforms of Vatican II. Here was a liturgical commission already established by Pope Pius XII in 1948—a full fourteen years before the first session of the Second Vatican Council took place.

31. The Assisi Liturgical Congress of 1956

1. *View of the city of Assisi and Saint Francis Convent.*

2. *William Congdon,* Saint Francis Basilica, *oil on wood. This work was created at the end of the 1950s in Assisi, which is still one of the world's great spiritual centers. The American painter had chosen to live in that Umbrian city.*

1

One significant pre-conciliar event was the international liturgical congress held at Assisi in September 1956. Indeed, if we wish to find a bridge between the liturgical movement itself and the Second Vatican Council, it was undoubtedly the Assisi Congress. This is so because Vatican II would later echo many of the same concerns voiced at Assisi when the council's Constitution on the Sacred Liturgy was eventually promulgated. Acknowledging liturgical developments around the world, the Vatican's Congregation for Sacred Rites convoked an international congress on pastoral liturgy in September, 1956. The invitation-only event drew more than 1,400 participants from every corner of the globe—eighty bishops and six cardinals among them. The host was Cardinal Gaetano Cicognani, Prefect of the Congregation, who made it clear that while the subject was to be pastoral liturgy, the only item not to be discussed was worship in the vernacular. Among the talks at Assisi, two were considered the most significant—both given by Jesuits: Josef Jungmann addressed the subject of "The Pastoral Idea in the History of the Liturgy" followed by the biblical scholar Augustin (later Cardinal) Bea who spoke on "The Pastoral Value of the Word of God in the Sacred Liturgy."

Cardinal Cicognani's address was consistent with the recent papal encyclical *Mediator Dei* (promulgated in 1947), expressing both praise for the accomplishments of the liturgical movement and caution against acting erroneously or too quickly. Thus, there were to be no "debates" during the Assisi Congress although "private and unofficial discussions might well result in . . . conclusions to be submitted to the ecclesiastical authority." Predictably, Cicognani upheld the continuation of Latin in the liturgy not only as "a splendid sign of unity and universality" but also to "clothe the sacred truths in their magnificence . . . effectively safeguarding them against the corruption of true doctrine." He continued that even though those in the assembly do not normally understand Latin, this was no reason for replacing it with the vernacular since they did not participate in the ordained priesthood: "The faithful are not the hierarchical priesthood, a chosen class who alone offer the sacrifice in the true and proper sense and who for that reason should understand fully the sacred formulas and expressions. In their royal priesthood, the faithful take part *aequo modo*, according to their station, in the sacrifice and the divine mysteries."

This strong reaffirmation of the unqualified use of Latin in the liturgy came as a shock, and the translators at this point fell silent. Cicognani was well aware of the grassroots support for the vernacular around the world, and did his best to see that the topic would carefully be avoided in the course

172

2

of the meeting; he did not succeed. There may have been no official "debates" at the congress, but unofficial debates and discussions abounded with the Prefect himself. And the topic, not surprisingly, was the vernacular. Indeed, despite the Cardinal Prefect's directive that the theme of the vernacular was not to be discussed, every speaker advocated the vernacular either directly or indirectly, beginning with the major addresses given by Jungmann and Bea. As Jungmann traced the history of the vernacular, he was interrupted several times with sustained applause, much to the chagrin of Cardinal Cicognani. In fact, translators had been forbidden to translate anything regarding the vernacular during public talks and discussions. Thus, when the topic was broached, the translators paused in shock not knowing what to do.

At a certain point during the congress, Cardinal Cicognani abruptly left Assisi and returned to the Vatican. Cardinal Giacomo Lercaro of Bologna then stepped in as President. Word soon spread that Cicognani was furious because of all the pro-vernacular discussions, and had to return to inform Pope Pius XII of the group's disobedience so that they could be duly scolded and reprimanded during the papal audience scheduled for Friday of that week. Actually, the reason for Cicognani's departure was much more benign: He was housed in the cardinal's suite in the bishop's palace,

which had not been used for some time. The bed was infested with fleas who took a liking to the Cardinal, so he returned home to seek a cure.

As the group prepared to travel to Rome at the end of the week for an audience with Pope Pius XII, at least some held out hope that the Pope might not scold them at all, but rather use the occasion to announce certain vernacular concessions. To their disappointment, he stated just the opposite: that it is the "unconditional obligation" of those celebrating the Latin Rite to use Latin; he also insisted that Gregorian chant should not be translated into the vernacular. Nevertheless, Pope Pius XII did affirm that the liturgical movement was "a sign of God's providence and of the movement of the Holy Spirit in the church, bringing people closer to the mystery of faith and the grace that comes through liturgical participation." It was from the list of participants at Assisi that the council's Preparatory Liturgical Commission was drawn up, and it was the pastoral vision exhibited at Assisi that would influence the shaping of the council's liturgical agenda.

32. THE CONCILIAR PREPARATORY COMMISSION

1

On January 25, 1959, in the Basilica of Saint Paul's Outside the Walls, Pope John XXIII announced the Second Vatican Council. On May 17 of that same year, it was announced that the Pope had instituted an ante-preparatory commission for the council which was to "trace the general lines of the matters to be discussed by the Council," after having listened to suggestions from the episcopate, from the Roman Curia, and from the theological and canonical faculties of the pontifical universities. The responses were tabulated and published in 1960–1961 in sixteen volumes entitled *Acta ed Documenta Concilio oecumenico Vaticano II apparando, Series Praeparatoria.* Replies on the topic of the liturgy were numerous and varied, including comments on the simplification of the rites; introduction of the vernacular; adaptations t o the cultural genius of various peoples; and participation of the faithful as suitable elements for fostering an intimate understanding of the Christian mystery on the part of the liturgical assembly itself.

On June 5, 1960, just a few weeks after he announced the establishment of the ante-preparatory commission, Pope John instituted commissions that were to prepare the sche-

mas of the documents to be presented for discussion at the council. Cardinal Gaetano Cicognani was appointed President of the Preparatory Commission on the Liturgy. The nomination of Vincentian Father Annibale Bugnini came one month later and the two began their work immediately. Bugnini was well qualified for the post, having acted as Secretary of the commission for Pope Pius XII's liturgical reform. The full preparatory commission consisted of sixty-five members and consultors with thirty advisors. A number of bishops and liturgical scholars were among those nominated, representing twenty-five countries and five continents. It held its first meeting in Rome several months later on November 12, 1960. The schema prepared by the commission included the areas that needed theological re-thinking and ritual revision and led to the formulation of thirteen subcommissions: 1) the mystery of the liturgy in relation to the church; 2) the Mass; 3) Eucharistic concelebration; 4) the Divine Office; 5) Sacraments and sacramentals; 6) Reform of the liturgical calendar; 7) the use of Latin; 8) Liturgical formation; 9) Liturgical participation by the laity; 10) Cultural and linguistic adaptation; 11) simplifica-

2

tion of liturgical vesture; 12) sacred music; 13) liturgical art. One of the most difficult subcommissions was Latin working group (*De lingua latina*) and it brought about a significant level of debate within the wider preparatory commission itself. At least some saw the issue of language raising a question of the relationship between the doctrinal (the use of Latin in the liturgy articulated Catholic identity) and the pastoral (the vernacular was the very symbol of what was meant by such a pastoral council to communicate with the modern world). A close look at the list of the thirteen subcommissions also reveals a hierarchical ordering beginning with the most important—the mystery of the liturgy in relation to the church—and concluding with the more ancillary topics to be treated—liturgical music and art. When the time came to nominate members to serve on the various subcommissions, many familiar names from Assisi could be found.

The Commission's last plenary session was held January 11–13, 1962. The final text of the schema was ready on January 22 and submitted to the council's General Secretariat soon after. Significantly, very little change was required in

the text. Just four days after the text was submitted to the Secretariat, Cardinal Cicognani died and was soon replaced by Cardinal Arcadio Larraona, CMF, both as Prefect of the Congregation of Rites and President of the Preparatory Commission. Once the opening date of the council had been set for October 11, 1962, and the preparatory period was over, those preparatory commissions were replaced with Conciliar Commissions. On September 4, 1962, Pope John appointed Cardinal Larraona President of the Conciliar Commission on the Sacred Liturgy. Soon after the council opened, the council fathers elected sixteen members of the Conciliar Commission and they began their work immediately with the help of two vice presidents appointed by Cardinal Larraona. Surprisingly, however, Cardinal Giacomo Lercaro of Bologna was not chosen as one of the two vice presidents, despite the fact that he had been elected a member of the Preparatory Liturgical Commission by an overwhelming majority precisely for his competence in the area of liturgy.

33. *Sacrosanctum concilium*: The Liturgy Constitution of the Second Vatican Council

The proposed draft of the Liturgy Constitution was the first item on the agenda as it was considered a fairly unproblematic subject which could be treated expeditiously. That was not the case. Aside from tensions over the content of the document itself, there were also internal conflicts: Not only was Lercaro not chosen as a vice president of the Conciliar Commission, but Annibale Bugnini, who had served as secretary of the Preparatory Commission, was demoted to *peritus* (expert) rather than remain secretary of the newly formed Commission. Both Lercaro and Bugnini would not be reinstated until the election of Paul VI, when they would be chosen to lead the post-conciliar international Commission *Consilium* charged with the task of implementation. Bugnini was also removed as Professor of Liturgy at the Pontifical Lateran University for liturgical ideas that were viewed as too progressive. The newly appointed President of the Conciliar Commission Cardinal Larraona was a very conservative canon lawyer who believed that Bugnini was the main protagonist in the Preparatory Commission's aversion to Latin in the liturgy. Bugnini was replaced by a staff member in the Congregation, Father Ferdinando Antonelli, OFM.

Between October 22 and November 13, 1962, council bishops spent fifteen general congregations discussing the draft document and the liturgical reform in general. Those discussions lasted about fifty hours with 328 oral interventions and 297 written proposals. Conservatives and progressives continued to lobby for or against the draft document—each camp trying its best to sway those bishops yet undecided. It was not until the end of the second session that the council's Liturgy Constitution *Sacrosanctum concilium* was presented in its final form, passed the general vote by a wide margin of 2,147 to 4, and was then promulgated by newly-elected Pope Paul VI on December 4, 1963. It was the first document to be promulgated.

Sacrosanctum concilium clearly established the general principles and norms that were to be observed in reforming the Roman liturgy: "The rites should be marked by a noble simplicity; they should be short, clear, and unencumbered by useless repetitions; they should be within the people's power of comprehension and as a rule, not require much explanation." As we have seen, it was precisely "noble simplicity" which characterized the Roman Rite as it grew from the fifth to the eighth centuries before it came into contact with the more dramatic, poetic, and verbose Gallican Rite.

The document contains seven chapters that treat the fundamental principles of liturgical reform; concrete directives on the Eucharist; sacraments and sacramentals; liturgy of the hours; liturgical year; liturgical music; and liturgical art. It is interesting to note that the liturgical reforms approved at Vatican II were some of the very things that Martin Luther and the other reformers had been asking for back in the sixteenth century, and yet again at the Jansenist Synod of Pistoia of the eighteenth century. Sufficient time had elapsed from the Reformation in order to revisit some of those delicate questions treated at the Council of Trent, and the collective wisdom contributed by the cross-fertilization of the biblical, ecumenical, liturgical, and patristic movements enabled Catholic bishops of the twentieth century to make more informed judgments on the matters at hand.

The Liturgy Constitution is a carefully worded document and needs to be read accordingly. While it allows for greater use of the vernacular, for example, it continues to uphold Latin as the official language of the church and therefore of its worship. Thus, despite popular misconceptions, the Catholic Church did not completely abolish Latin at the council. Indeed, the translations of post-conciliar liturgical texts (prayers, readings, and blessings) begin with the original Latin text (called the "typical edition") and from there the text is carefully translated into the vernacular. Essentially, the document strikes a careful balance between historical and theological foundations, between "sound tradition and legitimate progress." In many respects it was a *via media*—a compromise document that attempted to appease both conservative and progressive camps. Put differently, it reflects the mixed opinions of the drafters of the Constitution—some more traditional, others more progressive—and tries to find a middle ground that would be satisfactory to both sides.

At the same time, however, *Sacrosanctum concilium* was much more than a *via media*. In some cases, it called for a complete revision of liturgical books and not a mere superficial editing of what was present in the Tridentine liturgy. And while the Constitution did not use the term "inculturation," it did acknowledge the need to allow for "legitimate variations and adaptation to different groups, regions, and peoples, especially in mission lands." The conciliar principle of collegiality among bishops was clearly operative in the Constitution: liturgical matters pertaining to the local church were best dealt with by episcopal conferences or even by diocesan bishops themselves. The Constitution is both pastoral and juridical in scope, promulgated by the Pope himself, reflecting a combination of general principles and concrete liturgical reforms.

Sacrosanctum concilium reveals three fundamental bases in its reform of the Roman Rite: first, a historical consciousness and desire to return to early church sources. Thanks to its contact with the biblical, ecclesiological, ecumenical, and patristic movements, the liturgical movement recovered the church's foundational liturgical documents that

1. Pope Paul VI presides over a ceremony at Saint Peter's during Vatican Council II (Photo, Giuliani).

in Church. He is present, lastly, when the Church prays and sings. . . . Rightly, then, the liturgy is considered an exercise of the priestly office of Jesus Christ. In the liturgy . . . the whole public worship is performed by the Mystical Body of Jesus Christ, that is, by the Head and his members."

Like the entire Liturgy Constitution, the rich theological statement about the role of Christ in the liturgy and the assembly's liturgical role as living and active members of Christ's body was not invented at the council *ex nihilo.* Rather it was the fruit of the firm foundation laid by the work of German theologians at Tübingen in the nineteenth century and of scholars associated with the liturgical movement in the twentieth. Equally important here was the recovery of liturgy's eschatological dimension—the already and not yet—the earthly liturgy celebrated *in via* as the church continues on pilgrimage toward the heavenly banquet that will be celebrated in the new and eternal Jerusalem. This recovery of liturgical theology is notably superior to what one finds in Pius XII's encyclical *Mediator Dei.* This conciliar recovery included a renewed understanding of ecclesiology—the church's self-identity—as foundational for Christian worship. This is so since it is in and through the liturgy that the Christian community is more fully in communion with the mystery of Christ and the church, and is more clearly able to make that commitment manifest in the world through the living out of its worship in daily life.

Prior to Vatican II, liturgy was often looked upon as an object—a thing. However, the council challenged that view, speaking, rather, of liturgy as an event—an action which necessarily involves the whole church in exercising Christ's priesthood which they share through baptism. In this liturgical action, Christ unites the church to himself in associating it to himself in the worship that he renders to God. In so doing, the church as Christ's mystical body participates in this priestly act of Christ. Clearly, this is a very different perspective from the medieval or Tridentine theology, which located Christ's priestly activity solely in the person of the priest.

Thirdly, there was a strong pastoral desire to promote "full, active, and conscious participation," drawing the faithful from being passive spectators into the action of celebrating the Roman Rite together. The notion of "full, active, and conscious participation" was based on the Pauline theology of a common baptismal priesthood in Jesus Christ—a doctrine that would come to be articulated in the council's Dogmatic Constitution on the Church *Lumen Gentium.* This liturgical participation was not one option among many, but rather the "right and duty" of all Christians by virtue of their baptism. Thus, the council argued that to facilitate such participation, the rites should be accessible

we examined earlier in this text. Indeed, that historical consciousness had a huge effect on the council's agenda in reforming the Roman Rite.

Secondly, there was a recovery of liturgy theology and spirituality—that the heart of Christian liturgy is always the paschal mystery of Christ. In number 7, we read "Christ is always present in his Church, especially in its liturgical celebrations. He is present in the sacrifice of the Mass, not only in the person of his minister . . . but especially under the Eucharistic elements. By his power he is present in the sacraments, so that when a man baptizes it is really Christ himself who baptizes. He is present in his word, since it is he himself who speaks when the holy Scriptures are read

2. Pope Paul VI in the conciliar hall during a moment of prayer (Photo, Guiliana).

2

and unencumbered, within the grasp of people's comprehension; use of the vernacular was encouraged along with greater recognition of the role of the laity in exercising the different liturgical ministries. The faithful were to receive Communion consecrated at that particular Mass rather than taken from the tabernacle. The council affirmed that such participation at the moment of Holy Communion might even include the giving of the chalice to the lay faithful—at least on special occasions—depending on local norms and with the permission of the local Ordinary.

Even as we note the restoration of the active and participative nature of Christian worship, however, and even as we acknowledge the presence of Christ within one another and corporately in the liturgical assembly itself, *Sacrosanctum concilium* reminds us that Christian liturgy belongs to no one individual or group: it belongs to Christ. In other words, Liturgy is always God's work on us—God's gift to the church—given for our spiritual upbuilding and

nourishment. Thus, if the priest thinks that he is the center of the celebration rather than Christ—attempting to become the center of attention in his liturgical leadership and preaching—this attitude does not correspond to the council's Christocentric vision as expressed in the Liturgy Constitution.

Sacrosanctum concilium also gave attention to the importance of scripture—fruit of the twentieth-century biblical movement whose influence was felt also within the liturgical movement. More reading from the scriptures was encouraged during the liturgy along with the restoration of biblically based liturgical preaching, stating that the homily should not be omitted on Sundays and feasts "except for serious reason." The Prayer of the Faithful was also restored for Sundays and feast days, in which the liturgical assembly prays for the needs of the church and the world. The Divine Office was recovered as the public prayer of the church as a source of devotion and nourish-

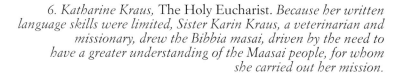

6. Katharine Kraus, The Holy Eucharist. *Because her written language skills were limited, Sister Karin Kraus, a veterinarian and missionary, drew the* Bibbia masai, *driven by the need to have a greater understanding of the Maasai people, for whom she carried out her mission.*

6

4

5

3–5. Jan van Eyck, The Adoration of the Mystic Lamb, *1425–1433, Saint Bavo Cathedral, Ghent. The polyptych (3) is thought of as a synthesis of the Christian doctrine of salvation centered on eucharistic worship. On the lower part, at the center, is an altar with the lamb, toward which Old Testament characters converge, along with Christ's soldiers, saints, martyrs, and pilgrims. Everyone is participating in the liturgy, by either praying, singing (4), or following along in their texts (5).*

ment in living out the Christian life. In all of this, we see the council's desire to recover the unity between Word and Sacrament—between the table of God's Word and the table of the Holy Eucharist—the two tables from which Christians are fed.

34. The International *Consilium* and the Implementation of the Liturgical Reforms

If members of the Preparatory Commission and the council fathers themselves found their task to be daunting, the greater challenge was yet to come. The reforms would need to be implemented and the universal church would have to be formed and catechized in a new worship style and language. On January 29, 1964, Pope Paul VI established a special commission to assist with the universal implementation of the newly approved liturgical reforms for dioceses and regions throughout the world. The commission, called *Consilium ad exsequendam Constitutionem de Sacra Liturgia,* was separate from the Sacred Congregation of Rites and ultimately suppressed it when it became the Sacred Congregation of Divine Worship in 1969. Its first chairman was the liturgically-minded Archbishop of Bologna Cardinal Giacomo Lercaro, later succeeded by the Congregation of Divine Worship's Prefect Cardinal Benno Gut; the secretary was Vincentian priest Annibale Bugnini, who had essentially been the chief architect of the council's liturgical reforms. The commission was comprised of sixty cardinals and bishops and over two hundred consultors from around the world.

The task given to the *Consilium*, and later to the Congregation for Divine Worship, was the implementation of the liturgical reforms which was marked by four vital stages: 1) the passage from Latin to the vernacular in the years 1965–66; 2) the reform of liturgical books begun in 1964; 3) the formulation of new liturgical books for all linguistic groups of the world; and 4) the delicate work of adaptation (later called "inculturation") of the Roman Rite to the uses and mentalities of different peoples and cultures. On September 26, 1964, the First Instruction, *Inter oecumenici,* was issued: *On the Implementation of the Constitution on the Sacred Liturgy*; it was to be put into effect on March 7, 1965. In addition to the mandate to revise all liturgical books so that they were in harmony with the directives of the council, those Latin texts would then be translated into vernacular languages by regional commissions. The *Consilium* also worked on composing new liturgical texts such as three new Eucharistic Prayers in 1968. That same 1964 document also gave the *Consilium* the task of instructing bishops and dioceses everywhere about the renewed liturgy and just what its call to "full, conscious, and active participation" would mean. Newly revised liturgical books followed. The Rite of Ordination was revised and published in 1968; the Rite of Marriage in 1969; the Roman Missal, Lectionary, and Rite of Infant Baptism in 1970; the four volumes of the Liturgy of the Hours and the Rite of Confirmation in 1971; the Rite of Christian Initiation of Adults in 1972 as well as the Rite of Anointing of the Sick and Pastoral Care; the Rite of Penance in 1973 and the Book of Blessings in 1984.

In his posthumous book *La Riforma Liturgica 1948–1975* (Roma, 1997), Annibale Bugnini discussed the opposition to the conciliar liturgical reforms, naming several groups that were especially vocal and influential. One was the international organization *Una voce*, for the defense of Latin and Gregorian chant as over and against the shift to vernacular worship and more contemporary forms of liturgical music. The second mentioned were a series of divergent groups of "Counter-reform" which were hostile to the decrees of the bishops and the Holy See. Among them, Bugnini refers to the American *Catholic Traditionalist Movement*, and some individuals like the Italian Tito Casini who aggressively defended the continued use of Latin in his book *La tunica stracciata.* Cardinals Alfredo Ottaviani and Antonio Bacci are also mentioned by Bugnini for their support of oppositions to the new Missal for its "heretical," "psychologically destructive" and "Protestant" elements, along with the French Abbot Georges de Nantes who called for Pope Paul VI to be deposed, and whom he accused of heresy, schism, and scandal.

To varying degrees, opposition to the reforms was also registered within the Congregation for Divine Worship itself, and tensions grew increasingly strong between the Congregation and the *Consilium*. The largely conservative Congregation viewed the *Consilium* as too progressive, gradually limiting its authority as a result, and impeded liturgical authority of episcopal conferences. For example, the council originally stated that liturgical translations and other texts could be approved at the level of episcopal conferences without the need to send those texts to the Holy See for final approval. The Congregation changed that rule, requiring that all proposed liturgical texts be sent to the Congregation for Divine Worship to receive the *recognitio* (final approval) after having been approved by the particular episcopal Conference.

Such tensions can be understood in part as the result of two conflicting systems that did not easily integrate with one another. The Roman Curia is that which was created after the Council of Trent. The forebear of our Congregation for Divine Worship and the Discipline of the Sacraments, for example, was the Congregation for Sacred Rites founded in 1588 to implement the Tridentine liturgical decrees. That council produced no liturgy constitution like *Sacrosanctum concilium*; rather it was the task of the Congregation of Sacred Rites to give the needed liturgical direction. Such Roman congregations did not exist prior to Trent, but dicasteries such as the Congregation of Sacred Rites were founded precisely to deal with issues of order and uniformity in the post-Tridentine church. Nowhere in the Tridentine Missal of Pius V is reference made to the "People of God." Rather, the problem of the day was unity—liturgical unity and the

1. Oscar Niemeyer, preparatory sketch for the Cathedral of Brasilia, 1970.

unity of the church—especially in light of the Protestant Reformation. Not surprisingly, therefore, the emphasis was on a common language, fixed rubrics, norms to be observed by everyone, and virtually no room for adaptation. The liturgy, like the Roman Congregations themselves, was shaped by the same circumstances.

Both the *Consilium* and Congregation for Divine Worship existed to facilitate implementation of the liturgical reforms of the Second Vatican Council on the international level, but the greater challenge would be implementation on the local and regional levels. For example, the Holy See initially found it difficult to understand why the Spanish-speaking churches of Latin America could not use the same vernacular liturgical books as the church in Spain. Linguistic issues—not to mention historic and cultural ones—soon made it clear that there were too many variances to support just one translation in Castilian Spanish from the Latin typical edition.

Change came quickly, which was not only the case with the vernacular but in other areas as well. Complex Latin liturgical texts were translated into the vernacular expeditiously. While the experts were quite familiar with the liturgical tradition and the sources, they could not have imagined in advance the extent of the change that the use of the vernacular would bring about. Today, almost three hundred and fifty languages or dialects are presently used in the liturgy. Within a few years after the council, the entire liturgical celebration would be in the vernacular. As a result, the council's directive that Latin should continue to

be used in the Divine Office soon became a dead letter. Indeed, as early as 1971, episcopal conferences were authorized to permit the use of the vernacular both throughout the Divine Office and the Mass.

As a result of the introduction of the vernacular, it became desirable to have a large number or prayers and songs, especially in the celebration of the Eucharist, available in the vernacular. The results were largely uneven and some texts were better than others. In various parts of the world, the church breathed the *bon aire* of liturgical experimentation with Masses celebrated in the home; unauthorized new compositions of Eucharistic prayers and other improvised liturgical texts. Much of the criticism against the liturgical experimentation of the 1960s and 1970s was not without justification, and mistakes were made. Be that as it may, as we look back at the work of the International *Consilium* and the implementation of the liturgical reforms at the local level, it was carried out as best as was possible at the time and we are in a far better place today liturgically than we were back in 1963 when *Sacrosanctum concilium* was promulgated. We need to remember that the liturgical renewal is not yet even fifty years old. Indeed, a mere four decades are but a brief moment in our tradition when one considers that it has been a millennium and a half since we last undertook vernacularization in the late fourth century, when Latin came to be introduced into the Roman Rite.

35. THE LITURGICAL ASSEMBLY IN THE POST-CONCILIAR CHURCH

1. Religious ceremony in the only village on Easter Island where, like in other parts of the world, Christianity has been welcomed and combined with local traditions, as the wooden Madonna bears witness to.

2. Preparations for the Feast of the Assumption, 1998, at the Tonantzintla church, located on top of the Mexican Plateau.

1

The Second Vatican Council recovered the understanding of the liturgical assembly as primary symbol of the liturgy—the subject rather than object of the liturgical action, providing the proper context for all liturgical ministry. Presiders and musicians, readers, servers, ministers of hospitality, deacons and Eucharistic ministers, are first and foremost members of the assembly and their servant-role only makes sense in relationship to the assembly. In his 1998 Apostolic Letter *Dies Domini,* Pope John Paul II spoke of the eccesial dimension of the liturgical assembly as "the privileged place of unity," (no. 36), and stressed anew the conciliar agenda of full and active liturgical participation. In the post-conciliar church, the liturgical assembly exercises its royal priesthood in the one sacrifice of praise, celebrating the sacrament of the body and blood of Christ—the mystical body of Christ convoked in holy assembly to receive "the gifts of God for the people of God" as Saint Augustine said.

Giving ourselves over to Christ's action in the liturgy implies the need for reverence in how we treat all of our liturgical symbols and how we pay attention to the places where Christ's presence is revealed: ambo and altar; Lectionary and Book of the Gospels; bread and wine; how we treat one another; how we form the procession at Communion with the ideal of moving together as one body—the mystical body of Christ. Christ's presence and action within the liturgical assembly are further encountered when members of that assembly exercise its various ministries with care and preparation—when the Word is proclaimed prayerfully and with reverence; when the homily is preached with integrity; when members of the assembly (including the priest) sing the hymns and acclamations and speak the prayers and responses aloud and with conviction.

Careful attention to gestures, movement, and posture encourages "mindfulness" so that what members of the liturgical assembly do is never done in haste, but rather in a manner that is intentional and deliberate. These nonverbal elements convey meaning and truth to such an extent that they are regarded as one of the basic languages of the liturgy. Indeed, careful attention to how we use our bodies within worship and the intentionality with which we use movement (how we form processions, for example)—along with the other nonverbal components—move us from worship as individuals to corporate worship in and as the mystical body of Christ. Such bodily gestures actually have the potential of becoming "doors to the transcendent."

Some years before the council, the great German liturgical scholar Romano Guardini wrote in his book *Sacred Signs* about the importance of relearning the forgotten way of doing things. One of the examples he gave was the importance of paying attention in making the sign of the cross: "When we cross ourselves, let it be with a real sign of the cross. Instead of a small cramped gesture that gives no notion of its meaning, let us make a large unhurried sign from forehead to breast, from shoulder to shoulder, consciously feeling how it includes the whole of us—our thoughts, our attitudes, our body and soul, every part of us at once—how it consecrates and sanctifies us . . . It does so because it is a sign of the universe and the signs of our redemption. On the cross, Christ redeemed mankind. By the cross he sanctifies us to the last shred and fiber of our being. We make the sign of the cross before we pray to collect and compose ourselves and fix our minds and hearts and wills upon God. We make it when we finish praying in order that we may hold fast the gift we have received from God." (St. Louis, 1956, p.13)

The General Instruction on the Roman Missal speaks of the gestures and postures of the assembly and liturgical ministers, stating that those gestures "ought to contribute to making the entire celebration resplendent in beauty and noble simplicity, so that the true and full meaning of the different parts of the celebration is evident and that the participation is fostered." (no. 42). That said, however, we must honestly admit that we are still finding our way not only regarding the mindful enacting of liturgical gestures, but also in general as local churches struggle to discover what the assembly's liturgical participation actually means and what such participation demands of them when taken seriously. We are often left with more questions than

2

least no longer attend Sunday Mass, many are present in our liturgical assemblies on Sunday morning. Indeed, many of these individuals live generous lives of service within the church in numerous ways. The fundamental question for clergy and other pastoral ministers is how best to reach these individuals and constituencies. How do we preach a word of hope to them in the midst of the challenges that they face? How do they recognize themselves in our words? There are also increasing numbers of ecumenical and interreligious marriages and it is increasingly common to find these interchurch families worshipping together on Sunday mornings. Of course, such marriages have always existed, but their presence today is more common and calls for greater pastoral sensitivity within the Sunday assembly. If we have learned anything in these post-conciliar years, we have come to understand the importance of hospitality within the liturgical assembly, making room for one another, especially for the newcomers among us. Indeed, every specialized ministry participates in that common ministry of hospitality in which the liturgical assembly engages in each time it is convoked. But it is the church as a whole that is the host and basic minister of hospitality as of liturgy in general. Liturgical hospitality will be crucially important as we look toward the future and failure to keep this in mind will be to our detriment. In Latin America, over 100,000 people leave the church each year in search of more intimate communities of faith that they often find in fundamentalist churches; they lament the anonymity and disinterest they experience in large, urban parishes. Clearly, if these various individuals are made to feel unwelcome for whatever reason, they will continue to look for a welcome and reception in other ecclesial communities and our church will be the poorer for their absence.

Increasing numbers of parishes in large cities around the world—even in Italy and Spain—find themselves in multicultural situations where a number of different cultural groups share membership in the same local parish. While this offers tremendous opportunities for a rich cultural exchange and a beautiful manifestation of the diversity of cultural gifts within the one body of Christ, it also presents concrete challenges. Moreover, as a microcosm of secular society, all the realities and challenges facing life in the wider world will be present, to a greater or lesser degree, within the church itself. Such pastoral situations could not have been imagined fifty years ago, but they will be an ever-growing challenge for church leaders as we look toward the future. The Second Vatican Council called the church to listen to the signs of the times. While the fundamental vision of "full and active participation" remains as much a goal today as it was almost fifty years ago at the time of the council, that goal will need to be reinterpreted again and again as the face of the Mystical Body of Christ continues to change. New models will need to be employed if we are to respond effectively to changing pastoral needs of the church in the twenty-first century.

answers. What is the proper balance between the universality of the tradition and the locality of the worshiping community? What is the relationship between the parish church and the local bishop; between the local church and the Bishop of Rome? Today we have a participative liturgy in most places, but the challenge remains to discover the full meaning of the liturgical assembly's central role in the liturgy and its relationship to the wider universal church. Even despite our best efforts, the individualism and narcissism within the cultures of the developed world can too easily find a way into our liturgical assemblies as well. As Pope Benedict XVI notes in *Deus Caritas Est,* love of God and love of neighbor is one inseparable reality. Assemblies need to look not only at the "neighbor" within the assembly itself, but beyond the confines of church buildings to the poor and needy, the immigrant and homeless "neighbor" who cries out for help.

While the conciliar agenda has not changed, we find ourselves in a very different place today than at the time of the Second Vatican Council fifty years ago. Of course, it is the same body of Christ—the same "one, holy, catholic, and apostolic Church"—but the faces have changed, and so have the issues and needs, the problems and tensions, that its constituents bring with them each time they gather together for worship. In much of the developed world, increasing numbers of Catholics find themselves in what the church calls "irregular situations"—divorced and remarried Catholics, for example. While some of those in "irregular situations" have left the church, or at the very

36. The Liturgical Year Revisited

1. This Virgin and Child icon, placed under a thirteenth-century painting, still has, on its two faces, the original paint. It dates back to the sixth century. Santa Maria Nuova, Rome.

1

The holy days, feasts, and seasons of the liturgical year are one of the primary ways through which most Christians celebrate their faith and mark the weeks and months of the year beginning with the First Sunday of Advent (four Sundays before Christmas) and ending with the thirty-fourth Sunday of the church year which falls toward the end of November. The year is made up of two overlapping cycles—the temporal (from the Latin word *tempora* meaning seasons), and the sanctoral cycle which refers to the feasts of individual saints. At first only local martyrs were commemorated by Christian communities, usually at the site of their burial and on the date of their death. But in later centuries after major persecutions ceased, the concept of sainthood came to include other Christians judged to have lived outstanding and virtuous lives in service of the Gospel along with numerous biblical figures, thus devotion to saints ceased to be purely local. By the late Middle Ages the majority of days of the year had at least one commemoration of a saint attached to it.

The temporal does not coincide with the civil year but is rather a combination of two spans of time—one based around the spring feast of Easter whose date is movable each year, and the other based around Christmas and Epiphany whose dates are fixed. Since the two annual cycles overlap, they affect one another as well as the weekly Sunday celebration of the Lord's resurrection, thus churches have clearly established rules for what to do in situations where the feasts coincide. Despite those rules, however, there can often be a tension between the church's official liturgy and expressions of popular piety. For example, in Italy when the Feast of Saint Joseph (March 19) falls on a Sunday which is always one of the Sundays in Lent, it can be difficult to persuade pastors or parishioners that the feast must be transferred to the Monday so that the Lenten Sunday observance can be kept. The temporal cycle also has two "in-between" times that the Roman Catholic Church refers to as "Ordinary Time," the shorter one from the end of the Christmas/Epiphany season until the beginning of Lent and a much longer stretch from the feast of Pentecost (celebrated in May or June) until the beginning of Advent in late November or the beginning of December.

There are occasions when the liturgical calendar intersects with the civil calendar presenting challenges for pastoral leaders and especially preachers, and January 1 is one such feast. Indeed, few feast days on the Christian calendar have undergone the sort of metamorphosis that this day has: Mary the Mother of God, the Feast of the Circumcision, the Feast of the Holy Name of Jesus, the Octave Day of Christmas. And of course, it is the beginning of the civil New Year. The historical evolution of the church's celebration of the beginning of the New Year is interesting. As an attempt to counter pagan practice, the early church advocated a more penitential celebration of fast and abstinence to welcome the New Year. A special Mass formulary evolved "For Protection against Idolatry." In the sixth and seventh centuries, the church in France and Spain witnessed further attempts in this direction, as an antidote to the excessive feasting that had become commonplace in secular society at the New Year.

The Roman Church's observance of the New Year registered a different approach from what had evolved in France and Spain. Rather than choosing penitential themes for the New Year's liturgy of the church, Rome chose to celebrate the anniversary of the Mother of God. So, by the second half of the sixth century, Christian Rome had begun keeping the feast *Natale Sanctae Mariae* on January 1, both to close the Christmas octave and also as a fitting way to ring in the New Year. This Roman practice represents the oldest Marian feast in the West and was probably influenced by the liturgy of Constantinople, where feasts dedicated to the Virgin Mother had already been in existence for some time. By the seventh century, a new wave of Eastern Christian immigrants arrived in Rome, bringing with them the Byzantine feasts of the Annunciation and Assumption (or "Dormition") of Mary. Those new feasts gradually overshad-

2

2. Presentation of Jesus at the Temple, illumination of Abbess Saint Hitda's Book of Gospels, Cologne, 1000–1020. Hessich Landesbibliothek, Darmstadt.

3. Clara Halter, Jean-Michel Wilmotte, Wall for Peace, *2000, expanded nighttime view, Champs de Mars, Paris.*

sistent overlapping of incarnational and Marian themes. In December 1967, Pope Paul VI introduced the "World Day of Peace" to be observed beginning on January 1, 1968, and repeated each year as a sign of hope and promise for a world healed of division and renewed by love. Two millennia after pagan New Year's celebrations and various Christian attempts at liturgical responses to such rivalry, we struggle to find the right balance in a proper celebration of this day, and tensions between cultural and religious traditions remain. Indeed, the striking contrast between civil and liturgical calendars is probably more evident on this day than on any other of the church year. When January 1 is considered in its secular context, some cultures use it as a day for political inaugurations and civic celebrations. For many, it is a day of traveling home after the Christmas holiday or New Year's Eve celebrations, or simply of resting from a night of revelry with family and friends. With that secular background, it is the Solemnity of Mary the Mother of God and the World Day of Peace on the church calendar.

While the liturgical year has occasionally been viewed as nothing more than a succession of historical commemorations that provide useful help in teaching the Christian faith, it is much more than that. It invites believers into a pilgrimage in which Christians celebrate the paschal mystery of Christ as it is lived out sacramentally in meditating upon the various dimensions of the life of Christ, the Blessed Virgin Mary, and the saints.

owed the *Natale Sanctae Mariae* and January 1 remained only a celebration of the Octave of Christmas.

It was at this point that the feast of the Circumcision of the Lord found its way into the Roman liturgy. Already in the sixth century, there was a growing observance of that feast in both Spain and France amid the penitential nature of the New Year observance mentioned earlier. With the arrival in Rome of French and Spanish pilgrims in the seventh century, the Gallican Feast of the Circumcision of the Lord came also to be observed in Rome, although some scholars suggest that it only really took hold there in the thirteenth and fourteenth centuries. Complicating the situation still further, yet another feast came to be celebrated on that day: the Feast of the Holy Name of Jesus. It was first celebrated locally toward the end of the Middle Ages, especially in England, but then elsewhere in Europe as well. That feast grew in popularity thanks to the efforts of the Cistercian monks in the twelfth century, the Franciscans and Dominicans in the fifteenth century, and the Jesuits in the sixteenth century. The Feast of the Holy Name was suppressed with the conciliar calendar reform in 1969. With the 2002 revision of the Roman Missal, it was restored as an optional memorial on January 3. As we look back at the liturgical history of New Year's Day, we can observe a con-

3

37. LITURGICAL INCULTURATION

1. *John Paul II during a ceremony at Saint Peter's Basilica, on the occasion of the Extraordinary Synod of Bishops in 1985 (Photo, Giancarlo Giuliani).*

Vatican II's Constitution *Gaudium et Spes* makes a significant statement about the role played by culture in the life and mission of the church. In number 58 it declares: "The Church has existed through the centuries in varying circumstances and has utilized the resources of different cultures in her preaching to spread and explain the message of Christ, to examine and understand it more deeply, and to express it more perfectly in the liturgy and in various aspects of the life of the faithful." Over a span of two thousand years the church has been integrating the cultural resources of regions and peoples so as to evangelize, to teach, and to celebrate the paschal mystery of Christ in the liturgy. Undoubtedly, one of the most significant accomplishments of

Second Vatican Council's liturgical reforms was a new awareness of the important relationship between liturgy and culture—what would come to be called "liturgical inculturation." This was due in large part to the important collaborative work done by cultural anthropologists, sociologists, and theologians both before Vatican II and especially in its aftermath. Before the twentieth century, when reference was made to culture, one normally thought of the great masters such as Caravaggio, El Greco, or Rubens, Michelangelo or Bernini, or the music composed by Bach, Beethoven, and Mozart, or the writings of Shakespeare. Thus, one would speak of those who were "cultured," often used as a synonym for educated and opposed to the "uncultured"—

2. Group of fathers at the Extraordinary Synod of Bishops session, 1985 (Photo, Giancarlo Giuliani).

3. Dance being performed at the Mututum Monastery, Mindanao, the Phillipines.

the Gospel in particular cultures over the centuries, precisely because the only valid cultural model presented was that of Western Europe. A good example of this incapacity can be found in the Chinese Rites Controversy, which lasted for about one hundred and fifty years from the beginning of the seventeenth century until 1742. Matteo Ricci and his colleagues dedicated themselves to encouraging and supporting positive elements in Chinese culture as an important strategy within the process of evangelization: to make the Christian gospel more credible and accessible to the Chinese. The approach of non-Jesuit missionaries, supported by civil and church authorities, was to employ the largely white, Western European classical model as the only valid approach, and the church's mission in China was lost as a result. Even in more recent times, the pre-conciliar or Tridentine Rite of the Roman Catholic Church reflected in large measure the classical model mentioned above. To be Catholic meant to celebrate Mass in Latin.

Thanks to the pre-conciliar writings of liturgical scholars like Edmund Bishop, Anton Baumstark, Gregory Dix, and Joseph Jungmann, to name a few, attention was drawn to the diverse cultural contexts in which Christian worship grew. Thanks to their scholarship, it has now become abundantly clear that Christian liturgy cannot be studied, much less celebrated, except within its cultural context. It was such cultural consciousness within the area of liturgical scholarship that contributed significantly to the Second Vatican Council's cultural awakening in relationship to worship, and the consequent need to adapt the liturgy to particular cultural contexts. Unlike culture, the term "inculturation" is

those incapable of appreciating the beauty of art and architecture, classical philosophy, literature, and music. This understanding fostered the conviction that there was but one culture into which people are initiated: the culture of arts and letters; of classical music and poetry.

With the advent of the social sciences in the twentieth century, and especially thanks to cultural anthropology, we have come to understand that the cultural reality is far more complex than had been believed. Rather than the one-culture model, we now recognize the multiplicity of cultures, each with its unique characteristics and rites of initiation. Indeed, the one-culture model can help us to understand the church's occasional inability to incarnate or inculturate relatively new in documents of the Roman Catholic Church. Indeed, it does not appear even once in any of the documents of Vatican II. The council does speak of the importance of culture and even of the necessity of adapting the Gospel and the church's worship to particular cultures (*Sacrosanctum concilium* 37–40), but the chosen term is "adaptation" rather than "inculturation." Introduction of the term "inculturation" came in 1962, through an article published by Gregorian University professor Joseph Masson, SJ ("*L'Eglise ouverte sur le monde*" in *Nouvelle Revue Théologique*, 84, 1962, p.1038). The term was used again in 1973 by a Protestant missionary in New York, George Barney, in which he urged prudence in the practice of inculturation lest the essentials of the Gospel message be lost. Two years later the Jesuits used the term in discussion during their 32nd General Congregation held in Rome in 1975 with a letter on the subject three years later written by their Superior General, Fr. Pedro Arrupe. The following year, 1979, Pope John Paul II used the term in his Address to the Pontifical Biblical Commission; this was the first time in which "inculturation" appeared in a papal document. John Paul further developed the concept in the document *Catechesi tradendae* (No. 53) promulgated that same year which treats the relationship between catechesis and culture. Also in 1979, Crispino Valenziano of the Pontifical Liturgical Institute spoke of the relationship between popular devotions and liturgy and suggested that inculturation was the best method to foster reciprocity between the two realities.

The Extraordinary Synod of Bishops held in 1985 offered its own helpful contribution, suggesting that inculturation is different from a mere external adaptation, as it signifies an interior transformation of authentic cultural values through their integration into Christianity and the rooting of Christianity in different cultures. In 1994, the Congregation for Divine Worship and the Discipline of the Sacraments issued a document "The Roman Liturgy and Inculturation," noting its preference for the term "inculturation" over "adaptation." It described inculturation as a more organic development in which the church seeks to incarnate the Gospel in particular cultures, but also in which the church is enriched by the cultural contributions of different peoples. This double-movement is significant in that it suggests that each entity has something to learn from the other; it implies a certain reciprocity. That being said, however, discernment is essential for balanced judgment as to what cultural elements should or should not be embraced for the liturgical rites or within the discipline of theological discourse.

While the Second Vatican Council did not use the term "inculturation," it permitted and even encouraged an adaptation of the Roman Rite to the particular cultural contexts where it was being celebrated, vigorously affirming that cultural plurality was intrinsically Catholic. Many justifiably defined numbers 37–40 of the Liturgy Constitution as the Magna Carta of the liturgical inculturation. In Number 37, *Sacrosanctum concilium* affirms that the church does not wish to impose a "rigid uniformity" in matters liturgical, but rather

4

respects and fosters the "genius and talents of the various races and peoples," provided that such cultural components are not linked to superstition or error, and provided that they are in harmony with the liturgy's "true and authentic spirit." The document then accentuates the possibility that provisions be made for "legitimate variations and adaptations to different groups, regions, and peoples," so long as the "substantial unity of the Roman Rite" is preserved (no. 38). The most advanced prospect comes at number 40, when it affirms that there are some situations and regions where an even more radical or substantial adaptation will be necessary. A good example of such radical adaptation can be found in the 1988 approval of the Holy See granted to the bishops of Zaire (now the Democratic Republic of Congo) for the publication of "The Roman Mass for the Dioceses of Zaire," popularly called the "Zairean Rite," which contains distinctively African and Zairean (Congolese) elements. All of this, of course, was a radical departure from what preceded it in the Tridentine period, which strove to maintain a rigid liturgical uniformity at all cost.

Fifty years after the council, our understanding of liturgical inculturation and how it functions continues to evolve. The situation is further complicated by the growing multicultural reality in urban parishes and dioceses around the globe that was mentioned earlier. Indeed, it is precisely our dedication to the furthering of the rapport between liturgy and culture that will enable Christians to be more competent dialogue partners in the world church.

4. *A moment during the opening ceremonies for the African Synod, carried out at Saint Peter's Basilica, Sunday, April 10 (Photo, Giancarlo Guiliani).*

5. *The bishops at the opening ceremonies for the African Synod, at the Vatican's Saint Peter's Basilica (Photo, Giancarlo Guiliani).*

6–7. *Easter rites at a Comboni mission in Africa (Nigrizia archives).*

38. Liturgical Art, Architecture, and Music after Vatican II

Vatican II's Constitution on the Church describes the community of Jesus' disciples as "a people brought into unity from the unity of the Father, the Son and the Holy Spirit" (no. 4). Our life as believers is grounded on the life which the Holy Trinity shares with us and which gives energy and purpose to our life of faith. The church is a visible sacrament of our communion with God and unity among one another. It is both a sign and an instrument of communication which functions vertically between God and human beings, and horizontally among human beings. Vatican II's recovery of the centrality of the paschal mystery of Christ in the liturgy and of the liturgical assembly's participation in the common priesthood of the faithful exercised in its public profession of faith through the liturgy needed to find appropriate and corresponding expressions in the realm of art, architecture, and music. Unlike the one-culture approach of the preconciliar church, the liturgical reforms of Vatican II encouraged inculturated art forms and architectural designs, with music now sung in the vernacular and often reflective of a distinct cultural form.

1

Liturgical architecture has a fundamental role in promoting full, conscious, and active participation in the church's worship. The United States Bishops' document on art, architecture, and worship, *Built of Living Stones*, expresses this very well: "Because liturgical actions by their nature are communal celebrations, they are celebrated with the presence and active participation of the Christian faithful whenever possible. Such participation, both internal and external, is the faithful's 'right and duty by reason of their baptism.' The building itself can promote or hinder the 'full, conscious, and active participation' of the faithful. Parishes making decisions about the design of a church must consider how the various aspects and choices they make will affect the ability of all the members to participate fully in liturgical celebrations" (no. 31).

In the years immediately after the council, proposals were introduced for the restoration of a more domestic ideal for contemporary Catholic parish communities. This concept led to a less formal arrangement, with an emphasis on functionality. The Eucharist shifted from sacrifice to meal; the altar of sacrifice became the table. In the redesign of church buildings with the assembly as primary subject of the liturgy, chairs (sometimes without kneelers) replaced pews or benches, and were often arranged around the principal liturgical symbols of altar, ambo, presidential chair, and baptismal font, to allow closer access to the liturgical center. It must be admitted that the years immediately after Vatican II did not yield a good deal in terms of artistic taste and good sense. It was a time of great experimentation; for example, neo-Gothic churches were renovated to correspond to the litur-

gical vision of the council. In some cases, renovations were minor: moving the altar out from the east wall so that it was now freestanding, allowing the presiding priest to face the assembly and walk freely completely around it. This often required the building of a platform to accommodate the freestanding altar. Communion rails were removed to further enhance the communitarian and domestic dimension of the post-conciliar liturgy. In other cases, however, the renovations were major: the access of the neo-Gothic church was changed with the altar now placed in the middle of the church (on the side wall) with chairs surrounding it on three sides.

Newly constructed church buildings had greater flexibility in exhibiting minimalist modern or postmodern designs: Some of these buildings were almost puritanical in their design. The liturgical assembly—now the subject of the ritual action—would bring the needed color and texture to the worship space, so the walls were often whitewashed with few devotional objects in evidence. Members of the assembly were to abandon their personal devotions in favor of a rich liturgical participation desired by the church. The problem, however, was that many people, especially older parishioners, were not accustomed to the changes. They missed their devotions, the kneelers, and were less than convinced that the liturgical space no longer needed the warmth and texture to which they had grown accustomed. It would take a number of years to rediscover the

1. Pier Luigi Nervi (with Pietro Belluschi), Saint Mary's Cathedral, San Francisco, 1967–1971.

2–3. View of the hall and the presbytery at the Madonna della Vena Church, Cesenatico.

2

3

equilibrium—the balance between liturgy and devotions especially as that balance is found in the relationship between liturgy and the arts.

This domestic emphasis on the liturgical space was also reflected in the area of art and liturgical music with varying results. In the United States, popular folk music of composers like Bob Dylan came to be employed in the liturgy with a more appropriate set of words. New composers came on the scene and made various attempts at their own liturgical folk music. However, it was often the case that such music paled in comparison with what preceded it, whether one considers the long tradition of Gregorian chant or the theologically rich hymnody of Charles and John Wesley, for example. Almost fifty years after Vatican II, the church continues to find its way in its search for beauty within the liturgy. In recent years, composers of liturgical music have come on the scene around the world, and some of them are producing music in different languages that is of a superior quality to what emerged immediately after Vatican II. Much, however, remains to be done.

In these post-conciliar years, the church now recognizes that, like the other arts, music is culturally conditioned and is hardly a "universal language" as had been thought in the past. Each culture has its own variation and style, tempo and form, which is quite distinct. Thus, musical participation can be challenging especially in multicultural parishes, where parishioners need to make the effort to learn one

4

4–6. Interior (with organ) and exterior of Our Lady of Angels Cathedral in Los Angeles.

7–8. Exterior views of the Church of Tor Tre Teste, designed by Jewish architect Richard Meier. It is located in the outskirts of Rome.

5

6

another's musical traditions. This is essential in order to foster mutual enrichment, precisely by the people of different cultural traditions with whom parish membership is shared. That multicultural reality is especially evident in the United States, and the United States Conference of Catholic Bishops commented on this need for musical "interculturality" in a 2007 statement *Sing to the Lord: Music in Divine Worship*: "When prepared with an attitude of mutual reciprocity, local communities might eventually expand from those celebrations that merely highlight their multicultural differences to celebrations that better reflect the intercultural relationships of the assembly, and that unity that is shared in Christ. Likewise, the valuable musical gifts of the diverse cultural and ethnic communities should enrich the whole Church . . . by contributing to the repertory of liturgical song and to the growing richness of the Christian faith" (no. 59).

Parishes also need to find a balance between the singing of contemporary liturgical music and employing the rich music of the church's ancient tradition that has endured for centuries. Today we recognize that sung participation by the assembly is no longer an option or something peripheral to the liturgy, but rather an intrinsic part of the celebration. As Latin remains the official language of the church and the liturgy, Gregorian chant remains its official musical form. Today, in various parts of the world, a renewed interest in Gregorian chant is emerging, not only in monasteries and other religious communities, but also in some parishes and other churches. Interestingly, the tradition was never lost in Anglo-Catholic churches where both

Gregorian and Anglican chant has continued to be sung by the liturgical assembly for years.

Clearly, there are situations where the Latin language does pose an obstacle for many individuals and the singing of Gregorian chant itself requires a certain degree of training in order to execute it well. However, the complete abandonment of Gregorian chant on the grounds either that it is too complicated or irrelevant would be unfortunate,

7

8

given the fact that it remains the church's musical form *par excellence*. Liturgical artists, architects, and musicians have been greatly assisted in these post-conciliar years by courses, institutes, and programs in liturgical formation, which have enabled them to understand the way in which the arts are intended to serve as a handmaid of the liturgy in its search for beauty. This has led to a significant improvement in quality and taste. Such progress is especially evident in the area of liturgical architecture.

Two recent church building projects come to mind. Both reflect worldwide searches for the best architects, designers, and artists to combine modern architecture and art in a place of great spiritual power. One is the Church of the Jubilee in suburban Rome designed by the Jewish-American architect Richard Meier and commissioned to celebrate Pope John Paul II's twenty-fifth anniversary of his papal election. The church is defined by three tall concrete shapes like sails that lead to the heights. The spaces between them and the ceilings are all glass, which allows light to flood the entire space. For Meier, the shafts of sunlight that penetrate the skylights dance in the interior as a metaphor for the presence of God and draw the assembly into the numinous and the holy. The second building is the Cathedral Church of Our Lady of the Angels in Los Angeles, California, begun in 1999 and dedicated in 2002. It was designed by the Spanish architect Raphael Moneo and includes huge cast bronze doors by the Mexican-born artist Robert Graham, in the tradition of the great medieval cathedrals, welcoming one into the building. The interior is lighted by the soft light of alabaster windows. The

worship space is further warmed and colored by twenty-five large tapestries lining both walls of the nave depicting the communion of saints. Five tapestries represent the baptism of Christ behind the baptistery, and an additional seven tapestries hang behind the altar. This group represents the streets of Los Angeles converging at the center to create an image of the New Jerusalem.

As we look back at the various artistic, architectural, and musical experiments of the 1960s and 1970s, we can see with clarity the limits of such a functional approach in a way that we were unable to back then. Today, we understand that liturgy's climate is one of awe, mystery, wonder, reverence, thanksgiving, and praise. It cannot be satisfied with anything less than the beautiful in its execution of art, architecture, and liturgical music. This is because the beautiful is related to the sense of the numinous, the holy. In a world dominated by science and technology, liturgy's quest for the beautiful is more urgent than ever. The use of the plastic arts within the liturgy, for example—painting, sculpture, and textiles—are all potential instruments for enhancing the assembly's experience of beauty within worship and potential "doors to the sacred" that lead worshippers into the transcendent and the numinous.

9

9. Josep Lluis Sert, Chapel of Peace, which is near the Carmelite convent in Mazille, Burgundy. It was built between 1977 and 1981.

10–11. Cloister and skylight in the Chapel of Peace, which is next to the Carmelite convent in Mazille, Burgundy.

12. Bell with ecumenical points of reference, designed by Paolo Soleri.

10

11

12

13–14. *Basilica of Saint Julien (Brioude), along the Santiago de Compostela pilgrimage route, between Puy and Clermont-Ferrand. It was built between the eleventh and fourteenth centuries, at the spot of the previous one from the fifth century, in memory of the martyr Saint Julian (Brioude), to whom it is dedicated. The Dominican Kim En Joong at work on the stained-glass windows at the basilica spot, which is rich in history and layers.*

13

15

14

16

15. *Stained-glass window depicting Saint Julien: the martyr is red and the water blue, under which lies the washed, cut-off head of the martyr.*

16. *Religious function taking place inside the basilica.*

17. *Stained-glass depiction of Saint Stephen that glorifies the first martyr.*

39. LITURGICAL VESTURE AND OBJECTS

1. Grape harvesting scenes, Saint Constance (Rome) mausoleum's ambulatory ceiling mosaic. The laborers are wearing short tunics.

2. Imperial family's cortege, Ara Pacis, Rome.

Much liturgical vesture of both Eastern and Western churches has its origins in the formal secular dress of the Roman Empire in the first six centuries of Christianity. After the legalization of Christianity in the early fourth century, the clergy were given important roles in the government as civil administrators and that was reflected also in their vesture. At the same time, wealthier members of the church gave ornate gifts of clothing for liturgical use on special occasions, both adding a degree of splendor to the liturgical celebration and at the same time distinguishing the one wearing the garment—the president—from the other members of the assembly. By contrast, in the earliest artistic representations of the Eucharist, no distinction can be found in the vesture worn by the one presiding and that of the others present. The earliest piece of clothing that was given special significance in the early church was the white baptismal garment, or alb, with which the newly baptized were clothed when they emerged from the baptismal pool.

In the West, the basic forms of historic liturgical vesture were three: the white alb; the outer garment (either chasuble or cope); and the stole, which served to mark the office or rank. The alb is the vestment common to all liturgical ministers whose design was taken from the long, sleeved garment worn by the Greeks and Romans. In the ancient Mediterranean world, it was essentially a secular garment in both long and short forms. The shorter knee-length form (called *chiton*) was worn by men, especially soldiers and workers, and was made both with and without sleeves. The longer form was called *talaris* because it reached to the feet,

3. Apsidal mosaic at Saint Agnes: detail of the saint and Pope Gregory the Great.

4. Saint Clement's Mass, *fresco detail, 1078–1084, Basilica of Saint Clement, Rome. The saint has a communion cloth in his hand and is wearing a black chasuble over his alb and a mantle around his neck. A chalice, paten, and open missal are lying on top of the altar.*

4

or *tunica* because of its white color. It normally had tight-fitting sleeves and was worn by women, elderly men, and officials, and girded with a cincture. Wealthier citizens and those of greater importance in the community wore a second tunic with wider sleeves, often made of wool from Dalmatia, which was worn over the tight-fitting tunic. This "dalmatic," as it came to be called, was often decorated with strips of purple cloth, initially to cover the seams of the garment, but then gradually more stylized.

The alb remained the basic garment of the clergy until the eleventh century when the looser-fitting "surplice" or *cotta* was introduced north of the Alps to fit over fur-lined garments worn by the clergy in the winter while chanting the Office numerous times each day in cold churches. This surplice began as a full and lengthy garment that was gradually reduced over the centuries. Thanks to the ecumenical collaboration in the twentieth-century liturgical movement, the alb has now become the standard ecumenical garment, worn by clergy and other liturgical ministers of various denominations, replacing the academic dress worn by the churches of the sixteenth-century reformation. Today, the alb tends to be made of heavier material than in the past, with wider sleeves, and often worn without a cincture. The amice (from the Latin *amicio*—to wrap around), whose origins are found in the eighth century, has traditionally been worn under the alb as a scarf, to protect more precious vestments from sweat. Its usage is not as common as in the past, although it is still worn by some liturgical ministers.

Both the chasuble and cope are vestments whose origins are found in the outer garment or cloak that was worn by all in the late Roman Empire world regardless of social level or gender. It was made from a large, semicircular piece of cloth—usually wool. It was either sewn into a single piece that hung like a bell or tent with a hole cut for the head, or it was left open as a cape and held together with a clasp. With its cone-like form, it was called the *casual* or "little house"; the cape was the antecedent of what came to be called the "cope." The chasuble was especially designed for travelers since its form as a sort of poncho (often with a hood) also provided warmth and protection for those who needed to sleep outdoors. The earliest testimony of its usage within Christian liturgy can be found in a letter of Germanus of Paris (+576), and then in the twenty-eighth Council of Toledo (633). Early on, its amplitude came to be symbolized as the garment of charity—appropriately worn by the president of the liturgical assembly. Even as the chasuble grew in liturgical usage, it continued to be donned as a standard item of clerical clothing even outside the liturgy. Only in the eleventh century when the cope was established as a liturgical vestment did the chasuble come to be reserved for the celebration of Mass.

The thirteenth century marked a significant turning point for the chasuble's shape and design. Concomitant with other liturgical changes in that period—the combining of liturgical books into the one *Messale Plenum*, for example, or the decline in the Offertory Procession—the chasuble became a more restricted garment so as to use less material and also be less cumbersome for the celebrant. That vestment's style and measure was further reduced in the post-Tridentine period and especially in the eighteenth century,

5

6

5. Detail of Pope Pius II's pluvial surplice, made in England circa 1300. Museo della Attedrale, Pienza.

7

cutting off the sides of the chasuble and creating what came to be called the *pianeta* or "fiddle-back" in English. Thus, gradually, the Gothic penchant for the oval-shaped chasuble gave way to the more minimalist Baroque vestment without sleeves, which tended to use heavier, stiff brocades.

Episcopal vesture also has its own unique history. The pallium was initially given to archbishops with no particular significance of papal authority or a link with the See of Peter. Only in the ninth century did it become official and obligatory for every metropolitan archbishop. Today it is a symbol of the fullness of the pontifical office and Episcopal participation as Metropolitan in that office. Its form is deliberately cruciform. In the first millennium in both East and West, its form was lengthy and worn over the chasuble. Today, its form remains lengthy in the East while its Western form has been sharply reduced. Soon after his papal election, Benedict XVI returned to using the more ancient form of the pallium but has now returned to the reduced form since he found it less cumbersome.

The Episcopal hat or *camelaucum* came to be worn in processions by elderly bishops as a way of keeping their heads

6. Illumination of the School of Angels, which depicts the capital letter "T" from a 1370 gradual. Biblioteca Medicea Laurenziana, Florence.

7. Detail of pluvial cowl, Botticelli's Florentine design, from the last quarter of the fifteenth century. Museo Poldi Pezzoli, Milan.

10

10. Chausable made of red fabric, decorated with grape clusters and gold brocade spikes. Treasure found in Salzburg's Saint Peter's Abbey.

9

8. Guido Reni, Saint Philip Neri's Vision, *Chiesa Nuova, Rome.*

9. Chasuble cape made in Milan in 1610. Milan Cathedral Treasury Museum.

warm as early as the eighth century in a simplified form. However, that style was more formalized in the ninth century with the introduction of the tiara. By the tenth century, the miter was established for all bishops in the West. A similar historical development can be noted in the East. The gold ring was originally worn by all Christians as a means of stamping or sealing a document with the possessor's name or with a symbol of the possessor. By the seventh century, it became traditional to give bishops a ring during their episcopal ordination as a symbol of being married to the local church for which the bishop was ordained. The episcopal cross began as a private ornament worn under the clothing. In the fourth century, the tradition of wearing a cross was also extended to the laity, first in the East and then in the West. Only in the fourteenth century did the church speak of the episcopal cross as an official ornament for bishops.

The history of other liturgical objects is equally interesting, with the evolution of the chalice and paten over the centuries, corresponding to different modes of celebrating the Eucharist. In the early church through the medieval period, one can note a wider and larger cup and larger

11. *Tassilo chalice made of finely chiseled gilt copper, from the eighth century, Kremsmünster Abbey Church.*

12. *Paten with engravings and precious stones from the eleventh century, Santo Domingo de Silos Abbey.*

plate as the lay faithful received Communion under both forms, drinking from the chalice as well as receiving the consecrated host. As the reception of Communion by the lay faithful waned in the late Middle Ages through the Tridentine and post-Tridentine period, the chalice and paten were reduced to a much smaller form, since it was normally only the celebrant who received the Sacrament during Mass—a Mass that was often celebrated privately with only the presence of a server.

The idea of reserving the consecrated Eucharist for the Communion of the sick or dying goes back to the second or third centuries. In that early period, the place of reservation (what would later be called "tabernacle") would have been in private homes, as witnessed by the North African third-century church father Tertullian. Once public basilicas were built for Christian worship after the

Peace of Constantine in the year 312, a special room (the sacristy) was built to store the sacred vessels and vestments, also allowing a place to reserve the sacrament in a sort of small cupboard within the sacristy wall. In the Medieval period, the sacrament was then moved to within the wall of the *presbiterium* or sanctuary itself, and in some cases suspended and hung over the altar in the form of a *colomba,* or dove, representing the Holy Spirit. In other cases, the Eucharist was reserved in a small freestanding box that came to be called a "sacrament house." It was also commonplace in this period that both the Eucharist and the holy chrism used for anointing in various sacraments and rites were reserved close by in the same vicinity. In the thirteenth century, as Eucharistic devotion increased, the desire to visit the sacrament also grew, and the place of reservation was thus moved to near the high altar. In the year

1557, Archbishop of Milan Charles Borromeo decreed that in his archdiocese the tabernacle should be placed directly on the altar—the altar which was now attached to the east wall.

The monstrance evolved in the late fourteenth century as an ornate vessel that could contain the consecrated host so that it could be adored by the faithful. It developed in response to a complex of liturgical and devotional trends, including the decline of the reception of Communion by the lay faithful and growth in Eucharistic piety. The *pyx* or small vessel for transporting the Sacrament to the sick and dying is the antecedent of the ciborium in which hosts for consecration were contained and then placed on the altar during Mass. This grew out of a pastoral need because of the reduced size of the paten, which was only able to hold the celebrant's host.

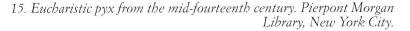

14. Precious Blood reliquary from the beginning of the fourteenth century. Treasure found at the Cathedral in Boulogne-sur-Mer.

15. Eucharistic pyx from the mid-fourteenth century. Pierpont Morgan Library, New York City.

16

17

18

16–17. Chasubles as drawn by Henri Matisse. Rosary Chapel, Dominican Convent in Vence, Provence.

18. Henri Matisse, Rosary Chapel altar, Vence.

19. Henri Matisse, detail of the furnishings, crucifix, tabernacle, and candlesticks on the Rosary Chapel altar, Vence.

40. Liturgy and Popular Piety in a Multicultural Church

1

Popular piety or religious devotions have an ancient tradition in the church and can be traced back to the second century. For example, in that period it was already customary that Christians in Rome took a Sunday afternoon *passeggiata,* or walk, along the Via Appia Antica to visit the tombs of the martyrs. After the Peace of Constantine and the tradition that his mother, Helen, had discovered the true cross in Jerusalem, pilgrimages to the Holy Land among wealthier Christians grew more frequent. One of the most famous of these was the Spanish pilgrim from Gallicia, Egeria, who made her own pilgrimage to Jerusalem toward the end of the fourth century where she remained for three years. Her published diary contains precious information about the liturgical and devotional life of the Jerusalem Church during that period.

Popular piety grew in the Medieval Period with pilgrim-

ages and other devotions, often serving as a spiritual substitute for liturgical participation, when the lay faithful were no longer able to take part fully in the celebration of the Mass. The Franciscans made an important contribution to the growth of popular piety in the thirteenth century, as they promoted a devotion to the humanity of Jesus along with that of his divinity. The origins of the Christmas *créche* introduced by the Franciscans can be seen within this context. Similarly, the introduction of the Angelus prayed at midday offered the laity a means of uniting with nearby monastic communities. Hearing the church bells ring at noon, calling the monks and nuns to choir for the midday office, they paused in their places of work to unite spiritually with the liturgical prayer taking place across the fields in monastic choirs. The Dominican contribution of the rosary, whose number of beads—150—deliberately

2

1. *Main portal's architrave, on the façade of Autin Cathedral; pilgrimage scenes.*

2. *Taddeo Gaddi's (1327–1366) panel painting faithfully reproduces the Mass at Greccio, based on Franciscan texts: on the left, wearing the dalmatic of a deacon, Saint Francis explains the prologue to the Gospel of Saint John; in the middle and toward the left, in priest's clothing, he consecrates the chalice and embraces the Christ Child. Galleria dell'Academia, Florence.*

corresponded to the number of 150 psalms chanted by monks and nuns as well as other religious orders, offers yet another example of such devotions. These various forms of popular religiosity—novenas included—had a special appeal as they were prayed in the vernacular when the Mass was now in Latin, so simple, uneducated people had little difficulty in taking part.

Vatican II's Constitution on the Liturgy said very little on popular piety, dedicating only one article to the subject. Number 13 of *Sacrosanctum concilium* states that popular devotions are highly recommended, provided that they are in agreement with those of the church: "These devotions should be so drawn up that they harmonize with the liturgical seasons, accord with the sacred liturgy, are in some fashion derived from it, and lead people to it, since in fact, the liturgy by its very nature far surpasses any of them." In his 1975 encyclical *Evangelli Nuntiandi*, Pope Paul VI noted that this form of religiosity is called "popular," because it is of the people, and "piety" because it is different from the more formalized means and structures of religious expression. The Pope continued that the word *piety* expresses a certain thirsting for God that only the poor and simple can experience, and thus fulfills a need that formal religiosity cannot meet. Such simple faith offers the possibility of appreciating God's compassion and goodness. Popular piety is clearly viewed here in a positive light and presented as an instrument of evangelization.

The Bishops of Latin America made an important contribution to the subject first at their meeting at Medellín, Colombia, in 1968, and then again eleven years later at their 1979 meeting in Puebla, Mexico. At Medellín, a serious, systematic study of popular piety was recommended along with the realization of a corresponding liturgical-catechetical program; a reinterpretation of devotion to the saints—not only as intercessors but also as models to be imitated; the formation of basic ecclesial communities in parishes built around families and with strong links to the Bible, sacraments, and the authority of bishops. The document published from the Puebla gathering provided further reflection on the topic, stating that popular piety offers the cultural and contextualized form of the Catholicity of that particular people. It also suggested that it contains a social dimension as well, offering the poor a means of understanding its own oppression and suffering. No other church document has offered such a precise analysis of popular piety as the Puebla text. While it does criticize some forms of popular religiosity, it speaks strongly in favor of the practice without giving a clear definition of the term.

When speaking of popular piety, we can note some general characteristics. It is linked to some of the most profound problems of the human person and expresses some of the

3

most basic human sentiments; it also has a spontaneous and creative dimension. At times, it has the tendency to distance itself from official church teaching and follow a separate path with or without church approval. One example of this would be the supposed sites of Marian apparitions (e.g., the weeping Madonna at Civitavecchia several years ago); even the popular Marian devotional site of Medjugorje has never been officially sanctioned by the Holy See and yet its popular appeal cannot be denied. Popular piety also tends to be traditional in its style, often attached to particular places and cultures, e.g., Our Lady of Guadalupe, in Mexico. Its practitioners tend to be the simple and humble.

Thanks to the initiative of the Bishops of Latin America and the significant study done in the 1970s and 1980s by theologians from Central and South America primarily, popular piety has returned to the church's vocabulary, and is now recognized as an important ingredient in the life of the faithful. As the official prayer of the church in its for-

3. Ubaldo Gandolfi, *Saint Dominic Guzmán and Saint Vincent Ferrer at the Feet of the Virgin and Child*, 1773. The Virgin Mary is handing the rosary to Saint Dominic. Museo della Basilica di San Domenico, Bologna.

4. A group of the faithful who belong to a sports association arriving at the large square in front of the Virgin of Guadalupe Sanctuary.

5. In the foreground, the old Mexican sanctuary's baroque outlines can be seen; on the right is the new Virgin of Guadalupe Sanctuary.

6. Towers at the Medjugorje Church, dedicated in 1969.

7. Pilgrimage on the Hill of Crosses at Medjugorje: the custom of placing crosses on high, with ribbons and ornamental decoration, is typical in Slavic countries.

8

9

malized and hieratic structure, liturgy is not capable of meeting all of the spiritual needs of the lay faithful. The warmth found in popular devotions responds more effectively to the sentimental and emotional needs of people that can be lacking in a properly celebrated liturgy. And it has been the bishops and theologians of Latin America who have helped the universal church to grasp this truth most profoundly.

The fundamental challenge that remains, however, is found in our attempts to understand how liturgy and popular piety interact. As *Sacrosanctum concilium* noted, the various forms of popular devotion should ideally lead its practitioners to a richer participation in the sacred mysteries—in the liturgical act itself—but this is often more the ideal than the norm. Indeed, at times, it can appear that liturgy and popular piety are in competition with one another. Given a less than clear understanding of how the two distinct realties were to interact, especially as various expressions of popular piety continued to grow in the 1980s and 1990s, the Congregation for Divine Worship and Discipline of the Sacraments published the *Directory on Popular Piety and Liturgy* in 2001.

That Directory was issued as a means of offering clarity and directives on the relationship between liturgy and popular piety, first establishing the historical and theological context, and presenting the subject in light of popular piety's relationship to the Magisterium of the church. In particular, the text had three main objectives. First, the Congregation wished to affirm and reinforce the pre-eminence of the liturgy in its relationship to all other forms of ecclesial piety and devotion. Second, it sought to evaluate and renew popular piety in light of biblical, liturgical, ecumenical, and anthropological research and developments. Third, it wished to posit popular piety both as distinct from the liturgy while at the same time in proper harmony with it.

The text is divided into two parts; the first part contains three chapters focused on historical-theological foundations of the subject, while the five chapters contained in Part II deal more specifically with various aspects of popular piety. Chapter 1 is entitled "Liturgy and Popular Piety through the Lens of History." Chapter 2 treats the subject in relationship to the Magisterium of the church. Chapter 3 offers theological principles for the evaluation and renewal of popular piety. Chapter 4 examines the not uncomplicated relationship between the liturgical year and popular piety. Pastoral tensions can arise, for example, when popular cultural feasts like Saint Joseph (March 19) or Saint Patrick (March 17) fall on a Sunday, as has already been mentioned. As a result, the liturgical norms in such cases are not always properly observed as they should be, and this chapter seeks to clarify the rationale.

A more recent challenge in this regard has been the introduction of the Feast of Divine Mercy (or "Divine Mercy

10

11

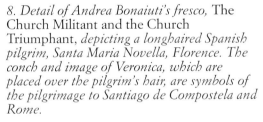

8. *Detail of Andrea Bonaiuti's fresco,* The Church Militant and the Church Triumphant, *depicting a longhaired Spanish pilgrim, Santa Maria Novella, Florence. The conch and image of Veronica, which are placed over the pilgrim's hair, are symbols of the pilgrimage to Santiago de Compostela and Rome.*

9. *Chartres Cathedral's south transept, detail of the right portal's lunette, with scenes of Saint Martin's life. The Pilgrimage to Tours, and some of the other illustrations that follow, are among those mentioned in the 2002 Directory of Popular Piety and Liturgy.*

10. *Saint Michael, gilt copperplate, from the eighth and ninth centuries. Monte Sant'Angelo, Foggia.*

11. *On high view from Sacra di San Michele Abbey, Piedmont.*

12. *Comprehensive view of the Mont Saint-Michel Sanctuary.*

12

13

15

14

16

Sunday") on the Second Sunday of Easter (*Domenica in albis*) which is often preceded by a novena that begins on Good Friday. Since the Second Vatican Council, the integrity of the Easter Triduum (Holy Thursday, Good Friday, and Holy Saturday) has been recovered and the church celebrates the three days as one seamless event—a memorial of the passion, death, and resurrection of Jesus Christ. Beginning a novena on Good Friday calls into question such a seamless celebration of the paschal mystery. Similarly, both the Council of Trent and the Second Vatican Council sought to keep major seasons such as Lent and Easter free of too many feast days to respect the integrity of the holy season. Indeed, the liturgical reforms of Vatican II recovered the great fifty days of Easter as one seamless feast of Easter meant to be celebrated and prolonged from Easter to Pentecost. The introduction of a feast on the eighth day of Easter presents fresh challenges for bishops and pastors. Chapter 5 treats the subject of the veneration of the Holy Mother of God while Chapter 6 explains the veneration of

saints and blesseds in the church. Chapter 7 examines the practice of prayers for the deceased and the final chapter presents the subject of sanctuaries and pilgrimages. Ten years on, it remains a pastoral challenge to strike the proper balance between popular piety and the liturgy. This is especially the case in the increasing numbers of multicultural parishes around the world in which each particular cultural group has its own unique expression of popular piety. Those various expressions represent very distinct traditions that do not always integrate well with those of other cultural groups sharing membership in the same parish.

17

19

18

13. *Crowd of faithful standing in front of Santa Casa Sanctuary of Loreto.*

14. *Nighttime procession through Our Lady of Fatima's sanctuary churchyard.*

15. *View of Our Lady of Lourdes Sanctuary.*

16. *Eucharistic procession at Lourdes.*

17. *Holy Friday procession in Caulonia, in the Province of Reggio Calabria, 1970.*

18. *Wedding celebration in Iruya, Argentina.*

19. *Corpus Christi procession in Cuzco, Peru.*

213

20

21

20–21. *Interior and exterior of the grand basilica dedicated to Our Lady of Aparecida, about 100 miles from Sao Paulo, Brazil, inaugurated in 1980 by Pope John Paul II.*

22. *Exterior view of the Saint Joseph's Oratory complex in Montreal, Canada. Two million pilgrims visit every year.*

23–24. *View of Le Puy-en-Velay, France, as well as the access road to Notre Dame Sanctuary.*

22

23

24

25

26

27

25. *Baroque façade, lit up by a torchlight procession of pilgrims from the Einsiedeln sanctuary in Switzerland, which is dedicated to Our Lady of the Hermits.*

26. *Crystal reliquary containing the remains of the Three Magi, which were transferred to Cologne from Milan and kept in the cathedral. For that reason, it became a pilgrims' destination at the end of the Middle Ages.*

27. *View of the Pannonia Sanctuary in Hungary, from the plain. The sanctuary is dedicated to Saint Martin of Tours, who was born in Hungary. He is a symbol of the Maygar people's national cdentity.*

29

28

30

28. *Comprehensive view of Saint Vitus Cathedral in Prague, a pilgrim destination. The Holy King Wenceslas (d. 983) and Saint John of Nepomuk (1340–1393) are venerated in this cathedral.*

29. *Another pilgrimage destination in Prague is Our Lady of Victory Basilica. A small statue of the Baby Jesus is venerated there.*

30. *The access door to the Sanctuary of Our Lady of Jasna Góra, in Czestochowa, Poland. The sanctuary is dedicated to Pope John Paul II. A 1430 image of the Virgin Mary is venerated there.*

31

32

31. Velehrad, Czech Republic: basilica complex at Our Lady of the Assumption Monastery, where Saints Cyril and Methodius, apostles of the Slavs, are venerated. Pope John Paul II, at the time of a 1990 pilgrimage, named the pair co-patrons of Europe.

32. Altötting Sanctuary complex in Germany. The small Church of Our Lady of Grace in the center.

217

41. Ecumenical Liturgical Cooperation: An Exchange of Gifts

1. Benedictine theologian Kilian McDonnell, founder of the Institute for Ecumenical and Cultural Research in Collegeville, Minnesota.

In order to understand the ecumenical liturgical cooperation of these post-conciliar years, we must return to the years of the twentieth-century liturgical movement that preceded the council. Just as the movement grew in Catholic monasteries and centers throughout Europe and the Americas, other Christian churches engaged in their own movements for liturgical renewal, often sharing information with one another and borrowing. For example, as was mentioned earlier, the Liturgical Movement in the United States Episcopal Church (Anglican) was founded in 1946. Called "The Associated Parishes for Liturgy and Mission," that movement collaborated closely with its Roman Catholic counterparts and Catholic speakers were often invited to address its annual conferences. One could note similar developments with Anglicans, Lutherans, Methodists, and Reformed on both sides of the Atlantic. Significantly, the ecumenical liturgical journal *Studia Liturgica* was founded in 1962 just as the Second Vatican Council was opening. Five years later in 1967, *Societas Liturgica* was founded—an ecumenical and international body of liturgical scholars. Today the organization has a membership of almost five hundred scholars and the journal continues to be published.

After the council, ecumenical liturgical cooperation played an increasingly larger part, especially with the need to revise liturgical books—a revision that was not limited to the Roman Catholic Church. Individual churches were well aware of what was going on in other churches and often drew on liturgical materials from one another's compositions. This led to the establishment of formal links among many of them. Some liturgical commissions invited other churches to send official observers to their meetings, and regional organizations composed of representatives from a number of churches were established in various parts of the world. For example, the Joint Liturgical Group was established in Britain in 1963 and produced a large number of texts in subsequent years that came to be incorporated into the liturgies of other churches. In North America, the Consultation on Common Texts was responsible for the 1983 creation of the *Common Lectionary*—an ecumenical adaptation of the Roman Sunday Lectionary; that text was later amended and published as the *Revised Common Lectionary*, which is now widely used throughout the English-speaking world. The working principle of this project was simple: just because we remain sadly divided at the Lord's Table when we come to celebrate the Holy Eucharist, we need not remain divided around God's Word, which we hold in common, proclaim, and profess together. Thus today, whether in Roman Catholic, Anglican, Lutheran, and other churches, the same three readings are read in most mainline Christian churches on Sunday mornings from the three-year Lectionary cycle. This has also led to the ecumenical prepa-

1

ration of the Sunday homily where ecumenical clergy groups are well established.

Ecumenical liturgical cooperation continues today in broader-based international organizations such as the *Societas Liturgica* mentioned above, and the North American Academy of Liturgy founded in 1973; today that organization includes Jewish members as well as Christian scholars representing a wide variety of denominations. From 1969 to 1974, the International Consultation on English Texts made an important contribution to the revision of common texts like the Nicene Creed and the Lord's Prayer. In 1983, the International Consultation on Common Texts (ICET) was replaced with the English Language Liturgical Commission (ELLC), which continues to this day.

That said, however, there have been some recent challenges to ecumenical liturgical cooperation that need to be mentioned. When the Congregation for Divine Worship

2. Foreshortened image of the main courtyard of the Bose monastic community, founded by Prior Enzo Bianchi.

2

3. The 1991 General Assembly of the World (Ecumenical) Council of Churches, Canberra, Australia.

4. A moment of interreligious monastic dialogue, Dzongsar Institute in Bir, India.

3

4

5

6

memorial	January 24	St. Francis de Sales, bishop and doctor of the Church (+CW)
memorial	January 31	St. John Bosco, priest (+CW)
	February 5	Martyrs of Japan (ELCA)
	March 2	John and Charles Wesley (ELCA
	March 24	Oscar Romero (CW+ELCA)
memorial	May 26	St. Philip Neri, priest (+CW)
memorial	July 31	St. Ignatius Loyola, priest (+CW)
memorial	August 4	St. John Vianney, priest (+CW)
	August 11	John Henry Newman (CW)
memorial	August 14	St. Maximillian Kolbe, priest and martyr (+CW+ELCA)
memorial	October 15	St. Teresa of Avila, virgin and doctor of the Church (+CW+ELCA)
	October 31	Martin Luther (CW)
memorial	November 3	St. Martin de Porres, religious (+CW+ELCA)
	December 1	Charles de Foucauld (CW)
memorial	December 3	St. Francis Xavier, priest (+ELCA)
memorial	December 14	St. John of the Cross, priest and doctor of the Church (+ELCA)

6. Diagram showing celebrations of Christian testimonies, as presented on the Roman liturgical calendar, which are common to the Church of England's Common Worship creed and the Lutheran Evangelical Church of America.

CW: Common Worship of the Church of England
ELCA: Lutheran Evangelical Church of America

5, 7–8. Holy Year of 2000, Rome. Miscellaneous moments during the solemn ceremony at the Coliseum on May 7, during which Pope John Paul II remembered twentieth-century martyrs from all over the world. Among the gathered were Lutherans, Orthodox, Anglicans, Protestants, Methodists, Pentecostals, and more; all told, nineteen different churches and Christian communities that are part of the World Alliance of Reformed Churches were present.

and the Discipline of the Sacraments issued the document *Liturgiam authenticam* in 2001, a new set of directives for liturgical translation were issued which placed new restrictions on the translation process, insisting on a more faithful and doctrinally sound translation at all costs. The text also presented fresh challenges for the issue of liturgical translation in the wider realm of ecumenism. Because of a stricter and more literal translation now required, the Catholic Church now has new translations of the *Gloria*, *Creed*, and *Sanctus*, for example, which no longer match those of the other churches. Language, of course, is itself symbolic, and holding liturgical texts in common communicates something quite profound about what we believe regarding common baptism. In other words, what we are able to do in common we must do in common, as the gospel of Christ commands, and this includes both the Word proclaimed and the texts we pray in common. Thus, our ecumenical partners find it lamentable that the Catholic Church has abandoned common liturgical texts, especially since those texts became common precisely because other churches generously adopted Roman translations in the revisions of their own liturgical books. They argue that, forty-five years after the promulgation of

9–10. Holy Year of 2000, Rome. Some other moments at the solemn ecumenical commemoration ceremony on May 7 at the Coliseum (Photo, Giancarlo Guiliani).

Vatican II's Liturgy Constitution, it is difficult to see this as progress.

Lest we be discouraged by such an ecumenical impasse, however, there have been some quite positive developments of late in the realm of ecumenical liturgical cooperation that bear mentioning. In recent years when the Church of England's Liturgical Commission revised its ordination rites, several Catholic liturgical scholars in Rome were invited to participate in the process of evaluating the revision. In November 2006, as the Archbishop of Canterbury Dr. Rowan Williams concluded an official visit to His Holiness Pope Benedict XVI, he presided at a solemn Anglican Eucharist in the Basilica of Santa Sabina on the Aventine Hill. He did so at the very altar where the Pope has traditionally celebrated Mass on Ash Wednesday since the fifth century, and in the presence of several Vatican representatives. Forty-five years ago the mere concept of an Anglican Eucharist in an ancient Roman basilica would have been unthinkable but is indicative of just how far we have come.

In the autumn of 2008, the World Council of Churches and Ecumenical Monastery of Bose cosponsored an in international ecumenical symposium at Bose. Called "A Cloud of Witnesses," the symposium, which drew more than 200 representatives from different churches around the world, explored opportunities for ecumenical commemoration of holy men and women in different churches. A mere glance at the Church of England's *Common Worship,* published in 2000, bears witness to the fact that such an ecumenical commemoration of Christian witnesses is already happening in some churches. On that liturgical calendar, one finds the names of Francis de Sales, Don Bosco, Martin Luther, Charles de Foucauld, Ignatius Loyola, Teresa of Avila, and John of the Cross. Similarly, in the Evangelical Lutheran Church of America's *Worship,* published in 2006, one finds the names of Martin Luther King, Jr., the Japanese and Ugandan martyrs, John and Charles Wesley, Oscar Romero, Martin de Porres, Francis Xavier, Teresa of Avila, and John of the Cross. Given the Catholic Church's long tradition of sainthood, with its complex process of beatification and canonization, it is obviously not in a position to lend its full support to such an initiative, but similar possibilities do exist at the local level even in Catholic parishes, for non-Eucharistic celebrations of ecumenical commemoration with other Christian denominations.

A precedent has been set for such ecumenical commemorations hosted by the Catholic Church even on the international level. It was Pope John Paul II himself who insisted that an ecumenical commemoration of witnesses to the faith in the twentieth century take place during the Great Jubilee Year, and that event took place at the Coliseum on May 7, 2000. The Pope was keen to affirm an

11–12. *Pope Benedict XVI and the Archbishop of Canterbury, Rowan Williams, in front of Westminster Abbey's (11) main altar, and praying in front of Saint Edward the Confessor's (12) tomb, on September 17, 2010.*

11

12

ecumenism lived in the giving of one's life in sacrifice for Christ regardless of one's ecclesial affiliation. Moreover, the ecumenical commemoration at the Coliseum was intended to be an invitation to all Christian communities to discern the effective presence of Christ and of the Holy Spirit even in the midst of persecution and violence. It was also intended to serve as a strong reminder to present and future generations to learn from the example of their forebears who bore witness to the gospel of Christ and suffered persecution even as they forgave their persecutors. That ecumenical commemoration initiated by the Catholic Church offers an eloquent example of ecumenical liturgical cooperation, and has set us on a path from which we cannot and will not turn back. Indeed, it offers a model for what is possible as we look toward the future—even despite our canonical and doctrinal differences.

42. LITURGICAL EDUCATION AND THE FORMATION OF LITURGICAL MINISTERS

1. Benozzo Gozzoli, Saint Ambrose Baptizing Saint Augustine, *1464, Saint Augustine Church, San Gimignano.*

Whether one considers the liturgical formation of clergy or laity, the concept is relatively recent in the church's history. The field of liturgical studies only emerged in the late twentieth century. This was due to the impetus of the liturgical movement prior to Vatican II where the study of the theology of the liturgy took its place alongside history, as the second branch of liturgical study. Indeed, it was these two already-established disciplines—the history and theology of the liturgy—that shaped Vatican II's liturgical reforms. Prior to the twentieth century, liturgical formation was popularly equated with rubrics. Thus, retired priests in seminaries and other houses of formation were employed to teach a course to seminarians on how to celebrate Mass. No special training was required for the teachers of such a course and there was little offered beyond the basic rubrical training. Such an approach, of course, largely left the lay faithful on the outside looking in since they had no need to learn such rubrics.

The liturgical movement gradually transformed such a limited approach to liturgical formation, not only in establishing foundations for the disciplines of liturgical history and theology, but also in the promotion of liturgical catechesis, and would come to be called "pastoral liturgical studies" after the Second Vatican Council. The liturgical weeks begun by Lambert Beauduin at Mont César in Belgium and the annual liturgical weeks in the United States begun in 1940 that drew thousands of participants did much to foster the sort of liturgical literacy ultimately advocated by the Vatican Council. Such liturgical formation led to the restoration of the role of the liturgical assembly and recovery of the importance of the whole complex of symbolic words and gestures. The liturgical pioneers who paved the way for the conciliar liturgical renewal recognized that the best way to encourage full and active participation in the liturgy was precisely to catechize people liturgically about their role as baptized members of the church, and their social responsibility as members of Christ's mystical body. Indeed, it could be said that the ultimate goal of the liturgical movement was education toward the worship of God since such education would lead to change in people's liturgical understanding and consequently their liturgical habits and participation as well. Liturgy's appeal to the senses and the emotions was precisely its richness, in that it was able to reach the depths of human experience far more profoundly than a catechism-based approach with its limited appeal only to the intellect. The liturgical pioneers were aware that feelings and emotions were often looked upon with suspicion, but they believed that such suspicion was often due to confusion between sentimentalism and a genuinely affective religious experience. Thus, teaching liturgy strictly as a

1

matter of questions to be memorized and soon forgotten was not the answer.

Liturgical pioneers were cognizant of the fact that when properly celebrated, the liturgy itself was the best teacher, not only in the words and how they were spoken, or in the content of the homily and its execution, but in the very rite itself. In other words, it was inherent in the use of symbols and communication of the nonverbal; the vesture; the music; the way the assembly was reverenced with incense and with a bow; the reception of Holy Communion. Ahead of their time, those pioneers were aware that when functioning properly, symbols do not need to be explained beforehand but are capable of communicating quite profoundly on their own. After their enactment or execution—after the liturgy itself—is the perfect time to reflect upon those symbols—upon the experience of the liturgical assembly. Returning to the language of the early church, today we refer to this as *mystagogy*—as a post-liturgical reflection on the rites themselves. The alternative is a more Western, analytic and intellectual explanation or interpretation preceding the rites, which can easily get in the way of the liturgical symbol's capacity to function effectively. The recovery of this mystagogical approach has been particularly effective in the post-conciliar restoration of the adult catechumenate—the Rite of Christian Initiation of Adults (RCIA). In the early church, the catechumenate was an extended period of training to live the Christian life. The great catechumenal teachers such as Tertullian, Ambrose, Augustine, Cyril of Jerusalem, and Theodore of Mopsuestia, engaged in an effective pedagogy that successfully integrated serious intellectual training in the faith and the intense challenge of living that faith in daily life. The catechumenal model, then, encourages a learning and liturgy that bears fruit in gospel living—in the "liturgy of the world."

Today, as we look back on the liturgical reforms launched by the Second Vatican Council, there is much for which we have to be grateful. Great progress has been made in the recovery of the assembly's role in the liturgical action, with the assembly now functioning as subject rather than object. That said, however, one of the greatest challenges that remains is found in the area of liturgical formation. Almost fifty years after Vatican II, those present on

2

Sunday mornings have yet to fully grasp just what their liturgical participation actually demands of them when it is taken seriously—the service of the poor and marginalized who stand at the fringe of church and society. In developed countries within Western Europe, North America, and Oceania, attendance at Sunday Mass has declined quite drastically, and among those who are present, teenagers and young adults often complain of boredom or feeling disengaged. Indirectly, the technological advances of the internet, iPods, iPads, DVDs, and the like have introduced fresh challenges for liturgists and pastors. People are accustomed to being entertained through the various devices mentioned above, and have often come to expect the same level of enchantment at the liturgy that they find in this postmodern world, whether or not they are aware of it. It is not uncommon to hear young people lament: "I don't like going to Mass because I don't get anything out of it." On the one hand, this can be a certain criticism of those charged with liturgical planning, or presiders or preachers themselves, for not effectively exercising the ministry with which they are charged. On the other hand, liturgy is not about entertainment, but rather about the awesome privilege of praising and worshipping Almighty God with heart and soul, mind and strength. Once again, the critical role played by proper liturgical formation for such individuals and constituencies cannot be underestimated.

The challenge of liturgical formation is not limited to the laity, of course, but can also affect the clergy as well. In 1979, the Congregation for Catholic Education issued an Instruction on Liturgical Formation in Seminaries, a document that provides both the background and rationale for the candidate's formation as one who will preside publicly at the church's sacred rites. The Instruction was an explanation of what is found in *Sacrosanctum concilium* 16, which states that the study of Liturgy "is to be ranked among the major and compulsory courses in seminaries and religious houses of studies," and that in theological faculties "it is to rank among the principal subjects." By properly forming seminarians in the ways of correct and creative liturgical practice, the faculty entrusted with such liturgical formation will ultimately assist the liturgical renewal of the whole church. But as always, there is often a gap between the ideal and the lived reality, and in these post-conciliar years, many have witnessed a certain degree of unauthorized liturgical experimentation on the part of clergy presiding at the liturgy. This is especially evident when some priests change fixed parts of the Mass with substitutions of their own invention, usually failing to understand exactly what they are changing.

Such uninformed experimentation can be found in priests who have chosen to improvise on the text of the Third Eucharistic Prayer in the Roman Missal: "So that from East to West . . . " adding "from North to South," clearly failing to understand the precise import of the text and mistakenly thinking that the reference was geographic. The reference "from East to West" refers to the rising and setting of the sun rather than geography. Happily, the new translation of the Third Edition of the Roman Missal will make this text explicit so that the reference is clear. To this end, the "General Instruction on the Roman Missal" found at the beginning of the Roman Missal with foundations dating prior to the Council of Trent, offers a helpful corrective to such liturgical idiosyncrasies. Indeed, the "General Instruction" offers a theologically based choreography—a guide or set of principles for a proper celebration of the liturgy, not only so that it is enacted with dignity and reverence, but also to better facilitate the unity of the body of Christ exhibited in the unity within the liturgical action. The purpose here is not to foster a rubrical rigidity on the part of the one presiding or other liturgical ministers, but rather to trust the wisdom of what the text prescribes—a text that has been tried and tested over the centuries and continues to be revised and adapted in our own day to respond to changing pastoral needs. Trusting such wisdom will also diminish the sort of liturgical idiosyncrasies mentioned above, in favor of a presider or other liturgical minister not calling attention to him- or herself, but rather serving the worship of Christ's Church in humility.

Related to the area of liturgical formation and education is the important relationship between liturgy and catechetics. While it would appear that the two realities should go easily together, the relationship has not always been an easy one. In the years immediately after the council, tensions arose between liturgy and catechesis regarding the precise role that worship was to play in the religious formation of children, teenagers, and adults alike, and there were very different answers to some of the same questions. At the risk of oversimplification, liturgists argued in favor of an exclusive living from the source of the liturgy and its rich symbolic system, while catechists defended a more didactic approach. In some parts of the world, for example, catechists advocated short introductions to each of the readings at Sunday Mass, which would help the members of the liturgical assembly to grasp what was about to be proclaimed. Liturgists, for their part, opposed such a practice, arguing that such introductions would overburden an already overly verbal liturgy. They contended that the homily was the appropriate moment to explain the readings, and that the key to

helping people grasp the readings was to properly train the lectors rather than add additional explanations. It would be better to let the people hear and experience the reading and then explain it later.

This same tension between liturgy and catechetics often presented itself in sacramental preparation programs, and in the celebration of the sacramental rites themselves. The subject of Confirmation offers an interesting example. In some parts of the world, catechists defended the practice of delaying Confirmation to the teenage years as a sort of Christian rite of passage into adulthood, so that the candidate could more knowingly commit himself or herself to effective Christian discipleship and witness. On the other side of the issue, liturgists lamented the separation of Confirmation from the ancient structure of Christian Initiation: Baptism, Confirmation, and Eucharist, as it has always remained in the churches of the East even in the initiation of infants into the church.

A third example of the post-conciliar tension between liturgy and catechetics has been in the relationship between liturgy and popular piety. Immediately after the council, liturgical purists began advocating the full, conscious, and active participation in the liturgy that left no room for popular devotions within the liturgical context. Liturgists argued that the council called the whole church to live from the wellspring of her worship, and therefore popular religiosity was to be limited to the home or church before or after Mass, but they were to remain two distinct realities. This was especially evident in the newly constructed church buildings and renovation of older buildings, as we saw earlier. Many of those newly designed churches removed kneelers, statues, and Stations of the Cross, creating worship spaces that conservative critics said looked more like Protestant churches than Catholic. Such an approach was soon challenged. Catechists and pastoral ministers argued convincingly that the liturgy actually needed the warmth of popular piety for its own well-being. Moreover, they contended that those devotions served importantly as the "gospel of the poor," forming and teaching those most simple and marginalized people in a way which the liturgy was not capable of doing.

Happily, the church has made great strides since those early days of the council in recovering that important relationship between liturgy and catechetics, greatly helped by the restoration of the RCIA mentioned earlier with its strong liturgical and formative components, especially regarding the important element of mystagogy. The *Catechism of the Catholic Church* offers a rich liturgical catechesis in part two of the *Catechism*: "The Celebration of the Christian Mystery." The *Catechism* states clearly that the liturgy is *opus Trinitatis*—the work of the Holy

3. The church at Saint Anselm's College in Rome, location of the Pontifical Liturgical Institute.

Spirit in which the Mystical Body of Christ participates, and also underlines the important role of the Holy Spirit in all liturgical celebrations—the epiclesis or calling down of the Holy Spirit not only over the gifts of wine, but also over the liturgical assembly for its own sanctification. But even with that rich presentation found in the *Catechism*, much remains to be done. Several years ago, the *Canadian Liturgy Bulletin* published an interesting observation on catechesis for the RCIA: "There is still an emphasis on knowledge over conversion, still program over process, still information over formation and transformation." Designing a *program* merely to give people *information* that leaves them with more knowledge may be the wrong approach as we consider the formative role that liturgy plays in shaping moral behavior, or in the task of mission and evangelization. Rather, we need to ask that deeper source that underlies true liturgical formation: the one whom we recognize in the breaking of the bread and the burning of our hearts.

Much progress has also been made at national, diocesan, and parish levels in terms of accredited programs in Pastoral Liturgy in the form of adult education. For many years now, the Pontifical Liturgical Institute at Sant'Anselmo has hosted a three-year accredited program in liturgy for lay Catholics within the Vicariate of Rome, many of whom work as catechists and pastoral ministers in Rome's numerous parishes. The fact that more than 170 lay Romans participate in this program each year offers great hope for the liturgical future in the Vicariate of Rome.

Similar programs can be found in various corners of the globe. With the growth of adult liturgical education programs, there has been a concomitant growth in graduate programs in liturgical studies. Those programs are no longer found only in the great liturgical centers of Rome, Paris, and Trier—well established since the time of the Second Vatican Council—but now also in North America, Australia, and the United Kingdom, as well as in the Philippines and elsewhere. These doctoral, licentiate, and masters programs in liturgics are often ecumenical in scope, both in terms of the students and faculty who make up the full constituency of that particular institution, but also in the manner in which the material is treated and taught. Indeed, the twentieth-century liturgical movement, which closely collaborated with the ecumenical movement, has led to unprecedented scientific collaboration across denominational lines, as evidenced in such organizations as the International *Societas Liturgica*.

43. Liturgical Preaching: The Sacramentality of the Word

1

1. Fra Angelico, Saint Peter Preaching in the Presence of Mark, *Linaioli tabernacle predella, 1434–1435.*
Museo di San Marco, Florence.

2. André Reinoso, Saint Francis Xavier Preaching in Goa, *seventeenth century, Sao Roque Church, Lisbon.*

3. Lucas Cranach the Elder, Martin Luther Preaching, *1547, detail of the altar piece of Wittenberg's Saint Mary's Parochial Church (Staadtkirche).*

4. Sano di Pietro (1406–1481), Saint Bernadine Preaching in Piazza del Campo, *mid-fourteenth century, Siena Cathedral.*

The verb "to preach" as used in the New Testament means to announce the coming of salvation, to solemnly proclaim that Jesus Christ is Lord and Savior. Christian preaching is always a proclamation of the Word and the ordinary way that leads to faith. Scholars have generally divided preaching into three areas: 1) evangelization: the proclamation of the Christian message to arouse faith; 2) catechesis: a more systematic teaching aimed at believers in order to make their faith more active and aware; and 3) the homily: special catechesis in the context of the liturgical action, closely connected with the Word and rites, what we now call "liturgical preaching."

Liturgical preaching grew significantly during the sixteenth-century Reformation. Martin Luther, for example, was insistent that vernacular preaching be a constitutive part of Lutheran worship not only on Sundays and feast days, but even at weddings and in other rites. Such preaching was to be biblical—based on the prescribed readings for the day, rather than a sermon on a pious topic that might have had little or nothing to do with the particular liturgical feast or assigned biblical readings for the day. Luther was known to be quite a forceful preacher himself, often following a classic Augustinian line of Eucharist leading to mission; and his preaching was effective because he used concrete imagery that members of the liturgical assembly could grasp. In responding to the Reformers, the Council of Trent needed to treat the subject of preaching as well. Interestingly, its pronouncements on the subject were not so far removed from those of the Protestant reformers. Preaching should be done at least on Sundays and feast days and it should be done in the vernacular so that people would be able to grasp the import of its meaning, and be drawn more fully into the richness of the sacred mysteries they were celebrating. Trent stipulated that if the homily could not be preached during Mass itself after the Gospel, then it was to be done either before Mass or after. The Jesuit Peter Canisius, who was a theological consultant to the Council of Trent, often encouraged the singing of a hymn in German prior to his preaching as a means of properly disposing the assembly to hearing his homily.

At the Second Vatican Council, both *Sacrosanctum concilium* and the Dogmatic Constitution on Revelation *Dei Verbum* offer a rich theology of the Word. Those documents highlight that the service of God's Word is the history of salvation; God is present in the Word and in the preaching; indeed, the Word of God has the power to communicate salvation. Thus, as we read in *Sacrosanctum concilium* 9, preaching is a call to both faith and conversion. The homily is part of the liturgy itself rather than something extraneous to it (*Sacrosanctum concilium* 35, 52). For this reason, the conciliar reforms dropped the sign of the Cross that was traditionally done at the beginning and end of the homily, as an attempt to integrate it more fully into the Liturgy of the Word as a constitutive element. The homily is descri-

bed as "the proclamation of God's wonderful works in the history of salvation, that is, the mystery of Christ, which is ever made present and active within us, especially in the celebration of the liturgy (*Sacrosanctum concilium* 35). Drawn from the scriptural and liturgical texts, the homily is an essential part of sacramental celebration, and should "apply to concrete circumstances of life and particular needs of hearers." (*Presbyterorum ordinis* 4).

It is significant that every liturgical rite revised after Vatican II contains a "liturgy of the Word" and a homily is usually called for, as well. Indeed, the new experience of the church in the years since the council has led both pastors and the lay faithful to reconsider the homily in all Christian rites, especially the Eucharistic celebration, where it is related to the two tables of the Word of God and the body of Christ, and where it points the way to moral transformation as the Eucharist is lived out in

5. Giusto de' Menabuo, fresco depicting The Universal Judgment, detail of Saint Augustine in a chair, last bay of the main nave of the Viboldone Abbey Church, close to Milan.

5

Christian mission. Such preaching is no longer limited to Sundays but increasingly normative at weekday Eucharists as well, especially in seasons such as Advent and Lent. The liturgical movement called renewed attention to the original meaning and practice of the homily, thanks to its collaboration with the biblical and patristic movements. One classic example of this is found at the Augustinian monastery of Klosterneuburg in Austria, and in the work of Augustinian Canon Pius Parsch (+1945). Parsch made it his aim to combine the academic with the pastoral in a common goal of biblical and liturgical renewal.

In 1926, Parsch founded the review *Bibel und Liturgie* to promote a more integral relationship between the Bible and worship, and to foster a greater awareness of the Scriptures among Catholics. All of this made a significant contribution to the recovery of biblically based preaching—radically different from what preceded it. Consistent with what was decreed at the Council of Trent, Canon 1345 of the 1917 Code of Canon Law stated that on Sundays and feast days there should be "an explanation of the gospel or some part of Catholic doctrine." This resulted in a number of dioceses around the world preparing "preaching syllabuses" designed to provide greater cohesion and organization to the preaching but often with no reference to the liturgy itself. The recovery of the homily as a constitutive part of the liturgical action would not arrive until

the Second Vatican Council. The introduction to the second typical edition of the 1975 *Roman Missal of Paul VI* states at number 42 that the homily "should normally be given by the priest celebrant" to further enhance the relationship between the preaching and its relationship to the liturgy itself.

Today in the Catholic Church of the twenty-first century, much work remains to be done in the area of liturgical preaching. Indeed, with a few notable exceptions, it is abundantly clear that our non-Catholic liturgical counterparts remain very far ahead in both the content and style of preaching within the liturgy. Some scholars have recently described the homily as a moment for "naming grace"—calling to mind the ways in which God is at work in everyday life—what God is doing for us here and now in this community and in the wider community of God's world. That is the "good news" that preachers are to proclaim, and allows liturgical preaching to be a means of grace given to us to transform and sanctify. It that sense we can speak of the Word itself as "sacramental" and the preaching from the table of God's Word as nourishment for the people of God as they strive to be the body of Christ in daily life. If liturgical preaching is to be authentic, it will need to address the concrete situations and problems in people's lives—naming their joys and sorrows. Effective preaching means speaking truthfully, so that people will be able to

6

6. Drawing from the portrait of a female singing a Bessie Griffin gospel-style song.

7. Catecheses in Saint Mark's Coptic Orthodox Cathedral, Cairo.

recognize their own lives in the words of the preacher. Such truthful and sacramental preaching will ultimately gather the liturgical assembly into a holy communion and will lead that assembly from the table of God's Word to the table of the Eucharist as a seamless garment.

One of the great gifts in these post-conciliar years has been the Revised Common Lectionary, which was mentioned earlier. With a significant number of mainline Christian churches reading the same Scriptural lessons on Sunday mornings, there is now the possibility of common homiletic preparation in an ecumenical context. Indeed, it has become increasingly common that local ecumenical clergy groups meet weekly to pray over the readings for the common Sunday, exchanging thoughts and reflections on how they intend to approach the preparation of the forthcoming homily. Such exchange is mutually beneficial because of the insights shared and discussed.

During the 2008 Synod on the Word, the topic of the homily figured prominently to the extent that one bishop suggested that the following year should be dedicated to "the Year of the Homily." Numerous bishops addressed themselves to the importance of the homily within the liturgical action, noting that this is often the one opportunity that pastors have each week to reach their parishioners. They suggested that three questions should be kept in mind regarding homiletic preparation: "What are the scriptures being proclaimed saying? What do they say to me personally? What should I say to the community in the light of its concrete situation?" Yet that synodal assembly was very much aware that forty-five years after Vatican II, those three questions are not asked often enough, and there is still much work to be done in the field of homiletics.

Pope Benedict XVI made this clear in his Post-Synodal Apostolic Exhortation *Verbum Domini* at number 59, where he calls for greater improvement in the preparation and execution of homilies: "Generic and abstract homilies which obscure the directness of God's word should be avoided, as well as useless digressions which risk drawing greater attention to the preacher than to the heart of the Gospel message. The faithful should be able to perceive clearly that the preacher has a compelling desire to present Christ, who must stand at the center of every homily." To this end, the Holy Father called for the preparation of a "Directory on Homiletics" as a practical text to assist preachers in carrying out this task (no. 60).

7

44. POST-CONCILIAR DOCUMENTS ON THE SACRED LITURGY

1

Despite the numerous documents published on the Liturgy since the Second Vatican Council, the Liturgy Constitution *Sacrosanctum concilium* clearly holds the highest ecclesial and magisterial authority. Thus subsequent liturgical documents are to be read and interpreted in light of the council's extraordinary Constitution on the Sacred Liturgy. It also should be noted that not all Roman documents carry the same theological import: Apostolic letters, Apostolic Constitutions, Instructions, Encyclicals, Post-Synodal Exhortations, all need to be interpreted and understood in terms of the particular genre in which they are generated. It is also important to recall that some documents are written for the whole church while others are written for a particular country.

In the years immediately after the Council there were several documents published to assist the universal implementation of the liturgical reforms. Immediately following the council in 1965, the letter *Le renouveau liturgique* was

published on furthering the liturgical reform following the previous year's Instruction *Inter oecumenici*. The year 1967 saw the publication of several documents that were of fundamental importance for the future of the reform. Particularly worth mentioning are the Instruction on Sacred Music in the Liturgy (*Musicam sacram*); a second instruction on the orderly carrying out of the Constitution on the Sacred Liturgy (*Tres abhinc annos*) which also opened the Canon of the Mass to vernacular usage; and an instruction on the worship of the Eucharist (*Eucharisticum mysterium*), which constituted a point of reference for the reform.

Two years later in 1969, a number of other liturgical documents saw the light of day, corresponding to the publication of a significant number of new liturgical books published in that same year including the *Ordo Missae* (Order of Mass) itself. Among the instructions published was the *Actio pastoralis* on celebrations for special groups and the

In 1988, the Congregation for Divine Worship and the Discipline of the Sacraments issued a Circular Letter *Paschale Soleminitatis* on preparing and celebrating the paschal feasts. Six years later in 1994, the same Congregation issued the document "Inculturation and the Roman Liturgy: Fourth Instruction for the Right Application of the Conciliar Constitution on the Liturgy" (nn. 37–40). In 1998, Pope John Paul II issued his Apostolic Letter *Dies Domini*: "On Keeping the Lord's Day Holy." In 2001, the Congregation for Divine Worship and the Discipline of the Sacraments issued a new instruction on liturgical translation *Liturgiam authenticam*, replacing the 1969 Instruction *Comme le prévoit*; those two documents will be discussed in the next chapter. The following year in 2002, the same Congregation issued the "Directory on Popular Piety and Liturgy" to further assist the proper relationship between expressions of popular religiosity and the liturgical celebration.

Apart from documents related directly to the liturgy and other sacraments, the Holy See has published at least eight documents on the Eucharist: the encyclical *Mysterium Fidei* (1965) of Paul VI; the *General Instruction on the Roman Missal* (2003); the encyclical *Ecclesia de Eucharistia* (2003) of John Paul II; the Instruction *Redemptionis Sacramentum* (2004) from the Congregation for Divine Worship and the Discipline of the Sacraments; the Apostolic Letter *Mane Nobiscum Domine* (2004) of John Paul II; the Post-Synodal Apostolic Exhortation *Sacramentum Caritatis* (2007); the Apostolic Letter (moto proprio) *Summorum Pontificium* (2007); and the papal letter accompanying *Summorum Pontificium* (2007) by Benedict XVI.

instruction *Memoriale Domini* on the manner of distributing Communion. The instruction *Comme le prévoit* on the subject of liturgical translation was also published that year. The Congregation for Divine Worship's third instruction *Liturgicae instaurationes* of 1970 on the orderly carrying out of the Constitution should also be mentioned. Many of these documents, especially the first two Instructions, issued concrete changes in the liturgy to further the reform envisaged by the Constitution. Some, especially the Third Instruction, were a response to abuses committed by individuals in the implementation of the Constitution in light of five years of experience.

1. Organ in the Chapel of Peace, which is next to the Carmelite Convent in Mazille, Burgundy.

2. The organ that was built during restoration work on the Stuttgart Collegiate Church.

3. Chronology of post-conciliar documents that address liturgy.

	Liturgy	Eucharist
1963	*Sacrosanctum Concilium*	
1965	*Le renouveau liturgique*	*Mysterium Fidei*
1967	*Inter oecumenici*	
1967	*Musicam sacram*	
1967	*Tres abhinc annos*	
1967	*Eucharisticum Mysterium*	
1969	*Actio pastoralis*	
1969	*Memoriale Domini*	
1969	*Comme le prevoit*	
1970	*Liturgicae instaurationes*	
1988	*Paschale Solemnitatis*	
1994	*Inculturazione e liturgia romana*	
1998	*Dies Domini*	
2001	*Liturgiam authenticam (Comme le prevoit)*	
2002	*Direttorio sulla pietà popolare e lla iturgia*	
2003		*Istruzione generale del Messale romano*
2003		*Ecclesia de Eucharistia*
2004		*Redemptionis Sacramentum*
2004		*Mane nobiscum, Domine*
2007		*Sacramentum caritatis*
2007		*Summorum Pontificum*

3

45. ON THE TRANSLATION OF LITURGICAL TEXTS

1. *Antonello da Messina,* Saint Jerome in His Study, *circa 1474–1475, National Gallery, London.*

"If I translate word by word, it sounds absurd; if I am forced to change something in the word order or style, I seem to have stopped being a translator." Those words of Saint Jerome express very well the dilemma that liturgical translators find themselves in as they engage in the process of translating liturgical texts in the service of the community's prayer. On the one hand, literal translation often results in texts that fail to convey meaning or appear stilted, while on the other hand, translating texts more liberally or "dynamically" can easily err on the other extreme, betraying the original meaning of the text. This task of translating liturgical texts is extremely delicate and this has been well documented in the numerous problems that various language groups and episcopal conferences have encountered in the years since Vatican II, as they have worked at preparing vernacular translations of the Latin typical editions of liturgical books.

At the Second Vatican Council, the move toward vernacular worship was not easy and discussions on the subject were often heated. Even among liturgical pioneers prior to the council, many in the liturgical movement distanced themselves from those pushing for vernacular reform since

they were convinced that it was a battle that could never be won. Nonetheless, after many long and often tense discussions, helped by the lobbying and gentle persuasion of some pro-vernacular bishops present at Vatican II, consensus was finally reached on December 7, 1962, during the council's thirty-sixth General Congregation, when the bishops approved the first chapter of the liturgy schema (what would become the first chapter of *Sacrosanctum concilium*), including the use of national languages within Catholic worship. Among the 2,118 bishops present, 1,922 voted in favor; 180 voted favorably but with some reservations; 11 were opposed; and 5 votes were void.

Nonetheless, there were some problems to be resolved. First, there was the question of the number of languages in which to translate liturgical texts from the Latin into the vernacular. For example, the Holy See originally wanted just one Spanish edition of the liturgical books for the entire Spanish-speaking world, but it soon became evident that the Spanish spoken throughout Spain was somewhat different from the Spanish spoken throughout much of Latin America. Similar questions arose regarding English translations and whether or not it would actually be possible to have one international English translation that could encompass both British and American English. Even today in Italy, one commonly hears Italians distinguish between *inglese* (English) and *Americano* as if to suggest that they are two separate languages.

A second problem involved the translation principles to be employed: should the texts be translated literally or rather more interpretively so that they captured the meaning of the word or phrase in a more dynamic way? Early attempts at translation produced mixed results and in hindsight, we can note the imperfections in those first vernacular drafts of the Roman Missal published in the immediate aftermath of Vatican II. When the International *Consilium* published the instruction *Comme le prévoit* mentioned in the last chapter, it was pastoral in tone and argued for texts that served the prayer of the people of God. The Instruction contended that a faithful translation cannot be judged based on individual words, but rather, translators needed to keep in mind the larger context and literary genre. And what did the larger context entail? According to the Instruction, it necessarily included the message itself, the audience for which the text was intended, and the manner of expressing the text. Thus, there was clearly much more involved than a mere literal translation of a word or phrase from Latin into the vernacular.

Comme le prévoit gave way to the recognition that liturgy itself is a symbol more than mere words; liturgy itself is about metaphor and rhetoric. In the twentieth century, thanks largely to the contribution of the social sciences, human speech came to be viewed through the lens of poetry, and language itself as a living entity that is constantly changing. Thus, liturgical translation came to be understood as an art form that would necessarily need to involve poets and linguists, anthropologists and composers, in the translation process. We came to understand the significant differences between language that is spoken and heard, sung, and prayed aloud, and language intended for private reading or scholarly precision.

Moreover, liturgical texts are meant to be performative and not simply communication or transmission of church doctrine. By their very nature, they are meant to be proclaimed within a living assembly. It was the desire of Paul VI that liturgical texts be accessible—understandable—even to children and the uneducated, while not being pedestrian by employing a language form too commonplace or banal. Putting those desires into practice and taking its cue from *Comme le prévoit*, different language groups came to employ the translation principle of "dynamic equivalence"— translating a text more dynamically so that it communicates meaning to the people of our own day and is contextualized within the particular celebrating community. So the Brazilian Episcopal Conference, for example, chose to translate the Latin phrase *Et cum spirito tuo* as "He is in our midst," rather than the more literal "And with your

spirit" and the Episcopal Conferences of the English-speaking world "And also with you."

In the year 2001 came the publication of the Congregation for Divine Worship's Instruction *Liturgiam authenticam*. As mentioned earlier, that new document suppressed the earlier instruction *Comme le prévoit* and was more restrictive in tone. Now a literal translation from Latin to the vernacular would be required at all costs. As many bishops and liturgical scholars have noted in the past ten years, this new instruction is not without its difficulties. Living languages, of course, change. Even if there was a golden age when liturgical Latin seriously influenced the local languages in contact with it, we are in a very different place now. Today, we would be unable to return to such a golden age even if we desired to, just as the Roman Rite of the twenty-first century would be unable to return to the classical epoch of that Rite's evolution from the fifth to the eighth centuries.

As we consider our liturgical future, we are faced with a fundamental question: what kind of translation—what kind of liturgical texts—serve the people of God in a new century and a new millennium and in urban liturgical communities across the globe that are increasingly multiracial and multicultural? In other words, we need liturgical translations that are both Catholic and contemporary. Liturgical texts that are "Catholic" implies theologically and doctrinally sound texts, firmly based in the universal tradition of the church. Also implied here are texts that fundamentally draw people into the mystery of God and of Christ's mystical body. For that is at the heart of what it means to be "one, holy, catholic, and apostolic." It is understood that Catholic liturgical texts in a post-conciliar church must also be ecumenically sensitive, since Vatican II made it abundantly clear that the search for Christian unity is not one option among many within the Catholic Church. These new liturgical translations must also be respectful of Jews, Muslims, and others who are not Christians.

Liturgical translations also need to be "contemporary"— not in a banal or pedestrian sense—but in such a way that they are contextualized and capable of communicating meaning in our own day. Thus, while maintaining "the substantial unity of the Roman Rite"—for those of the Roman Rite, obviously—liturgical translations need to be inculturated so that they foster the "full, conscious, and active participation" desired by the council. The Roman liturgy's vitality in our own day is contingent upon our capacity to produce liturgical texts that communicate their intended meaning to a contemporary audience. This means employing the expertise not just of Latinists, but also of cultural anthropologists and composers, linguists and poets, who understand the nature and genre of language and how it functions—meter and cadence—along with theologians and competent liturgical scholars.

46. RECOVERING THE TRANSCENDENT IN CATHOLIC WORSHIP

It is no secret that in the years immediately after the Second Vatican Council—in the second half of the 1960s and the 1970s—the universal church witnessed a significant amount of liturgical experimentation much of which was unauthorized, and much of which gave greater attention to the horizontal rather than the vertical; greater attention to the immanent rather than the transcendent. It has been argued that in the late 1960s and early 1970s, too much happened too quickly. Bishops returned home from the council enthusiastic to put into practice the new liturgical norms and principles, but few were sufficiently prepared to lead their dioceses in implementing the reforms. Complex Latin liturgical texts were translated into the vernacular expeditiously. Gregorian chant was abandoned in favor of newly composed contemporary music for guitar rather than organ; incense was abolished as something no longer appropriate in the reformed rite of Catholic worship; neo-Gothic and other traditionally oriented churches were quickly renovated to reflect the reforms and a more immediate access to the holy found within the liturgical assembly itself.

Much of the criticism against the liturgical experimentation of the 1960s and 1970s was not without justification and mistakes were made. The most conservative scholars referred to that time as a period of "complete liturgical anarchy." While other liturgical scholars might be a bit more muted in their assessment of those years immediately after the council, few would contend that the period was unproblematic. However, as Blessed John Henry Newman remarked after the First Vatican Council at the end of the nineteenth century, every church council has been followed by a period of turmoil and unrest. It would be enough to think of Nicaea and Chalcedon, but even the Council of Trent did not succeed in gaining unanimous adherence to its decrees. History is always instructive.

While there is much to be commended in the post-conciliar implementation of the liturgical reforms, there is also a significant level of reform—or full implementation of what the council desired—that has not yet been introduced, in the area of liturgical formation and catechesis, for example, as was mentioned earlier. And much has to do with how to redress the balance between transcendence and immanence; recovering a sense of mystery and the sacred; the custody of words with greater attention to silence and the nonverbal. Interestingly, by and large, our Anglican counterparts have done a far better job at this than Roman Catholics—maintaining a sense of dignity and reverence within liturgical celebrations; greater attention to mystery and the numinous without losing worship's participative dimension so characteristic of what was desired by the Second Vatican Council. Almost fifty years after that

council, we must state it honestly that attention to the transcendent within worship and the conciliar principle of "full, active, and conscious liturgical participation" are not mutually exclusive. Indeed, greater attention to recovering a sense of mystery within the liturgy might actually serve as a bridge to those who remain critical of the liturgy of Vatican II or the *novus ordo*.

Almost immediately after the council, an organized opposition led by Archbishop Marcel Lefebvre accused the Missal of Paul VI of being overly Protestant, and Lefebvre led the call for a return to the pre-conciliar Tridentine Rite of Pius V. Of course, we should not limit Lefebvre's criticisms to liturgy alone as his campaign was focused on the wider issue of church reform—what he saw as a mistaken progressive approach taken by the council that opened the church to the modern world. In the realm of liturgy, however, much of the criticism focused on the loss of the sacred and in particular, the sense of mystery and the transcendent within Catholic worship. Lefebvre and his followers eventually were excommunicated from the Catholic Church but his criticisms of the conciliar liturgical reforms found resonance with some conservative scholars. This has resulted in the publication of not an insignificant amount of books and articles critical of the conciliar reforms, published largely in English, French, and German. Those texts have called for a "reforming of the reform," and a "recatholicizing of the reform." Much of this criticism has focused around the question of the "hermeneutic of continuity." This refers to the extent to which the liturgical reforms of the Second Vatican II were meant to be interpreted as a continuation of what preceded them, thus suggesting an organic link between the pre- and post-conciliar rites. Or, rather, should the reforms indicate a sharp break with what preceded them in which Tridentine elements were absorbed into the new rite or replaced by the reformed rite of Vatican II? Not surprisingly, conservative scholars argue in favor of the "hermeneutic of continuity" while defenders of the conciliar reforms opt for the latter approach.

What has largely been at the heart of the conciliar criticisms, however, is precisely this loss of the sacred, the transcendent, and this, I believe, is a point of common ground that those on both sides of the issue have yet to realize. It is a well-kept secret that liturgical scholars of different stripes are essentially on the same page when it comes to critiquing worship that has become overly verbose to the point of banality, lacking in silence and attention to the church's rich symbolic system, and where the one presiding has become too central to the liturgical action. These same liturgical scholars would also agree on their critique of priests and bishops who take liberties on improvising on liturgical texts as in the Introductory Rite, choosing to

1. Apostles' Communion (1043–1046), detail of the intermediate space of the apsidal mosaic in the Saint Sophia Cathedral in Kiev.

begin Mass by saying "Good morning, everyone" rather than beginning with the greeting of Saint Paul "The Grace and Peace of God our Father . . . " as prescribed in the Roman Missal.

Liturgical scholars who defend the conciliar reforms would find it equally lamentable that certain presiders now find it fashionable to invite the entire liturgical assembly to pray the Apologetic Prayer before Communion together— "Lord Jesus Christ, you said to your Apostles, I leave you peace . . . "—just as their counterparts who criticize the conciliar reforms and argue in favor of the Tridentine Rite. So there is actually more consensus on post-conciliar liturgical problems than meets the eye between centrist and conservative critics, and even with ideological or reactionary conservative critics. What unites scholars on both sides of the issue is precisely a desire to restore the transcendent—the numinous—a sense of mystery— which is done by a custody of words in the liturgy and careful attention to the nonverbal and to the important role of silence where it is called for.

47. THE EXTRAORDINARY FORM OF THE ROMAN RITE

1. Eustache Le Sueur (1616–1655), The Mass of Saint Martin of Tours, 1654. Louvre Museum, Paris.

As we saw in the last chapter, a small but vocal and influential group that was critical of the *novus ordo* in the years following the council lobbied for a return to the usage of the pre-conciliar (1962) *Missale Romanum*. In fact, only seven years after the promulgation of *Sacrosanctum concilium*, Pope Paul VI granted an indult to elderly priests in 1970 who preferred to continue celebrating the pre-conciliar rite in private.

The schism launched by Archbishop Marcel Lefebvre and his traditionalist movement led Pope John Paul II to make several overtures at reconciliation. Indeed, during his pontificate, two indults were granted for a limited use of the Tridentine Rite—first in 1984 with the document *Quattuor Abhinc Annos*, issued by the Congregation for Divine Worship and the Discipline of the Sacraments. Four years later in 1988, Pope John Paul issued his own Apostolic

Letter *Ecclesia Dei*, which established the *Ecclesia Dei* Commission with the aim of facilitating "full ecclesial communion" with those among Lefebvre's followers who wished to remain in the Catholic Church. But with the motu proprio *Summorum Pontificium* of Pope Benedict XVI in 2007, the pre-conciliar rite received a new status. No longer restricted to limited usage, the 1962 rite could now be celebrated freely throughout the universal church. Indeed, in Pope Benedict's letter that accompanied the motu proprio, he suggests that the two forms of the usage of the Roman Rite can be "mutually enriching."

Both as Bishop of Rome and universal pastor, the Holy Father stated that he granted this universal permission for wider use of the Tridentine Rite out of his paternal love for the church and concern for that small minority of disenfranchised Catholics who felt excluded by the *novus ordo*. That said, however, the motu proprio has been read as victory by the church's conservative wing and a positive step in correcting or even negating the council's liturgical agenda despite the Pope's stating the contrary. Some have even suggested that the motu proprio actually offers a step forward for the church—part of what is called a "new liturgical movement." Be that as it may, while some conservative organizations and seminaries are now celebrating the 1962 rite regularly, and places where it is being celebrated draw crowds of young people often out of curiosity for experiencing what they never knew growing up, most bishops and liturgical scholars do not believe that the "Extraordinary Form of the Roman Rite" poses any significant threat to the Conciliar liturgy or its ongoing renewal. Among other things, few priests are capable of celebrating the pre-conciliar rite, despite various attempts at training seminarians and young priests to do so through short summer courses and DVDs. More importantly, statistics show a very small number of Catholics are actually desirous of the Extraordinary Rite. Indeed, in the past four years since the promulgation of the 2007 motu proprio there has not been a significant increase in those clamoring to have the pre-conciliar rite made available in their parishes. These statistics are consistent with results flowing from the 2009 Apostolic Constitution *Anglicanorum Coetibus* opening the door to the entry of traditionalist Anglicans—whether individuals, parishes, or dioceses. Despite that document, there has not been a large influx of Anglicans "crossing the Tiber" to become Roman Catholic, and the small group that has joined the Catholic Church tends to be more aligned with the sort of Tridentine-rite Catholics described above rather than mainstream Catholics who have largely accepted the teachings of the Second Vatican Council.

Pope Benedict's accompanying letter to bishops was an attempt to allay some disquiet among them, since the Holy Father was well aware that liberalizing the use of the pre-conciliar rite would not be without difficulty. Even despite the contentious debate over the two rites, and which is preferable, there are pastoral problems at the diocesan and parochial levels. For example, parishes that celebrate the Roman Rite both in its ordinary and extraordinary forms will find themselves in a certain quandary when it comes to establishing a stable liturgical calendar since the two calendars do not match. This is especially evident in the season of Advent. The 1962 Roman Missal has Ember Days on Wednesday, Thursday, and Friday of the third week with proper readings, prayers, and chants. On the other weekdays, however, the Sunday Mass texts are to be used except on feast days of saints. By contrast, the Missal of Paul VI specifies no Ember Days, but it does contain propers for all the weekdays of Advent as well as special Mass texts for the "O Antiphons" from December 17 to 24. Whereas the 1962 contains no Advent Preface and prescribes the Preface of the Holy Trinity for Sundays and a Common Preface for Weekdays, the Missal of Paul VI contains two newly composed Prefaces for Advent. Moreover, the 1962 Missal permits the chanting of the Alleluia on Advent Sundays but not weekdays, while the Vatican II rite allows the singing of the Alleluia throughout the entire Advent season.

There is also a problem in the realm of sacramental preparation and celebration, for example, in the sacrament of Confirmation where the sacramental formula differs between the old rite and the new. Some bishops have expressed the concern that the liberalization of the Tridentine Rite could be interpreted as opening the door to a pluralism of rites or liturgical styles in the church—appealing to the postmodern penchant for experience and variety that is constitutive of the present-day culture. These same bishops fear that rather than unifying the church, the existence of two forms of the Roman Rite in competition with one another will actually further divide it. In fact, both ecclesiologically and canonically, there can only be one "Roman Rite" just as there is one "Byzantine Rite" or one "Ambrosian Rite." While those desirous of the "Extraordinary Form" now have free access to this Rite for their spiritual nourishment, it remains the task for the rest of the Catholic Church in the West to take stock of the liturgical vision of the Second Vatican Council, properly implementing that vision in the careful preparation and celebration of the Roman Rite as discussed in the last chapter.

48. CHRISTIAN WORSHIP AND THE CHALLENGES OF GLOBALIZATION AND POSTMODERNITY

Since the 1930s, our world has undergone radical cultural shifts thanks to the process of globalization. These shifts have been seen in art, architecture, and music, as well as in literature, philosophy, and theology. We speak of this era as "postmodern." Architecturally, whereas the modern architectural movement emphasized organic integrity and functionality, postmodern architecture thrives on "multivalence," blending together various forms and styles, highlighting diversity and pluriformity through a hybrid of architectural designs. Similarly, postmodern art rejects the organic unity typical of modernity and argues for a more heterogenous blending of forms and shapes, with a preference for juxtaposing diverse and contradictory styles. Indirectly, such juxtaposition calls into question the tradition and validity of a single artistic director, arguing in favor of an eclectic mix of disharmonious styles and elements.

The world of postmodernism could be characterized—at least by some scholars—as pessimistic, holistic, communitarian, and pluralistic. Pessimism becomes a hallmark of this epoch as it underscores human fragility and negates the Enlightenment's emphasis on inevitable progress. Holism is mentioned in this description as a negation of rationality and an embrace of the emotions and intuition. The communitarian dimension within postmodernism serves as a corrective to the individualism so typical of modernity and advocates a community-based search for truth. Pluralism expresses the diversity of cultural traditions and the corresponding necessity of different truths representative of different yet equally valid communities. Thus, in the postmodern world, there is no one truth, no one objective reality, no one way of negotiating life in the real world. Rather, the world is a complex symbolic system that relies more on subjective interpretation than on absolute and demonstrable truth.

The church is not immune to these postmodern effects. Indeed, it would not be difficult to apply postmodern principles to the evaluation of Christian liturgy and how it is celebrated, and we would surely come up with some interesting results. Critics of the conciliar reforms have highlighted post-conciliar church architecture as consonant with the minimalist objectives of postmodern thought. Others might point to the eclectic combination of liturgical and non-liturgical elements in post-conciliar liturgy that stand in sharp contrast to the predictable and traditional framework of the pre-conciliar rite. With mobility and change as guiding principles in postmodernism, such transience is also indicative of the postmodern cultural construct. Tradition itself is challenged as change is introduced for the sake of change, whether the subject is the remodeling of a home, the restructuring of a business, or even the abandonment of responsibilities and commitments in human relationships in favor of new ones. Perfectly good systems are replaced whether or not such replacements are needed, because transience is good in and of itself. All of these cultural factors have a significant influence on the church's liturgy, and not necessarily for the better. In the early chapters of this book, we have seen how it was impossible for the church to worship outside of or apart from its cultural context, and the postmodern church is no exception as contemporary culture undergoes its own evolution.

Globalization itself is changing the face of the planet, and our churches and liturgical life along with it. We must now take note and respond appropriately. This is no short order, because while one can point to the positive effects of globalization, there are also quite negative effects. This process of globalization is essentially one of extension, in which the ideals of modernity and technological advance

2, 4. Hard Rock Cafe, Orlando, Florida.

3. Main entrance to Boston's New England Building's public spaces.
Architect Robert Stern designed the structure.

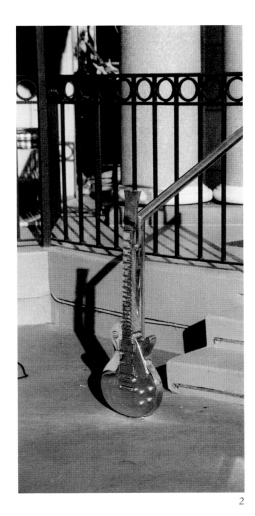

2

3

4

are spread or extended throughout the world. Such a process is helped greatly by a single economic system of neo-liberal capitalism and the rapidly expanding advances in communication technologies. This leads to the collapse of geographic boundaries which once defined cultural identity. In the concrete, we think for example of the risk of re-creating the "melting pot" theory that was common during the years of the United States economic depression of the 1930s, where all cultural diversity was blended into sameness as immigrants reached American shores. This remains a universal threat in our own day. Today, in places as far-flung as Kyoto and Manila, the U.S. coffee shop Starbucks can be found, all designed with the exact same décor as one could find at any Starbucks property in New York or London. Even the same jazz music of Miles Davis plays in the background! Thus, a homogenized culture is created, formed into a cohesion based largely on consumption.

5. Daily Banalaties is the title of this photograph by Architect Corrado Gavinelli.

6. Self-construction project by the studio of Mexican architects Carlos González Lobo and Maria Hurtado, detail of the neighborhood church.

7. Murals, San Diego, California. The Chicanos (Mexican-Americans) lay claim to their place in American society, in which they are no longer a minority.

8. Asian family in Boston.

6

5

7

8

Globalization has also had the effect of strengthening the "survival of the fittest" system where the stronger outlive the weak. In Rome, for example, small family-run food shops (*alimentari*) find it increasingly difficult to survive as big supermarkets have now opened in large number, offering cheaper prices and longer hours for shopping, including Sundays, when small shops close so that time can be spent at home with the family. Similarly, in Shanghai, the elegant new business district called "Pudong," built some years ago on landfill just across the city from downtown,

9–10. Donating one's time: volunteers help a handicapped person, and a doctor lends his services in an African country.

11–12. African immigrants participate in a mass that is celebrated in the Rosarno Maria Santissima Church, Calabria (Photo, Nino Leto).

9

10

11

12

had the negative effect of pushing out poor residents who'd lived in makeshift homes in the vicinity. One wonders where those poor people are expected to go without the necessary economic resources. A similar dynamic can be observed in other cities around the world, especially where projects of gentrification or urban renewal are under way. Thus, globalization has both positive and negative effects.

If liturgy is to be intimately linked to living as Christ's body in the world and within this particular culture—to being in solidarity with the plight of the poor and hungry; refugees and immigrants who are denied a just wage—then liturgists and pastoral ministers will need to face the problem squarely. They will need to consider carefully the challenges offered by globalization in this postmodern age so

that our liturgical communities foster cultural identity and model authentic human relationships based on equality and reverence, standing prophetically against claims within contemporary culture that promote a "survival of the fittest" mentality. In this sense, we can understand liturgy also as countercultural—standing together with those whom society rejects—the powerless and those who stand at the margins. Liturgy and culture must always be in dialogue but the Gospel of Christ proclaimed in Christian worship must also speak out strongly in its critique of contemporary culture.

49. Liturgy and Mission

2. *Masaccio,* Saint Peter Distributing Alms, *detail of the fresco in the Brancacci Chapel in Santa Maria del Carmine Church, Florence 1425–1427.*

1. *Jacopo Robusti, also known as "Tintoretto,"* Christ Washing the Disciples' Feet, *1547. Prado Museum, Madrid.*

3. *Theodor Rombouts,* Saint Augustine Washing the Feet of the Pilgrim Christ, *1636. Koninklijk Museum voor Schone Kunsten, Antwerp.*

1

One of the greatest gifts of the Second Vatican Council has been the recovery of the intrinsic link between liturgy and mission—liturgy and Christian witness within the world. Of course, the relationship had always been there in one form or another, but more often than not they were seen as two separate realities not meant to intersect. Upon entering church for Sunday Mass or devotions, the world was left behind for an hour or so. Stained-glass windows helped the faithful to block out those external and pedestrian distractions. Believers were evangelized and instructed in the Christian faith with the help of catechisms and other instructive materials. When there was one, the Sunday sermon offered its own admonition to observe the commandments and live the Christian life, but more as a spiritual exhortation than part of the liturgical act as was mentioned earlier. This pre-conciliar dichotomization between liturgy and mission, and, indeed, between liturgy and life, found its basis in the Enlightenment and the Industrial Revolution with a strong emphasis on rationality and reason. Even today in the post-conciliar church, clergy and other liturgical ministers must resist the temptation to offer explanations prior to and during the celebration itself, offering lengthy introductions and explanations.

The early church provides some clue as to how this intrinsic relationship between liturgy and mission was lived out concretely in the first centuries of Christianity. At the Last Supper, we do not hear of Jesus giving an extensive lecture to his disciples about the importance of loving one's neighbor. Rather Jesus stoops down, pours water into a basin, and with a towel wrapped around his waist begins to wash the feet of his disciples much to their confusion and astonishment. Only afterward does he explain his ritual behavior, and then concludes with the directive: "For I have set you an example, that you also should do as I have done to you" (John 13:15). Thus, beginning with the New Testament and continuing through the preaching and writings of church fathers like Ambrose of Milan, Augustine of Hippo, Cyril of Jerusalem, John Chrysostom and others, liturgy's relationship to Christian mission and witness in the world were part of the same reality.

In the fifth century, Prosper of Aquitaine (+463) expressed this very well as *lex orandi, lex credendi:* the law of worship establishes the law of belief. In other words, Christian worship expresses the fundamentals of what the church holds and teaches; catechesis and evangelization grow out of worship, not the other way around. This important link between liturgy and *caritas* or *diakonia* is also subsumed in

2

3

this same theological reality of *lex orandi, lex credendi.* As Saint Augustine reminded the church of North Africa in his sermons on the Eucharist, the commands "take and eat," "take and drink," implied a related obligation to become that holy food and drink, "the bread of sincerity and truth" for others as the church washed the feet of the poor and needy in daily life.

Thus, the theological axiom of *lex orandi, lex credendi* was merely an articulation of what the church's tradition had been from the beginning and of what membership within the church demanded. Witness to the mission of Jesus Christ within common worship always implied social responsibility within daily life. Indeed, the credibility of the church's worship depended upon its faithfulness to its mission in the ordinary routines of daily life whether at home, work, or in the marketplace. Augustine reminded the liturgical assembly of that indivisible unity of faith, hope, and charity that it shared one with another, and its call to recognize itself in the Eucharistic gifts upon the altar.

In September 1959, an international study week was held at Nijmegen and Uden in the Netherlands on the topic of "Mission and Liturgy." The meeting was an outgrowth of the famous Assisi Liturgical Congress of 1956, which gathered more than 1,400 bishops and liturgical experts. At the Assisi Congress, those missionaries present gathered to discuss the topic of the liturgical movement in their own unique missiological contexts, and the challenges they faced in trying to adapt Catholic worship to the diverse cultures where they lived and worked. The Planning Commission for the Netherlands Congress agreed that the primary focus should be "the particular missionary value of well-formed worship." They acknowledged that too often those engaged in missionary activity had failed to attend to the full import of Christian worship: its power to transform communities of faith. The Nijmegen gathering would promote worship in mission lands as a pastoral tool of evangelization and catechesis, leading to more effective witness in the world. Wisely, those who gathered at Nijmegen recognized that intrinsic link between liturgy and evangelical mission, and the tremendous potential within Christian worship to transform moral behavior. Given the fact that the thirty-seven missionary bishops and others who gathered at Nijmegen did so in 1959—three years before the Second Vatican Council had begun—they were well ahead of their time in calling for worship that was more integrated with the church's mission in the world.

In studying the documents of Vatican II, one can discern a clear convergence of both missionary and liturgical goals.

4. Andrei Rublev, The Trinity, *from the beginning of the fifteenth century. Galleria Tret'jakov, Moscow.*

5. Pentecost, hymnal from 1591. French Armenian Museum, Paris. The Holy Spirit leans over the bread and wine.

4

This is evident both in the Liturgy Constitution *Sacrosanctum concilium* as well in the council's Missionary Decree *Ad Gentes divinitus.* That council recognized that the church had now become what the Jesuit theologian Karl Rahner called a "world Church," marked by both pluralism and cultural diversity. Vatican II placed missionary activity at the heart of the church's life, whose natural source of energy and nourishment was the Eucharistic celebration. Just after the council in 1966, J. G. Davies published an interesting book entitled *Worship and Mission* (London, 1966), in which he addressed the problem of parallel structures that exist within the church when discussing the subject of liturgy and mission. He criticized liturgy that remained insular, isolated from the rest of life and, therefore, also from the task of mission and evangelization. At the same time, he also criticized that form of witnessing to the Gospel of Christ that seemed to lack the necessary grounding in the church's life of worship. Davies argued for a fundamental rethinking of both liturgical theology and missiology, which would then lead to a substantial transformation of both the theologies of worship and mission.

Forty-five years after Davies important work, I would venture to say that the tension between liturgy and mission has yet to be fully resolved. Today, church ministers who live in this complex postmodern world would do well to heed those words of Professor Davies, because the integration of liturgy and God's mission in the world is non-negotiable if the implementation of the Gospel message in diverse cultural contexts has a future. Indeed, it would be naïve simply to take such a future for granted. Pope Benedict XVI made this point explicit in his encyclical *Deus Caritas Est* and made even more explicit in his Post-Synodal Apostolic Exhortation *Sacramentum caritatis,* when he wrote of the inseparable relationship between love of God and love of neighbor, noting that the failure to link those two realities results in worship that is empty and incomplete. Ultimately, how we understand worship—the liturgy—will determine how we understand mission.

In the part of the Eucharistic Prayer called the Epiclesis, we are accustomed to giving attention to the Role of the Holy Spirit in transforming the gifts of bread and wine into the body and blood of Christ. Equally important is the role of the Holy Spirit in transforming us into becoming that which we receive: the body of Christ broken, the blood of Christ outpoured. Eastern Christians are much better acquainted with this reality than their Western counterparts, and the West has much to learn from the East in this regard. Indeed, our recovery of the importance of the epiclesis—the role of the Holy Spirit in transforming both the gifts as well as ourselves—has been

a significant ecumenical bridge between Catholics and the Orthodox. For it is only in the power of the Holy Spirit transforming us through the Eucharist we receive that we will be able to bear effective witness to the gospel and live as Christ's body in the world. As some theologians have put it, we ourselves need to be "transubstantiated"—consecrated—along with the bread and wine. In fact, the conciliar document *Lumen Gentium* speaks of our being "offered with the bread and wine."

Borrowing from the Lutheran World Federation's Nairobi Statement of 1996, I would like to highlight four themes that are of utmost importance if the relationship between liturgy and mission is to become a lived reality for the church of the twenty-first century. Liturgy must first be transcultural or universal—demonstrative of the communion *(koinonia)* of the church. This was the heart of Saint Paul's theology of the Eucharist and remains crucial for our own self-understanding as a eucharistic church. In our liturgical tradition, as we have seen, we speak of "the substantial unity of the Roman Rite" even as it offers room for cultural diversity and regional expression, but this is about more than the unity of the Roman Rite. We are speaking about

5

6. Dorothy Day recites Vespers at Saint Joseph House, headquarters for the Catholic Worker Movement. Catholic farm worker and intellectual Peter Maurin, and Dorothy Day, a leftist journalist and writer who converted to Catholicism, founded the movement in 1933. On May 1 of that year, Dorothy and some young people who were her supporters went to Union Square in New York City where they sold the first edition of The Catholic Worker, *a weekly publication, for one cent a copy (Courtesy of Jon Erikson).*

6

7

the unity of the church and its worship: the integrity between how we live this communion outside of the Eucharist, and how that "liturgy of the world" is offered back to God as we lift up our hearts in thanks and praise at the Eucharist. At the Second Vatican Council, the church recovered that ancient truth: "the Eucharist makes the Church and the Church makes the Eucharist." This is where church and Eucharist coincide: the church constitutes the Eucharist and is constituted by it. This expresses most profoundly the organic unity between our worship and the life of the church. But that organic unity does not happen automatically, and if the community is in some way divided outside of the liturgical celebration it will not miraculously be healed and recognize itself as Christ's body united within the liturgy. We are speaking here about a potential dichotomy between liturgy and life.

It is extraordinary, for example, to think that in Germany, in the years during the Holocaust, numerous SS officers went to Mass each morning before going about their daily chores of exterminating millions of Jews and Christians. A similar tension existed in the years of the Pinochet dictatorship in Chile where that tension was lived out between Eucharistic participation and adherence to the oppressive directives of that dictatorship. In India, it took the church more than three hundred years to declare that the caste system was "sinful and unchristian," yet even today there are still Indian villages and religious communities divided by caste and other conflicts, even as they continue to celebrate the Eucharist amid those social divisions. Similarly, the Catholic Church in the United States was quite slow in its own response to slavery. Today in Christian communities around the world, there are less dramatic examples of this disconnect where the community remains divided outside the Eucharistic celebration, but continues to gather for the Eucharist nonetheless, politely wishing "the peace of Christ" to one's neighbor.

Second, liturgy is always contextual. Thanks to the evolution of the social sciences in the twentieth century, we have come to understand how the cultural and material realities of our world shape our liturgical life and influence our understanding of mission. For this reason, the Roman Missal offers a great variety of choices in liturgical texts which can be chosen according to the particular context or celebrating community. The Eucharistic Prayers for Children that are found in the Missal offer a perfect example of this. With a more accessible language in which children can more easily enter into the action of the Eucharistic Prayer, those prayers exist precisely to be used in such con-

7. *A Filipino nun demonstrating alongside the people, in a peaceful show of force against the regime of General Ferdinand Marcos.*

8. *A welcoming missionary during an Eastern liturgical celebration (Nigrizia archives).*

8

ture might be affirmed within the liturgical assembly. The challenge today is no different. Worship and culture are always in dialogue but the Gospel of Christ must speak out strongly and prophetically in defense of the poor and powerless, the weak and the oppressed—those very individuals whom secular society has rejected. Where else but in the liturgical assembly are the poor treated as though they were rich, and the rich as no better than the poor—all reverenced with incense and fed with the Lord's body and blood, with no reserved seating and no special treatment except for the elderly and others whose physical condition require special assistance? Here, again, is the mission and will of Christ lived and enacted within the liturgy. The church must remain vigilant that its liturgical assemblies are places of God's hospitality, particularly for those whom our modern-day culture has rejected.

Fourth and finally, the reforms of the Second Vatican Council have opened our eyes to the many ways in which our liturgy is cross-cultural. This, too, has a great deal to offer to our discussion on the relationship between liturgy and mission, as this fourth theme deals with the fact that ours is a world church rich in cultural diversity. Happily, we are not all the same; rather, we are culturally and racially diverse, and such diversity makes the cultural mosaic that is the universal church rich and colorful. Taking God's mission seriously within our worship, then, means learning from one another's cultural traditions as they are expressed in the liturgy. It also means allowing ourselves to be taught by those whose traditions are not our own, and appreciating the fact that our own particular cultural approach is not the only one and not necessarily the best. As that cultural mosaic continues to evolve and expand our horizons, our church and its liturgy need to attend to how best to respond to this gift of cross-cultural identity.

Therefore, we are nourished at the Eucharist and sent forth into the world to serve those in need. We can only give what we have received ourselves: the bread of the Word and the Eucharist. In the Gospel, Jesus says to the disciples: "You give them something to eat" (Matthew 14:16). Herein lies the mission *Ite Missa Est:* "Go, you are sent." What you have been given, give as a gift. But that missiological dimension within liturgy cannot be limited to the sending forth: "The Mass is ended, Go in peace." Rather, it is a constitutive part of the liturgical act from start to finish, in not only the proclaimed Word and the preaching, but in way we treat one another in the liturgical assembly; in the gestures and use of symbols; in the prayers we proclaim and the texts we sing. In the words of the theologian Johannes Metz, faced with the "dangerous memory" of Jesus breaking bread with the broken people and outcasts of his culture and society, we are commissioned to share our bread with the broken of our own day. It is in this memorial of Jesus Christ and his paschal mystery that we are formed into God's people by the power of the Holy Spirit and strengthened to be sent on mission.

texts as Sunday Masses with children, school Masses, and the like. The two Eucharistic Prayers for Reconciliation serve a similar function for particular situations in which those prayers more effectively respond to the pastoral need of a given community. The way in which one preaches must also be contextualized. In other words, one needs to prepare the homily in a different manner if one is preaching within the context of a university community, a home for the elderly, a convent of religious sisters, a group of young adults, or a parish Mass on Sunday morning. However, even within parish Masses on Sunday morning, the particular community must be taken into account: a quiet Mass of older parishioners early on a Sunday morning has a different tone and style than the principal Mass of the day, which is still different from a Sunday evening Mass that may draw a larger number of young people who have different pastoral needs. All this has an effect on the way in which mission will be lived out through the liturgy and the potential influence that the liturgy will have concretely in the lives of the worshippers.

Third, liturgy is countercultural. From the earliest centuries of Christianity, the church engaged in careful discernment as to which cultural elements might be admitted into Christian worship, and which aspects of secular cul-

50. LITURGY AND THE FUTURE OF CHRISTIANITY

1. Pope John Paul II at the mass celebrated during Seville's "Campo de Feria," on the occasion of the closing of the 45th International Eucharistic Congress, which took place June 12–17, in 1993. Papal Master of Ceremonies Monsignor (later Archbishop) Piero Marini is next to the Pope (Photo, Giancarlo Giuliani).

The Second Vatican Council reaffirmed that the meta-narrative of the paschal mystery of Christ must be foundational for all ethical action. Yet for increasing numbers of people in the developed world, ethical questions and moral discourse take place without reference to religious practices such as devotional prayer or public worship. Many competing ethical viewpoints vie for attention. Within such a cultural mileau, the struggle to live faithfully in light of what the worship of God implies, and to interpret human life liturgically, becomes all the more acute. Today, we are challenged to discern the best means of inculcating that vision in others from the earliest years of religious formation, so that our religious practices—our worship in particular—might have a profound bearing upon ethical behavior and moral living, despite the obstacles. Questions about the conditions that generate and nurture human moral awareness draw us back again and again to questions about the relationships between the worship of God at Sunday Mass and life together as a community outside of it. As Methodist liturgical scholar Don Saliers has often said: "Liturgy is a rehearsal for the way we are to become related to one another and to the world." In other words, the just relationships exhibited within the liturgy offer a model for the sort of just relationships in which we should be engaged in the classroom or workplace.

As we face the future, we are ever more aware of the ecclesiological dimension of worship—liturgy's relationship to the church—and this is an important dynamic as we consider the future of Christianity. Indeed, several years ago in an address given in London, former Papal Master of Ceremonies Archbishop Piero Marini stated that "the future of liturgy is the future of the Church." He continued: "Celebrating the liturgy is itself the primordial source of renewal in the Church. We learn the liturgy by celebrating it. The more we succeed at celebrating the liturgy, the more we'll live the Christian life fully and the more we'll succeed in transforming the Church.... The great ideals of the Church are in crisis today in part because there's a crisis in the liturgy. The great ideals of ecumenism, of internal reform of the Church, are all connected. The crisis of the liturgy places in crisis these other great values, because the Council wanted to confront these challenges of the mission of the Church, of reform, of dialogue with the world, by beginning with the liturgy. If the liturgy is the source and summit, then we foster in the liturgy the kind of life we need to meet these goals. If these great movements of the Church are in difficulty today, we have to look to the difficulty in the liturgy."

Those words of Archbishop Marini are timely as we consider our current ecclesial and liturgical context and as we look toward the future. As he notes, liturgy's intimate link to ecclesiology is essential to understanding liturgy's role in the wider realm of the church, and as a catalyst and source of energy in our service of God's world. But as we look toward the future, we must also come to terms with the present. The church's face is radically different from the time of the Second Vatican Council in terms of where it is growing exponentially, and this has serious implications for our liturgical future and indeed, the future vitality of the church itself. At the beginning of the twentieth century, eighty percent of all Christians throughout the world were white and lived in the northern hemisphere. By the year 2020, we are told that eighty percent of all Christians will be people of color who live in the southern hemisphere. The average Christian in the world today is a very poor person, and in African and Asian countries, this Christian is often a minority living in a country dominated by other religions or secular ideologies. And while Christianity is on the rise in the global south, there is a growing secularism in the West with Christianity in sharp decline. Sociological surveys continue to be carried out, attempting to better understand the waning religious practice and liturgical participation in Western Europe, North America, and Oceania.

Another sociological reality that is not going away is the growing phenomenon of "priestless parishes" even in places like Catholic Italy. With the clergy shortage and vocation crisis of the developed world, increasing numbers of parishes find themselves without resident clergy and only occasionally have access to the eucharistic celebration. There are priests in Australia, for example, who serve as pastor of eight different parishes that were geographically

2. Pope John Paul II handing out communion to a group of young people during mass at Seville's "Campo de Feria" celebration (Photo, Giancarlo Giuliani).

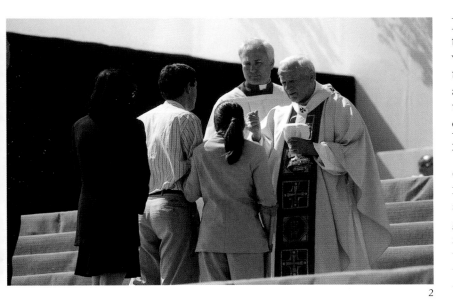

2

spread very far apart. Such parishes usually have a religious sister or lay leader who serves as administrator of the parish. Each Sunday and occasionally during the week, those administrators lead a Communion Service which closely resembles the Mass. They include an Introductory Rite and Liturgy of the Word (including a brief homily); Prayer of Thanksgiving (bearing a vague resemblance to the Preface of the Eucharistic Prayer); the Lord's Prayer; Invitation to Communion ("This is the Lamb of God…"); distribution of Communion from the tabernacle; Concluding Prayer; and Dismissal. But the structure appears so similar that the distinctions between Mass and the Communion service can easily be blurred.

Moreover, Communion Services are an inferior substitute to the celebration of the Eucharist—the church's lifeblood: its "source and summit." At the end of his summer holidays in 2005, Pope Benedict XVI expressed his concern about this growing reality, stating that Communion Services cannot be envisaged as a long-term solution or eventual substitution for the Mass itself. Saint Thomas Aquinas maintains that the Mass is and must be the center of the Christian life, and our church structures and other sacraments relate to it in a most intrinsic way. Aquinas, of course, was not saying anything new, but merely articulating what the church had recognized as its own tradition for centuries. Thus, as we look toward the future, the Roman Catholic Church will need to come to terms with what such centrality really means and how to resolve effectively this growing problem so that the eucharistic celebration continues to be given the utmost priority in the church's life and mission.

Fifty years after Vatican II, we are more aware than ever that Christian worship necessarily unites us in solidarity with those who suffer. We must constantly resist the temptation to think that our liturgical celebrations and preaching are only about us and our concerns. By their very nature, they are celebrations of the world church—the whole body of Christ—and that is what makes them Catholic. Karl Rahner's theological reflections on the "Liturgy of the World" are illuminating here. Rahner developed his liturgical theology around an understanding of worship that flows from the doors of the church into the care of the poor and needy within God's world. Illumined by Rahner's insights, along with the challenge of liturgy that is contextualized and inculturated, necessarily leads us to face squarely the task of Christian witness in the twenty-first century, and the role that liturgy plays within that process. This task takes on ever-greater urgency as we consider postmodern society as it is. As already mentioned, our world is increasingly secularized and, in much of the West, sadly post-Christian. Thus, our liturgical words and gestures must take on flesh and blood in daily life if the prophetic witness to the Gospel of Jesus Christ will bear fruit in the future.

In the concrete, this will mean taking our cues from the liturgy itself where the reign of God's justice and peace is celebrated time and again within the gathered worshipping assembly. As we long for that reign of God to be lived out within the world, this will mean a conscious and intentional commitment toward greater ecumenical and interreligious dialogue on the part of those who love the church and seek to give faithful witness to Christ's command "That all may be one." Ecumenical dialogue is first and foremost an essential item on the agenda because, quite simply, we can no longer afford to live and act apart. Effective proclamation of the Gospel message depends on our unity in witnessing to that message. Disunity within such proclamation will only weaken our common witness. Thus, respectful of the particular limits established by our churches and despite our sad divisions at the Altar of the Holy Eucharist, what we can do together we must do together, standing together as one—albeit broken—body of Christ before the cross.

It is even more imperative that we heed the call to Christian unity within our evangelical witness as we consider the growth of Islam in so many parts of the world.

Our common ecumenical witness must necessarily lead us from worship into serious efforts at interreligious dialogue. Political conflicts in Iraq and Afghanistan have only further strained relations between the Christian and Muslim world, causing great alarm as we consider our religious future both as separate religions but also together as people of faith who seek the face of the one God. But our com-

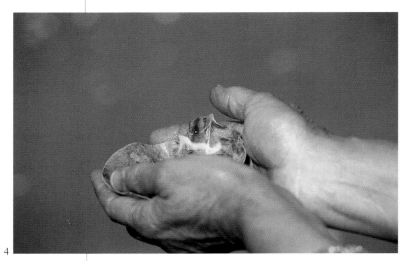

mon witness in Jesus Christ compels us to follow that path to dialogue ever more deliberately and intentionally. It is significant that in Indonesia—the largest Muslim country in the world—the Roman Missal used there now contains an optional Votive Mass which may be used during the Muslim period of "Ramadan"—a time of purification, prayer, and fasting, not unlike the Christian Lent. That Votive Mass offers the possibility for Indonesian Catholics to be united with their Muslim counterparts during that Muslim holy season, praying for their well-being and strength. Similarly, in India, one finds prayer texts in the Missal for Mass during the Hindu Feast of Lights ("Diwali"), as a way for Indian Catholics to be in spiritual solidarity with their Hindu counterparts. There are those who believe that efforts at common ecumenical witness flowing from our worship, and the determinate quest for greater interreligious harmony, are part of a past history that no longer holds promise. Indeed, in a world profoundly changed by acts of terrorism, the virtue of

Christian hope does not come easily. Taking our liturgical practice seriously, however, demands the kind of Christian witness in the work of justice and peace that remains open to embracing the whole of God's world.

As we consider the various problems around the globe in the twenty-first century, we are very much aware that ours is a broken world that is desperately in need of those who will offer themselves as instruments in its healing and restoration. But for Christians, dedication to such projects always begins in the eucharistic celebration—"the source and summit of the Christian life." It is precisely the eucharistic liturgy that offers the breaking of the bread as a sign of redemptive transformation for a broken world. This is what lies at the foundations of the Christian Eucharist and what remains our call if Christian worship is to be as authentic in the third millennium as it was in the first and second. This call to authentic worship is ultimately a call to greater holiness both corporately as the Body of Christ in the world and also individually: we receive the body and

6. Mass celebrated by Pope John Paul II inside Rome's Regina Coeli Prison, for the Jubilee, July 2000 (Photo, Giancarlo Giuliani).

7. 4th National Ecclesial Convention, October 2006. Pope Benedict XVI celebrated mass. Archbishop Piero Marini is next to him (Photo, Alessia Giuliani).

8. December 1, 2006. In the foreground, Pope Benedict XVI prays, the pastoral staff in his hand (Photo, Alessia Giuliani).

6

7

8

blood of Christ for our sanctification that we may be made holy. But here, too, in reflecting upon our Catholic tradition a half century after the Second Vatican Council, we are compelled to ask ourselves what that call to holiness means in our own day and what it will demand of us as we face the future.

In Pope John Paul II's Apostolic Letter *Spiritus et Sponsa* issued in the year 2003 on the occasion of the fortieth anniversary of *Sacrosanctum concilium*, he wrote: "In the Lord Jesus and in his Spirit, the whole Christian existence becomes a living sacrifice, holy and acceptable to God, genuine spiritual worship. The mystery brought about in the liturgy is truly great. It opens a glimpse of heaven on earth and the perennial hymn of praise rises from the community of believers in unison with the hymn of the heavenly Jerusalem…may a liturgical spirituality be developed that makes people conscious that Christ is the first liturgist who never ceases to act in the Church and in the world through the Pascal Mystery continuously celebrated, and who asso-

ciates the Church with himself, in praise of the Father, in the unity of the Holy Spirit." Such a liturgical spirituality is desperately needed as we consider the future of the Church and its worship in the twenty-first century. Ultimately, then, our goal is that the language of the Eucharist become the language and pattern of our own lives, as we participate in God's mission within the world as Christ would have us do.

THE ESTHETICS OF LITURGICAL EXPRESSION

Inos Biffi

The religious instinct of humankind requires that liturgical celebrations be marked by outward signs of distinction and propriety, distinguishing them from everyday activities. Moreover, we can immediately perceive that the "sacred" is an "anthropological" classification. This is demonstrated by the history of ritual, in which it appears that religious gestures aimed at showing devotion to God and worship are judged and seen as clearly different from what is "ordinary."

In our relationship with the Divine, attitudes are usually developed through the exercise of devotion. They can be transformed in many ways into different kinds of religious expression. Esthetic precision and rubrical exactness—which are not in other forms of human interaction—are characteristic of that expression. It is as if esthetic precision and rubrical exactness imbue religious symbols with divine, radiant glory, avoiding sloppy superficiality.

The fountainhead of divine worship, its main or most significant aspect, undoubtedly consists, as Saint Thomas Aquinas wrote, of interior acts. Nevertheless, "the human mind, so it can be led to God, needs perceptible realities," namely, of "signs that incite Man to carry out spiritual acts that will unite him to God" (*Summa Theologica*, II–II, 81, 7, c).

Because they are able to foster devotion of the mind, such perceptible realities are derived from their natural condition and converted into symbols. In one respect, they are meant to carry the concept of a "separate" and transcendent divine world back into our minds. Such symbols almost set themselves up both to contain and to reveal the mystery of God; in another respect, they create conditions favorable for the promotion of intimate communion with him, who is infinitely and forever beyond our reach.

It is precisely because theological symbolism is found in such liturgical expression that one talks about the sacred. It is a characterization that is often challenged nowadays—above all by worshipping believers and theologies considered prophetic and progressive. In reality, they are rather old; "the sacred" is distinguished from "the profane."

That is how liturgical style, marked by precision, is created: in a word, it arises out of Beauty. From time immemorial, liturgy has been characterized, possibly in its simplest, most elementary forms, by art, order, and light, the intent of which has not been to lay waste to the mind or scatter one's attention, but to elevate and bring harmony to it. Liturgical style is of value, too, when it comes to church furnishings, vestments, liturgical equipment, spaces, buildings, music, and song: everything that has to do with

such celebrations has to be "transfigured" in a certain kind of way, depending on both fluctuating sensibilities and prevailing tastes, during any given period.

One could talk about Beauty, in its purest form, as an ideal. Actually, one should not confuse it with pomp and splendor, which, instead of causing God to come into our midst, distances us from him, and instead of facilitating prayer, puts up barriers to it. In such cases, liturgical expression no longer acts as a symbol—which, because of its nature, is actively open and allusive—but as an anti-symbol, which minimizes and therefore reduces itself. In addition, since it might make things seem overly heavy in their religious aspects, pomp could scandalize God's people, who often live in poor and miserable conditions. However, those same people, in all their poverty, might agree that the "House of God" must never lack decorum, and that it presents a kind of elegance that points to a divine world, without diminishing or compromising in the least, the value of the Gospels, which, above all, is obvious in the practice of charity.

In that respect, we are familiar with the behavior of the more illustrious pastors, such as Saint Ambrose. The bishop of Milan even shattered the sacred vessels to rescue prisoners, for which initiative he was criticized. When he was forced to deal with his fellow clergymen on this issue, he did not hesitate to assert: "The Church possesses gold, which it should not hoard. It should distribute it, as a gift of aid, in the case of need. Is it not better for bishops to melt down holy chalices so the poor can be fed, if there are no other means to do so?" Although it is true that such vessels are sacramental ornaments, Ambrose thought that the swarm of freed prisoners "was a much more beautiful sight than that of beautiful chalices." Such an act did not compromise that shepherd of souls, in whom refinement and the conviction that the liturgical world should be the recipient of his grace were innate.

All one has to do is hear Ambrose's liturgical hymns, which are unsurpassed masterpieces of Christian poetry, and think about the despair that one of his servants, who moved about in an ungraceful and undignified manner during celebrations, must have brought to life in him.
One should be suspicious of preachers and Church ideologues who neglect the liturgy in pursuit of social issues. They often impoverish others spiritually because of the point of view they espouse, and they are quick to allow the undermining of divine worship.

Along the lines of what has already been expressed, special consideration must be given to liturgical language. It should be presented with literary elegance, contrary to the

254

opinion of many who believe it should be similar in style to spontaneous, popular, or journalistic expression. To write a liturgical piece based on the jargon of the moment would cause it to be quickly outdated, as always happens with language that is temporarily "in vogue"; within a very short time, it would be rendered intolerable.

Prayers, prefaces, and, in general, ritualistic expressions should, of course, be clear and straightforward. However, that does not mean that typical Christian terminology found in the rest of Scripture, with all its technical apparatus, which is not always immediately comprehended, should be excluded. Nevertheless, since there is a biblical exegesis that explains the holy pages, there should also be a liturgical catechesis that lays out the meaning of those texts.

All liturgical practice, with its symbols and activities, should be commented on immediately after it is presented. In that way, it becomes more transparent and is assimilated and enjoyed, so that no one will later feel compelled to request that it be explained, and it is done so in a manner devoid of clarity. This does not in the least mean that the mystery of Christianity is totally reflected by the enigmatic obscurity of different forms of liturgical celebration—and that transparency will "destroy" the mystery. Obscurity should not be one of the characteristics of liturgical celebration; nor should liturgy represent complications in one's relationship with God or the condition of being separated from him. It should speak of his light, closeness, and presence. This is based on an awareness that no symbol will ever be able to contain the mystery, and no voice will ever be able to express it, with adequate propriety.

In this respect, we find a clear lesson in the collections of old prayers. We can cite the case of the *Sacramentarium Veronense*, in which texts that date back to Leo the Great, the "Cicero of the Christian era," are not lacking. In them are revealed, as best as could possibly be—as a first-rate expert in the subject, Francisco di Capua, writes—"the marriage between lyrical effusion and eloquent exhortation."

They were compiled by looking at the architecture of words and phrases, that is to say, at the *concinittas* [tn: "beauty of style"]—as it was called—and at the *cursus*, which is based on quantity and accent, so that the beauty and harmony of the cadences allow one to hear the "latent melody (*cantus obscurior*)" of discourse in a pleasurable manner (Cicero, *Orator, 57*). In this kind of sacramentary (to return to di Capua)—Leo the Great's "thought, rhythm, and song are based on a homogenous, harmonic whole."

Every language has its own unique characteristics, in the same way that literary tastes vary, based on the times and the individual reader. A perfect version, immune to criticism, does not exist. Perhaps even the Ambrosian Missal does not even attain such a level. But that wonderful wordsmith, Cardinal Giovanni Colombo, lent it his felicitous, heaven-inspired touches; they shine forth through the document's newfound linguistic lucidity.

It was necessary, however, inside the context of liturgical esthetics, to point to the grace that must constantly accompany rituals, without, moreover, indulging in vain affectation. Flat, sloppy language would, in essence, be disrespectful to God and distasteful to Christians, who are more sensitive to form than one might imagine. For perhaps, in the end, what matters above all else is that when the Church prays, it is they who worship the Holy Father "in spirit and truth."

In the end, we are confident that, because God is compassionate, he hears all lamentations and praises, even though they seem inarticulate or incoherent.

BIBLIOGRAPHY

Ascani,Valerio, E. Bianchi, E. Borsotti et al. *L'evangeliario: nella storia e nella liturgia*. Magnano: Edizioni Qiqajon, 2011.

Augé, Matias. *Liturgia: storia, celebrazione, teologia, spiritualità*. Milan: San Paolo, 1996.

Baldovin, John F. "The Urban Character of Christian Worship: The Origins, Development, and Meaning of the Stational Liturgy." *Orientalia Analecta* 228. Rome: Pontificium Institutum Studiorum Orientalium, 1987: 45–104.

———. *Bread of Life, Cup of Salvation: Understanding the Mass*. Lanham, MD: Rowman and Littlefield, 2003.

———. *Reforming the Liturgy: A Response to the Critics*. Collegeville, MN: Liturgical Press, 2008.

Baumstark, Anton. *Comparative Liturgy*. Westminster, MD: Newman Press, 1958.

Bishop, Edmund. *Liturgica Historica: Papers on the Liturgy and Religious Life of the Western Church*. Oxford: Clarendon Press, 1918.

Boselli, Goffredo. *Il senso spirituale della Liturgia*. Comunità di Bose (Biella): Qiqajon, 2011.

Boselli, Goffredo, and Frédéric Debuyst. *Spazio liturgico e orientamento*. Magnanao: Ed. Qiqajon, 2007.

Boselli, Goffredo, Giuseppe Busani, et al. *Assemblea santa: forme, presenze, presidenza*. Magnano: Edizioni Qiqajon, 2009.

Boselli, Goffredo, et al., *Chiesa e città*. Magnano: Edizioni Qiqajon, 2010.

———. *Liturgia e arte: La sfida della contemporaneità*. Magnano: Edizioni Qiqajon, 2011.

Botte, Bernard. *From Silence to Participation: An Insider's View of Liturgical Renewal*. Washington, DC: Pastoral Press, 1988.

Bradshaw, Paul. *The Search for the Origins of Christian Worship: Sources and Methods for the Study of the Early Liturgy*. Oxford: Oxford University Press, 1992, 2002.

Bradshaw, Paul., Bryan D. Spinks, et al. *Liturgy in Dialogue: Essays in Memory of Ronald Jasper*. London: SPCK, 1993.

Brovelli, Franco. *Ritorno alla liturgia: Saggi di studio sul movimento liturgico*. Rome: CLV-Edizioni liturgiche, 1989.

———. *Liturgia: temi e autori: Saggi di studio sul movimento liturgico*. Rome: CLV-Edizioni liturgiche, 1990.

Bugnini, Annibale. *The Reform of the Liturgy (1948–1975)*. Collegeville, MN: Liturgical Press, 1990.

Calatayud Gascó, Rafael. *Beso humano y ósculo cristiano: Dimensiones histórico- teológicas del beso litúrgico*. Valencia: Edicep, 2003.

Calivas, Alkiviadis C. *Aspects of Orthodox Worship*. Brookline, MA: Holy Cross Orthodox Press, 2003.

Cattaneo, Enrico. *Il culto cristiano in Occidente: Note storiche*. Rome: CLV-Edizioni liturgiche, 1992.

Chauvet, Louis-Marie. *Symbol and Sacrament: A Sacramental Reinterpretation of Christian Existence*. Collegeville, MN: Liturgical Press, 1995.

Chupungco, Angar J. *Liturgical Inculturation: Sacramentals, Religiosity, and Catechesis*. Collegeville, MN: Liturgical Press, 1992.

———. *What, Then, Is Liturgy? Musings and Memoir*. Collegeville, MN: Liturgical Press 2010.

Collins, Paul. *Renewal and Resistance: Catholic Church Music from the 1850s to Vatican II*. New York: Peter Lang, 2010.

Congar, Yves. *At the Heart of Christian Worship: Liturgical Essays of Yves Congar*. Edited and translated by Paul J. Philibert. Collegeville, MN: Liturgical Press, 2010.

Corbon, Jean. *Liturgia alla sorgente*. Magnano: Edizioni Qiqajon, 2003.

Daly, Robert J. *Sacrifice Unveiled: The True Meaning of Christian Sacrifice*. New York: T & T Clark, 2009.

Dix, Gregory. *The Shape of the Liturgy*. Westminster (London): Dacre Press, 1945.

Farhadian, Charles E. *Christian Worship Worldwide: Expanding Horizons, Deepening Practices*. Grand Rapids, MI: Eerdmans, 2007.

Ferrone, Rita. *Liturgy: Sacrosanctum Concilium*. New York: Paulist Press, 2007.

Foley, Edward. *From Age to Age: How Christians Have Celebrated the Eucharist*. Collegeville, MN: Liturgical Press, 2008.

Foley, Edward, Nathan D. Mitchell, Joanne M. Pearce, et al. *A Commentary on the General Instruction of the Roman Missal*. Collegeville, MN: Liturgical Press, 2007.

Foley, Edward, John F. Baldovin, Mary Collins, et al. *A Commentary on the Order of Mass in the Roman Missal*. Collegeville, MN: Liturgical Press, 2011.

Francis, Mark R. *Shape a Circle Ever Wider: Liturgical Inculturation in the United States*. Chicago: Liturgy Training Publications, 2000.

Francis, Mark R., Keith F. Pecklers, et al., *Liturgy for the New Millennium: A Commentary on the Revised Sacramentary*. Collegeville, MN: Liturgical Press, 2000.

Gamber, Klaus. *The Reform of the Roman Liturgy: Its Problems and Background*. San Juan Capistrano, CA: Una Voce Press, 1993.

Gerhards, Albert. *Licht—Ein Wegdurch Räume und Zeiten der Liturgie*. Regensburg: Schnell und Steiner, 2011.

Gray, Donald. *Earth and Altar*. Norwich: Canterbury Press [for] Alcuin Club, 1986.

Grillo, Andrea. *La Nascita della Liturgia nel XX secolo*. Assisi: Cittadella, 2003.

Hall, Jerome M. *We Have the Mind of Christ: The Holy Spirit and Liturgical Memory in the Thought of Edward J. Kilmartin*. Collegeville, MN: Liturgical Press, 2001.

Hebert, Arthur G. *Liturgy and Society: The Function of the Church in the Modern World*. London: Faber and Faber, 1935.

Hovda, Robert W. *Strong, Loving, and Wise: Presiding in Liturgy*. Washington, DC: The Liturgical Conference, 1976.

Johnson, Cuthbert. *Prosper Guéranger, 1805–1875: A Liturgical Theologian; An Introduction to His Liturgical Writings and Work*. Rome: Pontificio Ateneo S. Anselmo, 1984.

Johnson, Clare V., et al. *Ars Liturgiae: Worship, Aesthetics and Praxis; Essays in Honor of Nathan D. Mitchell*. Chicago: Liturgy Training Publications, 2003.

Jungmann, Josef A. *The Mass of the Roman Rite: Its Origins and Development*. Westminster, MD: Christian Classics, 1992.

Kilmartin, Edward J. *The Eucharist in the West: History and Theology*, edited by Robert J. Daly. Collegeville, MN: Liturgical Press, 1998.

King, Thomas M. *Teilhard's Mass: Approaches to "The Mass on the World."* New York: Paulist Press, 2005.

Klauser, Theodor. *A Short History of the Western Liturgy*. New York: Oxford University Press, 1979.

Klomp, Mirella. *The Sound of Worship: Liturgical Performance by Surinamese Lutherans and Ghanaian Methodists in Amsterdam*. Walpole, MA: Peeters, 2011.

Lang, Uwe Michael. *Turning Towards the Lord: Orientation in Liturgical Prayer*. San Francisco: Ignatius Press, 2004.

Lathrop, Gordon W. *Holy Things: A Liturgical Theology*. Minneapolis: Fortress Press, 1993.

———. *Holy People: A Liturgical Ecclesiology*. Minneapolis: Fortress Press, 1999.

———. *Holy Ground: A Liturgical Cosmology*. Minneapolis: Fortress Press, 2003.

Longhi, Andrea, and Carlo Tosco. *Architettura: Chiesa e società in Italia (1948–1978)*. Rome: Studium, 2010.

Marini, Piero. *A Challenging Reform: Realizing the Vision of the Liturgical Renewal 1963–1975*. Edited by Mark R. Francis, Keith F. Pecklers, and John R. Page. Collegeville, MN: Liturgical Press, 2007.

Mazza, Enrico. *Continuità e discontinuità: Concezioni medievali dell'eucaristia a confronto con la tradizione dei Padri e della liturgia*. Rome: CLV-Edizioni Liturgi, 2001.

Murray, Paul D., and Luca Badini Confalonieri. *Receptive Ecumenism and the Call to Catholic Learning: Exploring a Way for Contemporary Ecumenism*. Oxford: Oxford University Press, 2008.

Neunheuser, Burkhard. *Storia della liturgia attraverso le epoche culturali*. Rome: CLV-Edizioni Liturgiche, Roma 2009.

Nichols, Aidan. *Looking at the Liturgy: A Critical View of Its Contemporary Form*: San Francisco: Ignatius Press, 1996.

Palazzo, Eric. *A History of Liturgical Books from the Beginning to the Thirteenth Century*. Collegeville, MN: Liturgical Press, 1998.

Palazzo, Eric. *Liturgie et société au Moyen Age*. Paris: Aubier, 2000.

Pecklers, Keith F. *Dynamic Equivalence: The Living Language of Christian Worship*. Collegeville, MN: Liturgical Press, 2003.

———. *The Genius of the Roman Rite: On the Reception and Implementation of the New Missal*. Collegeville, MN: Liturgical Press, 2009.

———. *The Unread Vision: The Liturgical Movement in the United States of America 1926–1955*. Collegeville, MN: Liturgical Press, 1998.

———. *Worship*. Collegeville, MN: Liturgical Press, 2003.

Pecklers, Keith F., et al. *Liturgy in a Postmodern World*. London: Continuum, 2003.

Post, Paulus Gijsbertus, and R. L. Grimes, et al. *Disaster Ritual: Explorations of an Emerging Ritual Repertoire*. Dudley, MA: Peeters, 2003.

Pott, Thomas. *Byzantine Liturgical Reform: A Study of Liturgical Change in the Byzantine Tradition*. Crestwood, NY: St. Vladimir's Seminary Press, 2010.

Raffa, Vincenzo. *Liturgia eucaristica: Mistagogia della Messa; dalla storia e dalla teologia alla pastorale pratica*. Rome: CLV-Edizioni liturgiche, 2003.

Ratzinger, Joseph. *The Spirit of the Liturgy*. San Francisco: Ignatius Press, 2000.

Rosso, Stefano. *La celebrazione della storia della salvezza nel rito bizantino*. Vatican City: Libreria Editrice Vaticana, 2010.

Santi, Giancarlo. *Architettura e teologia: La Chiesa committente di architettura*. Trapani: Il pozzo di Giacobbe, 2011.

Sartore, Domenico, Achille M. Triacca, and Carlo Cibien. *Liturgia*. Milan: Edizioni San Paolo, 2001.

Schmemann, Alexander. *The Eucharist: Sacrament of the Kingdom*. Crestwood, NY: St. Vladimir's Seminary Press, 2003.

———. *Liturgy and Tradition: Theological Reflections of Alexander Schmemann*. Edited by Thomas Fisch. Crestwood, NY: St. Vladimir's Seminary Press, 1990.

Schmidt-Lauber, Hans-Christoph, Karl-Heinrich Bieritz, et al. *Handbuch der Liturgik: Liturgiewissenschaft in Theologie und Praxis der Kirche*. Leipzig: Evangelische Verlaganstalt, 1995.

Senn, Frank C. *Christian Liturgy: Catholic and Evangelical*. Minneapolis: Fortress Press, 1997.

Skelley, Michael. *The Liturgy of the World: Karl Rahner's Theology of Worship*. Collegeville, MN: Liturgical Press, 1991.

Smyth, Matthieu. *"Ante Altaria": Les rites antiques de la messe dominicale en Gaule, en Espagne et en Italie du Nord*. Paris: Les Éditions du Cerf, 2007.

Smyth, Matthieu, and Marcel Metzger. *La Liturgie oubliée: La prière eucharistique en Gaule antique et dans l'Occident non romain*. Paris: Les Éditions du Cerf, 2003.

Spinks, Bryan D. *The Worship Mall: Contemporary Responses to Contemporary Culture*. London: SPCK, 2010.

Taft, Robert F. *The Byzantine Rite: A Short History*. Collegeville, MN: Liturgical Press, 1992.

———. *The Liturgy of the Hours in East and West: The Origins of the Divine Office and Its Meaning for Today*. Collegeville, MN: Liturgical Press, 1986.

———. *Liturgy: Model of Prayer—Icon of Life*. Fairfax: Eastern Christian Publications, 2008.

———. *Oltre l'Oriente e l'Occidente: Per una tradizione liturgica viva*. Rome: LIPA, 1999.

———. *A partire dalla liturgia: Perché è la liturgia che fa la Chiesa*. Rome: LIPA, 2004.

Turner, Paul. *Let us Pray: A Guide to the Rubrics of Sunday Mass*. Collegeville, MN: Liturgical Press, 2006.

Underhill, Evelyn. *Worship*. New York: Crossroad, 1989.

Van Dijk, Stephen Joseph Peter, and Joan Hazelden Walker. *The Origins of the Modern Roman Liturgy: The Liturgy of the Papal Court and the Franciscan Order of the Thirteenth Century*. London: Darton, Longman & Todd, 1960.

Vogel, Cyrille, William George Storey, Niels Krogh Rasmussen, et al. *Medieval Liturgy: An Introduction to the Sources*. Washington, DC: Pastoral Press, 1986.

Vogel, Dwight W., ed. *Primary Sources of Liturgical Theology: A Reader*. Collegeville, MN: Liturgical Press, 2000.

Wainright, Geoffrey, and Karen. B. Westerfield Tucker, eds. *The Oxford History of Christian Worship*. New York: Oxford University Press, 2006.

Wegman, Herman A. J. *Christian Worship in East and West: A Study Guide to Liturgical History*. New York: Pueblo, 1985.

White, James F. *Protestant Worship: Traditions in Transition*. Louisville, KY: Westminster/John Knox Press, 1989.

———. *Roman Catholic Worship: Trent to Today*. New York: Paulist Press, 1995.

INDEX OF NAMES AND PLACES
References in italics refer to captions.